The Gardens
of
Cambridgeshire

A Gazetteer of over 400 Gardens

CAMBRIDGESHIRE GARDENS TRUST

ISBN No 0 9538542-0-5
Copyright © Cambridgeshire Gardens Trust, 2000
Typeset by Axis Design, Over, Cambridgeshire CB4 5QE
Printed by Colin King Printers, 43 High Street, Over, Cambridgeshire CB4 5NB

Published by the Cambridgeshire Gardens Trust,
The Grange, Easton, Huntingdon PE18 0TU.
2000
Drawings and maps © John Drake

Sponsored by:

STANLEY SMITH (UK) HORTICULTURAL TRUST

THE DOVEHOUSE TRUST

THE VICTORIAN SOCIETY (GREAT ANGLIA GROUP)

Who would have thought that when Gilly Drummond launched the Cambridgeshire Gardens Trust on 7th November, 1996 that so much would be achieved in the space of four years. The driving force behind this achievement is John Drake and his team of enthusiastic researchers.

The publication of this Gazetteer will fill a void and will I am sure be of great interest to any serious gardener in Cambridgeshire, whether professional or amateur.

LORD FAIRHAVEN

President, Cambridgeshire Gardens Trust

FOREWORD

When I first came to Cambridgeshire some thirty-five years ago gardens were the last things that I noticed. I saw the county then, quite unjustifiably, as one of fens and flatness. Now I view it through very different eyes as a place with wonderful scenery, tremendous skyscapes and, most of all, as a fascinating and exciting historic landscape. And from somewhere with very few recognizable or accessible gardens and parks, Wimpole and Anglesey Abbey then being still in private hands. Cambridgeshire for me has become a land of modest but pleasing parks and beautiful and cherished gardens. Furthermore, at a personal level, the large number of relict or abandoned gardens it contains led me to the study of garden archaeology.

In this book the Cambridgeshire Gardens Trust has for the first time pulled together the wealth of information on Cambridgeshire parks and gardens both public and private. The result should surprise even the most ardent Cambridgeshire gardener, inform the interested visitor and encourage appreciation of the county's landscape.

Christopher Taylor

CONTENTS

ACKNOWLEDGEMENTS

The Cambridgeshire Gardens Trust would like to thank the following for their support in preparing this Gazetteer:

The staff of Cambridge University Library, Cambridge College Libraries, Cambridge University Department Libraries, Homerton College Library, The Royal Horticultural Society Lindley Library, Cambridge City Library, and the Libraries of Ely, Huntingdon, March, Peterborough, St. Ives, St. Neots, Soham, Swavesey, Whittlesey and Wisbech.

The staff of the Record Offices at Cambridge, Huntingdon, Northampton and Surrey.

The staff of the Cambridgeshire Collection.

The staff of Bidwells Record Office.

The staff of the Museums at Ely, St. Ives, St. Neots, Whittlesey and Wisbech.

Cambridge City Council and Cambridgeshire County Council.

Cambridge College Garden Committees, Archivists and Head Gardeners.

Cambridgeshire National Trust Properties.

Cambridgeshire Garden Owners and Head Gardeners.

Pamela Abbott, Lady Adrian, Daphne Astor, David Cozens, Jane Brown, Sydney Davidson, William Dawson, John Dejardin, Hazel Fryer, Mary Gillingham, Diane Haigh, Phyllis Hetzel, Terry and Margaret Lynch, Sibyl Marshall, Michael Neddo, Lady Nourse, Margaret Oldfield, Andrew Peters, Lady Rhodes James, Anna Pavord, Howard Rice, John Ruest, Gavin Smith, Elizabeth Staziker, John Strafford, Alan Strutt, Geoff Stebbings, Christopher Taylor, Liz Thompson, Tim Upson, Christopher Vane-Percy, Norman Villis and Alexis & Thomas Zavros for their help and suggestions.

Jon Burgess, Catriona Campbell, Jill Cremer, Brian and Sandra Dickinson, Sandra Easom, David Edgar, Elizabeth Mitchell, Jane Nicholas, Audrey Osborne, Peter Reynolds, Mansel Spratling, Emma Stapleton all members of the research team.

INTRODUCTION

The Cambridgeshire Gardens Trust was launched in November 1996 at Wimpole Hall. The aims of the Trust are twofold: 1. To conserve, enhance and recreate the historic landscape, parks and gardens that exist or may have existed in the county for the education and enjoyment of the public: 2. To raise public awareness and understanding of the value of landscapes, parks and gardens as part of our local and natural heritage.

Most people think that only three gardens exist in Cambridgeshire: Anglesey Abbey (NT), the Cambridge University Botanic Garden and Wimpole Hall (NT). This conception is a blinkered one and the Trust seeks to redress the balance by listing over 400 parks and gardens in this Gazetteer.

The county possesses fine examples of every style of historic gardens. There are over 300 moated sites in Cambridgeshire, many around properties built by yeoman farmers who proudly exhibited their wealth by constructing water gardens. The landed gentry laid out formal canals, often from existing fishponds, inspired by the drainage of the Fens. Around the precincts of two cathedrals a range of gardens give an indication of the importance of horticulture to the church. At Peterborough, records reveal that gardening was well established by the year 1200; at Ely a plane tree from the Oxford Botanic Garden was planted in 1674 and in 1787 the Bishop's garden contained a large range of newly imported South African plants. In 1109 the Bishops of Ely established extensive landscaped grounds at Somersham around a palace where they stayed on their journey to the capital. Similarly the Bishops of Lincoln whose diocese stretched to the River Thames developed Buckden Towers in the centre of the town.

Not surprisingly several gardens have connections with Oliver Cromwell and his circle. Thorpe Hall, built by his Lord Chief Justice is the finest Commonwealth house and garden in the country. 'Capability' Brown's scheme for the Backs of the Colleges in Cambridge was never carried out, but his plan for the park at Burghley is the most complete example of his work. Brown retired to take up the Cambridgeshire Manor of Hilton and Fenstanton and is buried in the graveyard of Fenstanton church. Visitors from all over the world always stop on King's College bridge to take photographs of the renowned views of the river and the college chapel. The Victorians established private and public parks; Town Councils of Cambridge, Chatteris, Ely, Huntingdon, March, Peterborough, St. Ives, St. Neots and Wisbech undertook the management of commons, new recreation grounds and cemeteries. By 1880 dons were permitted to marry and reside away from their college. Consequently a new residential area of detached houses in large gardens appeared beyond the Backs.

In 1924 a slim booklet entitled 'The Village College: Being a Memorandum on the Provision of Educational and Social Facilities for the Countryside with Special Reference to Cambridgeshire' was produced by Henry Morris, Secretary for Education in the County. His conviction was that 'a school exists to confirm man's essential worth, his human dignity and his sense of significance. The fundamental morality of the Village College is that it stands for truth, beauty, knowledge, wonder and mutual human concern'. Morris had a clear appreciation of the effect of good architecture. This led him to place great importance on the siting of a building in the landscape and its immediate surroundings. Morris's ideals have been our inspiration whilst undertaking the research for the Gazetteer which has been produced to bring to the reader's attention the wealth of parks and gardens that are to be found in Cambridgeshire.

For ease of reference the sites have been arranged in 33 tours which cover the whole county.

Entries written in italics inform the reader that only the remains of an historic garden exist today.

All the sites included in this Gazetteer have been visited by The Cambridgeshire Gardens Trust who wish to advise that **an entry does not mean that there is a right of access unless the property is separately advertised by the owner as being open to the public.**

Opening arrangements each year for many of the gardens listed can be found in *The Gardens of England* published by The Blue Guide, *The National Gardens Scheme Yellow Book, The Good Gardens Guide* and other charity publications.

During the preparation of this Gazetteer a room in my house has been given over to reference books and several hundred files filled with a wealth of published references and maps from various sources. This extensive research has been masterminded by Audrey Osborne. Without her enthusiasm and patience this Gazetteer would not have been produced. It has been my pleasure to refer to her research team's findings whilst writing the Trust's first Gazetteer.

John Drake
Chairman, Cambridgeshire Gardens Trust.

The Cambridgeshire Gardens Trust would be glad to receive details of other gardens and parks which could be included in future editions.

TOUR 1
CENTRAL CAMBRIDGE

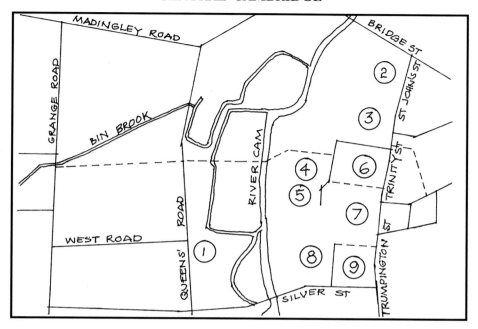

1.1 Cambridge, The Backs   OS445585

Until 1750 this world famous landscape acted as the town drain and a commercial waterway for barges. To the east of the River Cam, the colleges turned their 'backs' to it. By the time the Gibbs Building at King's was built in 1724, rooms were planned to look over the river when Charles Bridgeman proposed 'no place is capable of better Improvement, by cutting vistas through the Grove, and laying out the Waste Ground about it in regular Walks and Canals'. In 1741 James Essex produced a 'Prospect of King's College' with a symmetrical basin carved out of the west river bank and a circular temple terminating the main axis. In 1749 Essex erected the timber bridge at Queen's College (the first college access across the river) and in 1752 made alterations to the Grove opposite the College. In 1761 Harrison, the Head Gardener at Trinity College, was paid for planting North American poplars, weeping willows and other aquatics under the wall next to the river.

In 1779 Lancelot Brown (whilst working on garden plans for St. John's College) presented a scheme to the University for the complete remodelling of the Backs. His plan was based on the assumption that the individual Colleges would be prepared to abandon their old boundaries west of the river in the common interest. In essence the scheme provided a unified park with its centrepiece, the Gibbs Building as a 'great country house'. Sadly this concept was not realised probably because Brown did not distinguish between a nobleman's pleasure grounds and the needs for the health and exercise of students.

Today the Backs comprises land individually owned and laid out by the Colleges affording picturesque views of meadows, playing fields, lawns and riverside walks overhung with trees. Cattle graze in front of King's College Chapel where the river acts as a ha-ha when viewed from Queens Road. As a whole the Backs can never have been as superb as they are today, now that the groves and avenues have grown to a splendour possibly exceeding the boldest visions of those who planned and planted them.

1.2 Cambridge, St. John's College   OS4475887

David Loggan's view of St. John's College of c.1690 shows the three enclosed courts to the east of the river all laid out on an axis, with grass lawns surrounded and crossed by paths. To the west of the river the College owned extensive land which at that time consisted of a High Walk bordered by trees extending over the Bin Brook, (elegant cast-iron bridge c.1822) to the gateway at Queens' Road. South of this walk was a formal garden for the Fellows with hedged paths with seating recesses and lined with trees planted in lawns and nearby a bowling green. Immediately to the north of the walk was a walled enclosed real tennis court, extensive fishponds and a large field for grazing cattle.

In 1765 Charles Miller (son of Philip Miller, head gardener at the Physic Garden, Chelsea) was paid '2 guineas for his advice and plans for the improvements for the gardens'. By February 1773, Dr. William Powell, Master of the College was concerned at the expense of 'new-casing of the first Court and the laying out their Gardens under the direction of the celebrated Mr. Brown who had told him that his plan would cost them at least £800'.

In the previous year records mention that it was 'ordered that the bank be repaired under the direction of Mr. Brown'. In 1778 it was 'agreed that a piece of plate of the value of £50 be presented to Mr. Brown, for his services in improving the walks'. Lancelot Brown's improvements involved the simplification of the formal walks in the Fellows' Garden, with dense planting of trees and enlarging the Bowling Green into a spacious lawn. This area is now known as The Wilderness. Access to the Backs is through the wrought iron gates (which were removed from Horseheath Hall in 1777 – see 16.2). Today there are spring bulbs flowering in drifts under the trees which are followed later by naturalised martagon lilies and the outer walk has box bushes at regular intervals. The Bowling Green is now a croquet lawn with a small pavilion.

Opposite The Wilderness is the Scholars' Garden laid out to plans by Dame Sylvia Crowe in 1952, with yew hedges enclosing a rectangular garden with a central pavilion. The garden is edged with shrub and herbaceous borders and the six island flowerbeds have now been replaced by clumps of junipers.

To the north of the College, the Master's Garden overlooks the river and is dominated by a large plane tree and a chestnut both planted c.1868. The terrace is thickly planted with herbaceous perennials. Overlooking the river is a formal rose garden enclosed by yew hedging.

1.3 Cambridge, Trinity College   OS446586

Trinity Great Court was laid out between 1597-1605 by Thomas Neville. The stone fountain was erected in his time and is set today within one of six shaped lawns surrounded by paths. David Loggan's etching of 1690 shows the six lawns edged with stone balustrading with taller stone piers at each corner 'Add to this the ingeniously and delightfully composed variety of climbing plants and you will have some picture of the eminently English diversity of Great Court'. To the west is Neville Court built in 1612 and enclosed by Wren's Library in 1676. Here a simple lawn enhances the cloister atmosphere where again according to Pevsner, "From the Botanical point of view the climbers are even more rewarding". The Bowling Green, fitting tightly between the College and St. John's College, was laid out in 1647 and now comprises a rectangular lawn, an herbaceous border below the boundary wall and a long 20' high beech hedge. The College still has the original box of bowls. Loggan also shows a range of small gardens between the college and Trinity Street with elaborate parterres with a range of plants. To the south-east corner of the Chapel is a chequer-board layout of square beds each with a tree or shrub.

Between the College and the river is a short avenue of lime trees planted in 1780 when they were saplings 5 years old. Three are now missing and some branches have been removed and have lead cappings. James Essex designed the Cam Bridge in 1746 before the riverside walk was laid out in 1760 and the weeping willows planted by Harrison the Gardener in 1761. The lime avenue replanted in 1949, but set behind a central cherry tree avenue, is underplanted with crocus and red tulips in grass and continues over the bridge to the gates at Queens Road (removed from Horseheath Hall in 1777 – see 16.2). The avenue is centred on a vista of Coton church, which is no longer visible today.

To the west of Queens Road is the Fellows' Garden. The garden is protected from the noise of the road by three rows of yews, and is known as the Roundabout, so called after the perimeter path that existed around a field in 1803. In 1871, when the College bought the land, the cornfield disappeared and the informal layout of mixed borders, lawn and specimen trees was undertaken by W. Broderick Thomas (who also worked at Sandringham). Features include the rose garden with a memorial sundial dedicated to three Fellows of the College killed in World War 1; a pattern of paths in the wild flower area attributed to Wittgenstein, a Fellow in the 1930s; and a summer house on a mound erected by a Fellow as a romantic spot in which to propose.

Following the loss of an elm avenue in 1972, Richard Bisgrove redesigned the entrance to the Fellows' Garden with an avenue of plane trees which now links the garden, via a paved octagon, to Burrell's Field. Within a secluded part of the Fellows' Garden is Duffs Garden originally rented by J.D.Duff, a Fellow in 1889. Here a timber summer house is constructed in a hawthorn hedge and a mulberry tree has been planted in memory of Trisilian Nicolas (Bursar of the College).

The Fellows' Garden is approximately one-sixth of the College's 36-acre grounds, now extending from Sidney Street to Grange Road. Recently completed is accommodation in Burrell's Field by MacCormac Jamieson and Prichard set in a landscape designed by Cambridge Landscape Architects. Here, formal pergolas and conical yews link existing houses to the new design, a semi circular lily pool floats over the natural landscape beyond, and by a new bridge golden catalpas are planted amongst agapanthus. Existing houses overlooking Grange Road have been connected by paths leading to the octagon. Their intimate gardens, a small formal box edged herb garden and an Arts and Crafts Garden, nestle between extensive lawns under the shade of mature trees.

1.4 Cambridge, Trinity Hall   OS440580

The Principal Court of Trinity Hall was built gradually during the C14th, and is disguised behind the ashlar-faced external treatment of the walls. The scale is domestic and the combination of carefully chosen annuals at the base of the walls and the use of wall climbers is restrained and as successful as its grand neighbour. Loggan's view of 1690 shows Principal Court with a topiary yew and a struggling conifer in the centre. To the north were four small gardens bounded by Garret Hostel Lane.
Hidden away is South Court, with its diagonal path which was replanted in 1994 to Andrew Peter's designs. It contains box edged flower beds containing scented plants where small roses, philadelphus and herbs bask in the courtyard's heat .

The other gardens slope towards the river. The Fellows' Garden is enclosed by a brick wall and along the boundary wall with Clare College is a row of horse chestnut trees thought to have been planted in 1710 and one large copper beech. Along the opposite wall was an herbaceous border, which was replanted in 1990 as a wide mixed border with shrub roses, again to Andrew Peter's designs. A further lawn with herbaceous planting in Latham Court has been complemented by the planting around the new Jerwood Library which overlooks the river. The river terrace was re-landscaped in 1998 with a fine pear tree, and hot and cool loving plants have been chosen to continue the display of foliage for which the College is renowned.

1.5 Cambridge, Clare College   OS440580

Clare College consists of two courts – Old Court to the east of the river and Memorial Court to the west of Queens' Road.

The College entrance is in Trinity Lane through fine iron gates made by Warren in 1713 supported by stone gateposts of 1675 carved by Pearce. To either side of the path are lavender hedges. Old Court still retains the four lawns crossed by paths as shown on the Loggan map of 1688, and in his view of 1690 each lawn has a central tree. An enclosed walk of the same date survives between the Master's Garden and the Scholars' Garden shaded by a giant beech tree. Access to these gardens is through C18th gates. The river is crossed by Thomas Grumbold's balustraded bridge of 1639-40, for which he received 3 shillings for his drawing, the first bridge in Cambridge to be designed in the Classical style.

To the west of the river, further fine gates give access to the path now bounded on both sides by lime trees underplanted with crocus and other spring bulbs. At a lower level is the Fellows' Garden, designed by Professor Willmer for surprise and colour harmony. An outstanding wide herbaceous border backed by yews, sweeps diagonally across the lawn towards the river. There are two beds filled with red flowers along the river frontage, and a mirrored pair of blue and yellow borders either side of a grass path, that leads to a sunken formal water garden surrounded by clipped yews. Along the Garrett Hostel Lane boundary is Dean's Walk with white flowers and scented philadelphus edged with box. The garden was laid out under Willmer's supervision by Walter Barlow between 1946-47. The garden is also noted for its fine collection of trees.

To the west of Queens' Road is a further garden around Memorial Court (1923-24) containing a fine cedar and a Wellingtonia surrounded by evergreen and conifer planting.

1. 6 Cambridge, Gonville and Caius College   OS447586

Gonville and Caius was founded twice, once by a country clergyman, Edmund Gonville, in 1348, and by the celebrated Dr. Caius in 1557. Loggan's map of 1688 and his etching of 1690 show the gardens of the college clearly. The Gate of Honour, designed by Dr. Caius but built after his death in 1575, reflects his interest in Italian architecture. He had studied medicine in Padua and visited Rome, Florence and Bologna prior to his return to England in 1544. His design uses motifs from Alberti and Serlio's Fourth Book of Architecture of 1537. The scale of this architectural gem should be twice as large. This leads to Caius Court crossed by paths with simple lawns, the etching shows a stone column mounted on a series of circular stone steps. To the north is Gonville Court with a central lawn with a tree in each corner. To the west is the Master's Garden enclosed on three sides by a high brick wall. The garden was laid out with six small rectangular plots, two for vegetables and two were planted with different trees. Each plot was enclosed by low hedges. Tree Court consisted of an avenue of trees between parallel walls leading to Trinity Street, a tree walk within a rectangular enclosure and a partially walled lawn.

Custance's map of 1798 showed that the gardens had been simplified but the avenue of trees to Trinity Street remained. The first OS map of 1888 shows further changes as the College had built more accommodation on their compact site. The Master's Garden has been reduced in area by new buildings and the formal layout has been simplified to a central lawn with shrubberies to the east and west. Tree Court still has three compartments: One to the east of the Chapel has a lawn surrounded by trees and shrubs; a smaller enclosure with a rectangular lawn and path is entered from the Porter's Lodge nearby; and the avenue of trees has been reduced by the new building incorporating the Gate of Humility.

Today, the main change to the garden is the re-planning of Tree Court. This is now treated as one court, with a fine avenue of whitebeams within a strip of cobbles either side of the path leading from the Porter's Lodge to the Gate of Virtue. The lawn to the north is dominated by a cedar. Caius Court has a low raised bed planted with various conifers along the wall either side of the Gate of Honour. Gonville Court no longer has a tree at each corner of the lawn, but in summer the window boxes and annual bedding plants produce a colourful display.

To the east of Trinity Street is the college's St. Michael's Court extending round the north, east and south side of St. Michael's Church. The garden here has been planted with shrubs chosen for their dark foliage.

1.7 Cambridge, King's College   OS447584

King's College was founded by Henry VI in 1440. Loggan's map of 1688 shows the college hidden behind buildings along Trumpington Road. King's Bridge built in 1627 crossed the river mid-way between the boundaries of Queens' and Clare Colleges. Between the river and the entrance there were unequal plots of grass divided by straight avenues and crossed diagonally by footpaths; along the river ran a wall, and in the north-west part of the ground was a bowling green. West of the river the land was divided in two by a raised walk flanked by water courses and double rows of trees. In the thickly planted southern division, called King's Grove, was an oblong island surrounded by a moat.

Bridgeman's plan of 1724, 'improvement by cutting vistas through the Grove and laying out the waste ground in regular walks and canals', was only partly implemented. In 1741 James Essex published his *'Prospect of King's College'* showing a formal layout with the symmetrical basin carved out on the west side of the river and a circular temple terminating the vista. Again the College made no attempt to implement Essex's 'Prospect'. The layout of the grounds remained substantially unchanged from Loggan's map until 1749 when a new walk along the west bank of the river was begun. By 1751 the walk had been turfed and planted with limes and a second new walk had been made along the south side of the ground on the east bank. William Custance's map of 1798 shows the Fellows' Building by Gibbs (1723) overlooking a vast sloping lawn to the river edged by a perimeter path, with the central bridge leading to an avenue of trees to the west.

This formality was abandoned in 1818 when the land to the west of the river was altered by making two mounds set on the lines of the former avenue. A new bridge by Wilkins was erected to the south of the original bridge, and the gate to Queens'

Road erected by Wilkins in 1819. From the Backs Gate a path winds beneath trees to the new bridge without giving any clue of the vista that is in store. This element of surprise when reaching the bridge offers superb views to the College buildings and Clare College.

In 1823 Wilkins won a competition for the design for the hall and screen along the Trumpington Road entrance which encloses the main court. Today the two large expanses of lawn to the east and west of the Fellows' Building distinguish King's from other Colleges. In the centre of the east lawn stands a fountain with bronze figures by H.A.Armstead (1874).

To the west of Queens' Road is the Fellows' Garden which was laid out in the early 1850's. The garden has a perimeter walk through evergreens and two large island plantings of specimen trees, which include a 140 year old Wellingtonia, a Chinese Thuya and the best example of a Golden Rain Tree in Cambridge. A further island bed of herbaceous perennials divides the garden, and successfully maintains its Victorian atmosphere. The tall Wellingtonia in the Fellows' Garden balances the fine specimen horse chestnut immediately to the east of the King's Chapel.

1.8 Cambridge, Queens' College   OS446582

The College was founded in 1446 by Andrew Docket, Rector of St. Botolph's on the site of an old priory. It was re-founded by Margaret of Anjou in 1448 and again in 1465 by Elizabeth Woodville, Edward IV's Queen.

In 1690 Loggan's view shows the Principal's Garden divided into four plots enclosed by a wall with trained fruit trees, and a summerhouse along the wall overlooking the river. The Fellow's Garden next door has two plots arranged in a more elaborate manner edged with small shrubs, which then gave access to the Bowling Green also with a corner summerhouse. The College also gardened two further enclosed large formal orchards with raised perimeter walks edged with low hedges, to the north of Principal Court. To the west of the river the College owned further land reached by a bridge, consisting of four further formal orchards and a densely planted Grove but without any paths.

In 1749 James Essex erected the Mathematical Bridge without any nails, purely by pegging the timbers together (copied in 1902). Between then and 1752 various changes to the Grove were made. These improvements were due to John Forlin, the college gardener, who thinned the tree planting. By 1798 William Custance's map shows some of the orchards divided into small vegetable plots.

On the north wall of Principal Court is a sundial which dates from 1642 and since repainted more than once (e.g. 1733). There are narrow shrub borders including some conifers against the walls. To the west is Cloister Court with its brick cloister arcades and half-timbered President's Gallery above overlooking irregular lawns. Walnut Tree Court contains a newly planted walnut, and the Erasmus Building by Sir Basil Spence (1959) has a flat roof terrace giving fine views of King's and the Backs through a concrete pergola.

Across the bridge is Fisher Building which curves along Silver Street and hid the Fellows' original large walled garden from view. This garden is now the site of a new residential block by Powell, Moya and Partners. The landscape and planting around the building are designed to complement the architecture; no longer are the college gardens required to produce vegetables and fruit for the Fellows and students.

1.9 Cambridge, St. Catherine's College   OS448581

St. Catherine's College was founded in 1473 by the then Provost of King's College, Robert Woodelarke. The original buildings formed a court with an entrance from Queens' Lane, and to the south were three small square gardens with a tree in each corner. By 1680 this court had been rebuilt with no central lawn and a narrow medieval passage connected the college to Trumpington Street. This is shown on the Loggan map of 1688. Custance's map of 1798 shows Principal Court open ended to the east, with a central lawn set back from but looking through a double row of trees towards Trumpington Street. The medieval buildings have now been demolished and this gap along the street frontage is contained by new buildings. The fine gateposts set back from the street with iron gates and railings date from 1779. The college has changed its entrance, from the west to the east of Principal Court. The three small gardens to the south still remain.

The OS map of 1888 shows Principal Court with wide paths around the central lawn and two rows of trees between the iron railings; and Trumpington Street with posts at the back edge of the pavement. The three small gardens have changed to become the Fellows' garden with one lawn banked towards a shrubbery. At the corner of Queens' Lane and Silver Street is a new Master's garden with a central lawn edged with a path and two borders of trees and shrubs to the south.

Today the entrance to the college has been modified, Woodlark and Hobson's Buildings have both narrowed the space along Trumpington Street. A central path leads to the main gates, flanked either side by lawns each with a fastigiate beech. The posts along the pavement have been replaced by stone posts with chains. Immediately behind the gate are formal beds of shrubs, edged with low box hedges.

Sherlock Court and Chapel Court have recently been landscaped, both have circular beds filled with plants. Some fine cedars appear over the Master's Garden wall.

TOUR 2
CAMBRIDGE NORTH CENTRAL

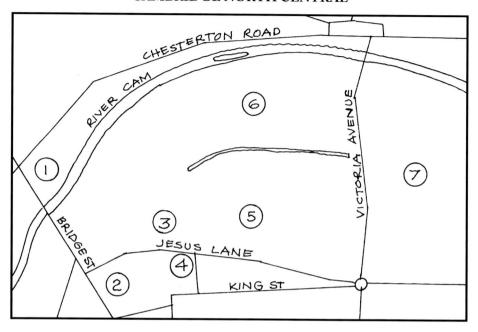

2.1 Cambridge, Magdalene College   OS446590

Magdalene College was founded in 1482 and again in 1542. The first foundation was as a Cambridge hostel for Benedictine monks from Crowland Abbey, to the north of the bridge over the river, under the shadow of Castle Hill. After the dissolution of the monasteries in 1538, Lord Audley of Audley End, founded the present college.

Loggan's map of 1688 shows First Court completed and the lawn divided by a central path. To the north of First Court are three rectangular plots with trees and a Bowling Green, and to the east of the court a small garden with trees. A path in this garden leads to a building standing where Pepys Building is today. This building is in the south-west corner of a large field called Magdalene Close which overlooks the river. It was enclosed by trees along the perimeter, with an avenue on higher ground along the track to the north (now Chesterton Lane). Custance's map of 1798 shows the Pepys Building on the site of the earlier building; and the plots with trees have been replaced by grass and the Bowling Green has been planted over. Adjacent to the Pepys Building is the brewhouse along the river frontage, which dates from 1629. Magdalene Close now becomes the Fellows' Garden with a wide path around a central lawn, but the trees remain.

In 1835 the Master's Lodge was built to the north of First Court. The Master's Garden was laid out over the Bowling Green. By 1888 his garden led directly into the Fellows' Garden, where the perimeter walk had been changed at the north-west corner to allow views through the trees which had been planted at random in Magdalene Close. Here there were narrow beds for flowers and a summerhouse below the earthwork's terrace. Second Court has trees planted against the walls parallel to the central path. Along the river frontage between Magdalene Street and the brewhouse is a garden and Tennis Court. After 1925 the college expanded by acquiring existing medieval cottages to the west of Magdalene Street, and in 1931 Edwin Lutyens designed Benson's Court with its back to St. John's College.

Today there is an exotic display of annual bedding plants along the river frontage of First Court. In Second Court the walls support climbing plants with herbaceous plants beneath. The Fellows' Garden has a fine view through mature trees (the oak was planted to commemorate Queen Victoria's 1887 Jubilee) to the river and beyond. In the north-west corner is a Victorian pets' cemetery. Flower beds filled with more herbaceous plants and heathers slope towards the lawn.

The spaces between the medieval buildings in Benson's Court are sympathetically planted with wall shrubs and are connected by raised paths and lawns. The view to the river is dominated by a large weeping willow.

2.2 Cambridge, Sidney Sussex College   OS450587

Sidney Sussex College is built on the site of a friary dating from 1240, of which nothing remains. The church was destroyed in 1547 and the stone used to build Trinity College Chapel. The College was founded by Lady Francis Sidney, Dowager Countess of Sussex, in 1594.

Loggan's map of 1688 shows the College consisting of two adjacent open ended courts facing the road, with an entrance through an Arch into the northern court. This had a central path with a lawn to each side. The southern court had a short avenue of trees along the street side. Between the north court and Jesus Lane was a Bowling Green overlooked by a summerhouse, a knot garden and an orchard. This became the Fellow's garden.

To the east of the College buildings was a bank containing the King's Ditch with a double avenue planted alongside and then the extensive grounds of Sidney College Close, bounded by a wall. By 1789 only the summerhouse and knot garden had been lost, and a copy of the Arch in a classical style was made in 1749 and erected in the corner of the Close towards Jesus Lane. The Close Garden was landscaped in the latter part of the C18th, and became the Master's Garden. Following the completion of the Cloister Court the Master's garden was reduced in size to incorporate the Fellows' Garden to the north.

Today the courts facing Sidney Street are enclosed by a high brick wall surmounted by railings, through which climb wisterias and cotoneasters with

Solomon seal beneath. Cloister Court to the north is built over the Bowling Green, but the lawn is edged with a narrow border of evergreen shrubs. The main garden is reached through a gateway at the end of Cloister Court. Here are mature chestnuts, beech and planes underplanted with spring bulbs. Yew hedges in the far distance enclose a secluded garden dominated by the Arch on a raised terrace, with its ginkgo surrounded by golden foliage plants. There are two flower borders with a central path forming the division between the Master's Garden and the College Garden, but the eye travels over a low yew hedge to admire the Master's fine weeping ash.

New buildings along the southern boundary have allowed a more adventurous solution to landscaping. Walkways and flights of steps present varied viewpoints over lawns and shrubberies. Clumps of evergreens have been used to give some enclosure and reduce the impact of new buildings over the garden. In summer there is dense shade from the trees and in spring there are drifts of bulbs beneath the mature trees throughout the gardens. Then there is the scent from the wisterias.

2.3 Cambridge, Wesley House   OS451588

In 1925 Sir Aston Webb designed three sides of a quadrangle, open to Jesus Lane in a Neo-Tudor style for a post-graduate theological college, on a site purchased from Jesus College. By 1948 the quadrangle was crossed by paths edged with lavender, leading to a statue. In 1972, a southern range along Jesus Lane completed the quadrangle and allows views in from the street. Today the garden has been simplified. The central lawn has various specimen trees, birch, Judas tree, ginkgo and a weeping pear. The walls are clothed in climbers especially clematis and vines. The annual bedding is much appreciated by summer residents. The grounds are maintained by retired clergy.

2.4 Cambridge, Westcott House   OS450587

Westcott Theological College lies to the south of Jesus Lane and to the west of All Saints' Church, and was founded in 1881. The College built a range of accommodation along Jesus Lane in 1899 by Grayson and Ould, which was added to by other architects over the following 30 years. This resulted in a relaxed enclosed Main Court with terraces on various levels and a cloister in the south-west corner. The central area is dominated by the spire of All Saints', and is used as a croquet lawn and part orchard with wild flowers in long grass (the wilderness). Around Main Court are herbaceous borders edged with lavender. The south facing terrace has fine shrubs backed by wisterias and passionflowers in abundance. A new court has been formed to the east on the site of the vicarage with lawns and children's play facilities.

2.5 Cambridge, Jesus College   OS452589

Jesus College was founded in 1497 by Bishop Alcock of Ely. He obtained leave from Henry VII to suppress the Benedictine nunnery of St. Radegund outside Cambridge and replaced it by Jesus College. The nunnery had at the time only two nuns. The

College is set back from the road and approached between high parallel brick walls along a paved path known as the Chimney.

David Loggan's etching of 1690 shows part of the Fellows' Garden to the west of the Chimney with a lawn edged with alternating trees and shrubs (the trees drastically pruned). First Court, with a mature walnut tree in the centre of the larger lawn, is closed in by a high wall along the west side. To the north of this court is a formal garden enclosed by shrubs. In the centre of this garden is a topiaried yew within a small circular bed with narrow parallel plots arranged around the central circle. To the east of the Chimney is the Master's Garden which is laid out with formal lawns each with a central trimmed tiered yew. One of these lawns has a complicated knot pattern edged with low box hedges. To the north is the land once owned by the nunnery, and the sweep of Jesus Close towards the boundary planting along the stream that separates the College from Jesus Green.

Loggan's map of 1688 does not marry with the view of 1690. The Fellows' Garden is shown divided into four square lawns edged with trees with a Bowling Green to the west. First Court has the walnut tree but the lawn is dissected by six paths almost forming a star pattern across the grass. The formal garden with its circular centre remains the same, but the Master's Garden is shown with a series of rectangular plots growing fruit and vegetables. Outside Jesus Close to the north west is an area of six fishponds and a dovecote owned by the Master.

By 1789 Custance had noted that the fish ponds and dovecotee were no longer owned by the Master, but had become Clarke's Nursery, although the dovecote still remained. The Fellows' Garden was now planted with several trees but the four formal lawns had been swept away.

Today, First Court is given over to lawns with a wrought-iron screen replacing the west wall. The walnut tree has been removed and a narrow border along the screen is planted with pelargoniums and also yews trained into bottle shapes. The Fellows' Garden contains fine examples of evergreen oak, mulberry and a magnificent cut-leaved plane, grown from seed in 1802 brought back from Thermopylae by Edward Daniel Clarke. Along the east wall is a shrub border containing *Aristololochia durior* commonly known as 'birthwort', thought to have been planted by the nuns. Along the west wall is a small timber summerhouse with pediment, placed between evergreens, which overlooks the bowling green lawn.

West of First Court is the Orchard which is really an arboretum containing a range of conifer, cedars, chestnuts, beech and yew. The grass is kept rough as it was historically grown for fodder. Amongst the trees are Second World War concrete shelters below ground which the gardeners use today for over wintering cannas and other half hardy bulbs. The Orchard leads round to Back Court where until recently the formal garden was planted with roses. These have now been replaced by lawn but the pairs of bottle shaped yews and the central walnut survive as a reminder of the C17th layout. Along the northern accommodation range are four small beds planted separately with grasses, ground cover plants and the remaining two with conifers. To the south-east corner a new St. Radegund garden has been planted with the apothecary's rose, bay and fruit trees. This is backed by a wide north facing border with viburnums, hellebores, box elder, ferns and bamboos.

Cloister Court is simple with a lawn and virginia creeper covering the cloister walls. In summer the cloister arches support fine hanging baskets.

To the east of this court is Chapel Court, another open ended space where pollarded limes along the wrought-iron screen have had to be removed because of disease. The large central lawn has variegated hollies at the corners and a cedar in the centre. The shrub border along the east facing range is now over 20 years old and to the south a lawn has a mature lime and sycamore tree. Around the east end of the chapel gravestones are to be found in the lawn.

Recently the College has built a new Library which is reached through a small garden off Chapel Court. This was part of the Master's Garden where a new path, evergreens and a curved yew hedge create an enclosed garden. The Master's Garden, now reduced, no longer serves as the College's vegetable, fruit and cut-flower source. There is an east facing herbaceous border along the drive and a lawn with long narrow island beds containing flowering cherries and roses, dominated by a large plane tree.

Along the Chapel wall is a herb garden where between the beds are rectangles of gravel with planted terracotta pots. A secret garden has been established by the south transept with circular paving made from clay flower pots. A Gothic seat is sheltered beneath a eucalyptus tree.

Jesus Close around the College buildings is used as a sports field. In a clockwise direction hockey pitches, tennis courts, cricket pitch, football and rugby pitches are laid out. Against the perimeter planting to the north is a thatched timber sports pavilion surveying the action.

2.6 Cambridge, Jesus Green   OS453592

On Maundy Thursday 1556, Cambridge's only martyr, John Hullier, a scholar of Kings College, was burnt on Jesus Green.

Before 1890 Jesus Green, Midsummer Common and Greencroft were effectively one large common (these names overlapped). The name of Jesus Green existed before Victoria Road and the bridge were laid out in 1890. Then the common was divided and the land to the west of the road was named Jesus Green. A proposal to enclose this common in 1841 applied to other commons in the city. A misinterpretation of the Council's Powers given in the Cambridge Corporation Act led to Jesus Green being mistakenly classified as a recreation ground in 1923. In 1965 the Commons Registration Act omitted Jesus Green from the registration. Thus today it is no longer common land.

The footpaths relate to the routes established after Jesus Lock was completed in 1832. The drainage channels (Middle Ditch) disappeared by 1890 in preparation for the 1894 Royal Agricultural Show. 1890 saw the planting of the horse chestnut avenue along Victoria Avenue, these were subsequently removed for the Royal Agricultural Show in 1894 and then replanted. In 1913 the diagonal avenue of London planes were later augmented by other avenues of ornamental fruit trees. By 1926 the swimming pool, tennis courts and bowling green were opened. Then by 1951 a putting green and a sports pavilion had been provided by the lock bridge. Recent changes have meant the loss of the putting green and a band stand, but the dead elms have been replaced by beech, lime and horse chestnuts. The river bank has now been planted with willows and the swimming pool has been upgraded.

2.7 Cambridge, Midsummer Common   OS455588

Following the re-siting of Barnwell Priory away from the castle to common land to the north-east of the town, Midsummer Common was named after the fair that had been granted by King John to the Priory in 1211. Together with Butts Green (the area to the south along Maids Causeway) they had been commons since at least 1189, and combined with Jesus Green they were also know as Greencroft. In 1232 Henry III granted that the Fair could be held over 4 days from 22nd-25th June. This meant that proceeds became an important source of income for the Priory. The Barnwell Chroniclers recorded that "boys and lads met to amuse themselves in the English fashion by wrestling matches and other games". In 1235 the town burgesses came to an agreement that the Priory would pay for any damage caused by the fair, and by 1506 the organisation of the fair was taken over completely by the burgesses. Goods for the fair were shipped along the River Cam until the middle of the C19th.

In 1714 the fair included a Punch and Judy, a giant, a dwarf, wild beasts, dancing dogs, three-legged cats and a female rope dancer, and by the late C18th it was extended to a fortnight each year and became more profitable to the town than Stourbridge Fair. Between 1810 and 1812 the site of Barnwell Priory was completely levelled and in 1821 permission was given to build a footpath along the edge of the common on the site of Brunswick Walk. In Victorian and Edwardian times there were 'Mammoth Shows' on August Bank holidays with balloon ascents and parachute descents performed by the Spencer family. A Rustic Sports day was held in 1838 to mark Queen Victoria's Coronation and more sporting events were held for the Jubilee in 1887.

An application for 17 houses with gardens was proposed on the common in 1870, reducing the area by 3 acres. This was rejected by the Council.

In 1945 Midsummer Common was the site for Victory in Europe celebrations. While not used for fairs and other events the land was grazed. During a period after the Second World War the common ceased to be grazed, but during the mid 1990s the cattle returned. They are removed when the common is used for Midsummer Fair, Strawberry Fair, circuses, funfairs and the annual fireworks display.

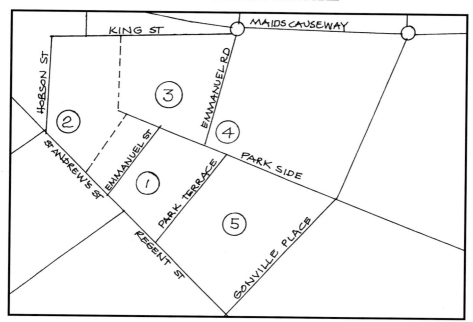

3.1 Cambridge, Emmanuel College   OS453583

Emmanuel College was founded in 1584 by Sir Walter Mildmay, Chancellor of the Exchequer. The College entrance was originally from Emmanuel Street to the north. This is illustrated on Hammond's map of 1592. The Loggan view of 1690 shows this entrance with a path bordered by low fencing between two lawns. There is a bathing pool in the Fellows' Garden surrounded by trees and to the south in The Paddock, enclosed by walls and backed by trees, is a larger pool. To the south of Front Court is Chapman's Garden, thickly planted with trees with an open culvert along one side, bringing water from Hobson's Conduit to the pond in the Paddock, and then on to Christ's College.

James Essex's plan of 1746 shows the Fellows' Garden pool to be formalised and brick lined with moulded stone edges, in a slightly different position, and to the west is a small Bath House. Chapman's Garden has been laid out with a series of walks between parallel beds and the open conduit now has curved ends.

Today the entrance to the College is along St. Andrew's Street passing through the narrow frontal strip of lawn with flowering cherry trees and shrubs against the College walls, sometimes planted out with dahlias. There is no planting in Front Court, which gives easy access to other courts and gardens.

New Court, formerly the entrance court, was enclosed in 1824 and now has a perennial herb garden designed by John Codrington in 1960, consisting of low raised brick beds set in the brick and cobble pattern of the court. The beds are edged with box and the soil is covered by coloured stones, including coal. The beds are triangular and intersected by paths diagonally crossing the court. The Paddock to the east of the Chapel was also designed by Codrington in the 1960s with the first view from Front Court deliberately confined by shrub planting. The long pool now has serpentine edges and an island dominated by a Swamp Cypress. Around the pool are bamboos, and other moisture loving plants. A winter garden was planted at the east end of the pool in 1985 with several conifers.

The Fellows' Garden seen over a low wall, is dominated by a mature Oriental Plane with branches sweeping the lawns, thought to have been planted in c.1835, and a fine Purple Beech. In the corner is the pool used for swimming since 1690, the present thatched hut dates from the mid C19th. There are outstanding C20th herbaceous borders along the north-west boundary.

Chapman's Garden is named after the Reverend Arthur Chapman, a Hebrew scholar who until 1913 had the whole garden to himself. To one side of the pool is an extensive collection of trees. Along a path is a white and red flower garden. The tree planting in this garden gives some indication of the 120 tree species, some rare, planted in the College garden.

Access to North Court is by a tunnel from New Court. Here in a sunken oval lawn are three magnificent trees; *Paulownia tomentosa*, *Fraxinus ornus* and *Cedrus libani*, providing the perfect foil to the Baroque pediments of the dormer windows.

3.2 Cambridge, Christ's College   OS451585

Christ's College was first established as 'God's-house' in 1437 by William Byngham, a London parish priest. Shortly after receiving its Royal Licence from Henry V1, God's-house was forced to move from its original site, as it was needed for the King's new project (what was to become King's College Chapel). God's-house moved to its present site in 1448 where it was re-founded as Christ's College by Lady Margaret Beaufort in 1505. The garden was leased in 1507 but purchased in September 1554.

Loggan's map of 1688 shows First Court with two rectangular lawns dissected by a path from the St. Andrew's Street Gateway. To the north of the Hall was the Master's Garden with three plots enclosed by a wall and a garden structure in a corner. Access to the Fellows' Building (1640-43) is along a narrow walled path. The path continues through the building, into a further walled garden, the Fellow's Garden with a tennis court and two paths. One path leads to a summerhouse in one corner, the other to a larger enclosed garden, divided into four rectangular areas each edged with trees and one given over to a Bowling Green. A further garden building is shown directly opposite the south entrance on the north wall. The culvert from the pond at Emmanuel College is diverted along the west edge of Christ's Pieces.

There is a reference by Thomas Salmon in 1748 to the Bath, a bathing pool set in paving, terminated to the south by a stuccoed loggia or summerhouse in the Fellows' Garden. Around the pool are three carved busts set on tapering pedestals, of the blind Professor of Mathematics, Nicholas Sanderson, John Milton and the philosopher Ralph Cudworth; a 4th pedestal carries an urn in memory of Joseph Mede; all C18th. Today the Bath is backed by a screen of shrubs, and overhung by beeches and plane trees. A memorial urn containing the ashes of the author C.P. Snow has been positioned on the east side of the pool.

The Custance map of 1798 shows a circular lawn in First Court, five plots in the Master' Garden and a short avenue of trees to the north of the Fellows' Building. The large enclosed garden to the north has been simplified by combining the two northern areas into a grove, and one further area has been cleared of its perimeter tree planting. This garden was combined with the garden immediately to the north of Fellows' Building into a larger Fellows' Garden, and its present form adopted in c.1825 with lawns, winding paths, shrubberies backed by trees to a style influenced by J.C. Loudon. In this garden is an old mulberry now propped, reputedly dating from 1609.

By 1888 the College grounds had extended to the north-west of the existing Master's Garden by a gateway leading to a larger enclosed space also called the Master's Garden. This rectangular area was indicated on the Loggan map. From both these gardens a narrow pathway led to glasshouses along the Hobson Street boundary. Here three buildings were constructed to form Third Court, within which is a large sunken oval lawn surrounded by a wide border of iris. In the early part of the C20th the Masters' Garden was revised to incorporate the end of Hobson's Conduit before it flowed beneath Hobson Street. The design subtly reduces the width of the water canal when it flows in the distance under an arch in the perimeter wall, until it reaches the Darwin Shrine built in 1920 to commemorate the centenary of Charles Darwin's birth. A fine *Pterocarya x rehderana* stands guard over the shrine and canal.

In 1969 Sir Denys Lasdun designed New Court, which is approached through plantings of juniper; and along King Street the new gateway incorporates a wrought iron daisy ('marguerite'), a further allusion to the founder, inspired by the daisies and red roses carved on the Gatehouse in First Court.

The College possesses a large collection of specimen trees, of which many can be seen from Christ's Pieces. Recently there has been a subtle change in emphasis in reducing the extent of annuals throughout the gardens and new plantings of shrubs and perennials have been carefully nurtured. First Court is a feast for sad eyes, the window boxes decorate the court and exotic half-hardy plants grow happily amongst wisteria, chimmonanthus, hydrangea and magnolia.

3.3 Cambridge, Christ's Pieces   OS453585

Despite what the name suggests and its proximity, Christ's College never owned the Piece. It was sold to the town by Jesus College in 1886 for the purpose of recreation.

Lyle's map of 1574 indicated what is now Christ's Pieces as a field growing corn. The Hammond map of 1592 shows strips which indicate the land was still used for arable crops; the map also shows the north south paths now known as Milton Walk and Pikes Walk. Loggan's map of 1688 shows the diagonal north-east south-west path across it. By 1815 proposals to enclose this land failed. The land has been used as a public open space ever since.

In 1887 a lake was proposed at the northern end of the site and in 1926 further proposals for a new open-air swimming bath were discussed. In the 1950s, Holford's Report recommending a spinal relief road through the site was rejected, as were proposals in 1956 for a Floral Hall to hold at least 2000 people.

The cross paths still are edged with fine lime trees, although the eastern path has been diverted at Emmanuel Road. The bandstand and the performance area with stage for evening concerts has been removed, as have some of the island planting beds. The Bowling Green is well used and the twice yearly displays of bedding plants are greatly admired. Gone are the days when families doing laundry for the colleges used Christ's Pieces to hang the laundry out to dry, and for cleaning carpets during the Long Vacation.

In September 1999 the Diana, Princess of Wales, Rose Garden was planted with over 200 roses.

3.4 Cambridge, Emmanuel Road, No. 2   OS454584

Charles Humfrey (1772-1848), a pupil of James Wyatt, practised as an architect in Cambridge from c.1800 onwards. His best works were the admirable speculative building developments carried out between 1815 and 1828 in the area south-east of Christ's Pieces. By the 1840s his annual income from property was over £1000. His Doll's Close development comprised the fine houses overlooking Midsummer Common in Maid's Causeway, Willow Walk, Short Street and Fair Street.

He built his home, Clarendon House and a range of mews in Miller Lane (now Emmanuel Road) facing Christ's Pieces in 1825-8. His garden was extensive and divided into three areas. A drive from Parker Street approached the house from the south. To the west, forming a backdrop to the Mews Range, a large lawn was divided by paths into two formal areas with central topiary. Immediately to the east was a large lawn with specimen trees surrounded by thick boundary tree and shrub planting, and beyond was a grassed enclosure of similar size again with boundary planting and a serpentine path.

By the early 1840s he was in financial difficulties and was forced to sell all his Cambridge properties to satisfy his creditors. The sale particulars record "a desirable Mansion House in the Elizabethan style, beautifully situated in the centre of its own grounds, walled garden newly planted, beautiful pleasure grounds with highly ornamental timber trees and shrubs of 30 years growth and highly ornamental paddock. It offers an advantageous speculation to the capitalist for the erection of villas etc from its contiguity to Parkers Piece which is an open and unenclosed ground and will always remain so".

The house is now demolished, but in the rear garden of 2 Emmanuel Road is a circular cast-iron glazed garden summerhouse which originally stood in Charles Humfrey's garden. It has recently been saved from total collapse with a grant from the City Council.

3.5 Cambridge, Parkers Piece   OS455581

Originally part of Middlefield in the Open Field of Barnwell situated between two tracks Hintuneweie and Hadestokweye. This important open space is named after Edward Parker, a cook, who had leased part of the land from Trinity College. In 1612-13 a transfer took place between the City Corporation and the College. The City acquired land which included the major part of Parkers Piece, giving some former common land to the west of Trinity College in exchange. During the Civil War Cromwell erected defensive earth banks through Parkers Piece and along Lensfield Road. Prior to 1831 the site was struggling to accommodate a range of uses, a grassed open space still with ridge and furrow divided into two fields by a hedge, and a pond dug for cattle and horses near the south-west corner, which became a hazard for children who played near it. In 1827 permission was given to fill in the pond and in 1831 for the levelling of a 60 yards square for a cricket ground so long as it was used by 'town and gown'. Mr. Watford of Gonville Place produced a layout in 1832 proposing a Horseway 22 yards wide around the perimeter when the ditches were filled.

In 1839 Charles Humfrey proposed further improvements by making proposals for a broad footpath on all four sides of the Common and a single row of elms spaced 40 feet apart along three sides, omitting the Park Terrace side to the north. Henry Charles Malden, an undergraduate of Trinity College in 1847, introduced football games with other undergraduates, as an alternative to the popular hacking games on Parker's Piece. To overcome the ensuing chaos, Malden and his colleagues agreed to a set of rules for the game, which were printed as *'The Cambridge Rules'*. In October 1863, these were adopted by The Football Association at their meeting at Freemason's Tavern, Great Queen Street, London, and have been used ever since.

In 1868 the Council thanked Mr. John Odell Pain for planting the 30 lime trees along Parkside at his own expense. These trees still stand today. By 1878 the Commons Committee resolved that Parkers Piece was to be kept solely for recreation and no horses were to be exercised or cattle grazed there. An attempt to surface the cross paths and install a perimeter iron fence was vigorously opposed by 2,014 people in 1880.

It was agreed in 1881 that the turf should be maintained by grazing sheep from May to November. A 'Curator of Parkers Piece' was appointed to take charge of cricket and other games. A horse mower and roller were obtained in 1890 to be shared with Christ's Pieces. In 1893 the Council agreed to the installation of an electric light in the centre of Parkers Piece which was refurbished in 1999.

Parkers Piece was used throughout the C19th for religious services, public meetings, election hustings, celebrations and games; and soldiers' drill during the First World War. A feast for over 5000 people to mark the peace following the entry of the Allies into Paris was held on 12th July 1814, the year Napoleon abdicated. On 28th June 1838 the coronation of Queen Victoria was celebrated by another dinner for 15,000 in the presence of 25,000 spectators. They consumed 1,608 plum puddings, 1,013 stones of meat, 72lbs of mustard and 99 barrels of best ale each of 26 gallons. In 1840 Parkers Piece was the location of the first ever Royal Agricultural Show. Queen Victoria's Jubilee Year celebrations were held over several days in 1897, culminating with a Treat for School Children of tea and amusements for 5,000 children.

Over a long period Parkers Piece remained a Common for recreation. As with Jesus Green it is listed in the Corporation's Year Book as Recreation Grounds. Before 1846 all County and University cricket matches were played on Parkers Piece and in 1930 a cricket pavilion was opened in honour of the famous Cambridge cricketer Jack Hobbs.

There was much local unrest towards a series of proposals: in 1951 to widen Regent Terrace for a car park; in 1957 to build a car park for 800 cars beneath Parkers Piece later revised in 1968; ramps for a multi-storey car park on Queen Anne Terrace. Subsequently the Council was asked to confirm the status of the land. After much deliberation the County Council as the Registering Authority recognised the validity of the claim for common status even though time for registration of the category of existing commons had expired. Ena Mitchell's research and commitment to various open spaces in Cambridge will hopefully ensure that the County and City will continue to respect Parkers Piece as a world famous town-green.

TOUR 4
CAMBRIDGE SOUTH CENTRAL

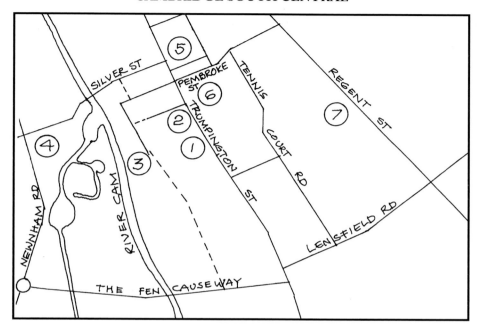

4.1 Cambridge, Peterhouse   OS448579

The first scholars of the Bishop of Ely arrived in 1284. But when Hugo de Balsham, the founder, died in 1286 he left money to build a Hall, and by the end of the century the College had expanded to Coe Fen and south from the adjacent churchyard of Little St. Mary's. Hammond's map of 1592 shows Old Court and outhouses where Gisborne Court stands, perhaps the cook's garden. The Fellows' Garden is shown containing eight trees and is enclosed by walls, and a Grove to the south has trees planted along some of its boundaries.

Loggan's map and view of 1688 shows Old Court with four grass plots centred on the Chapel entrance. Their planting is unusual: Trees are planted in rows running east-west. The outer side of the plots have fastigiate trees forming four rows and between these a further two rows of conifers in the centre of the grass plots. All the trees are 8 ft high. The Fellows' Garden also has four plots with trees and an Arbour. In the Grove a Tennis Court has been constructed (1571-2) along the west wall, as well as a Dovecotee and above the Water Gate a Spectaculum with an upper floor to look out over the Fen Wall. This structure was demolished by 1859. To the south of the Grove, the College owned a large garden divided into four parts by wide cross paths, all filled with orchards and rows of vegetables, known as Volye Croft, but shown as 'Peterhouse Garden' in 1688. This became the 'Far garden' in the C19th and is now known as the Scholars' Garden. Since 1795 the two parts along Trumpington Street were let to Christopher Pemberton who resided in Grove Lodge which is shown on the Custance map of 1798.

By 1755 Old Court was simplified by omitting the crosspaths, but lamp posts were installed at the four corners of the lawn, new lamps were erected in 1830 and later electrified. In 1985 new lamps replaced those removed during the war. The ground's garden ambiance was achieved by 1841, when after the completion of the Fitzwilliam Museum the College commissioned William Sawrey Gilpin (nephew of William Gilpin) to draw up plans. Gilpin's major work was at Scotney Castle in 1836 to create a picturesque landscape for Edward Hussey.

Today the Grove is called the Deer Park. Deer were introduced possibly in Gilpin's time and were kept until 1935. Its 1.5 acres became the smallest Deer Park in the country. In 1940 the College turned the Deer Park into a vegetable garden and felled the limes along the path. Since the war shrub beds and fruit trees have been planted with drifts of daffodils, aconites and crocuses beneath them. The Scholars' Garden continues with limes behind the Fitzwilliam Museum and then opens around the eight storey 1963 brick building by Sir Leslie Martin and Colin St. John Wilson, with lawns leading down to shrubberies. Nearby is the strange *Laburnocytisus adami* which seems an appropriate addition to this Victorian garden. The rear gardens of St. Peter's Terrace have been removed and laid down to lawn. The window boxes in Old Court still contain *Pelargonium 'Galilee'*, and an interesting collection of shrubs and herbs are to be found in and around Gisborne Court.

4.2 Cambridge, Little St. Mary's Churchyard   OS448581

St. Mary The Less was originally called St. Peter-without-Trumpington-Gate, and was appropriated by Peterhouse to serve as the college chapel until 1632. The church is surrounded by a graveyard which has been divided into two contrasting parts. The first is to the north and east which has been cleared, levelled and grassed over and kept tidy by the City Council. It contains a memorial area and trees commemorating individuals and events. The bird bath is a memorial to Burns Singer, the Scottish poet and marine biologist.

A gate in the iron railings marks the transition to the second 'garden' area which lies to the south and west of the church. This area is gardened by parishioners and volunteers who with Constance Babington-Smith have kept the garden accessible for over 20 years. The transformation into a semi-wild garden was devised by Robert Lachlan, a distinguished mathematician and Fellow of Trinity College. The churchyard had been closed to burials for 80 years and was derelict with some gravestones broken. Unmarked graves include the German Painter, Valentine Ritz (d.1743) who painted Isaac Newton and other Cambridge worthies, and the exiled

Dutch composer Pieter Hellendaal (1721-1799). The 'garden' is further sub-divided into the 'nearer' and 'further' garden separated by raised ground which supports tall trees and shrubs.

As most of the garden is within the shade of the church and Peterhouse College, sun loving plants are rare. But in spring aconites, snowdrops and celandines carpet the ground. Along the Peterhouse wall grow Asiatic teazles and in summer white comfrey, a native of Turkey appears amongst green alkenet. The comfrey was first identified in this churchyard by Charles Cardale Babington in his 1860 *'Flora of Cambridgeshire'*. A camomile lawn has been planted near the south porch.

4.3 Cambridge, Garden House Hotel   OS447578

In 1888 Garden House stood on the river front in Granta Place adjacent to the four houses which made up Coe Fen Terrace. To the south, the garden stretched along the River Cam, across the sluice and was then bordered by a ditch to the east along Coe Fen. To the north was a narrow alley which gave access to the river for residents in Little St. Mary's Lane to wash their laundry.

In 1933 the Garden House was converted into a Hotel by George Reynolds using the existing garden. During the Second World War prisoners of war built a small rock garden with Westmorland stone which has now been extended. The hotel was redeveloped in 1972 following a fire. The present landscaping of the garden fronting the river and the grounds was carried out in 1973 and still incorporates the evergreen oak, the horse chestnut and limes of the original garden. Recently hedges have been planted to screen the leisure facility and extended car park. One fine oak tree remains of the original garden at the southern tip of the grounds. The view of the garden from the public footpath on the other side of the river is to be increased by removing some shrub borders.

4.4 Cambridge, Darwin College   OS445579

Darwin College was founded in 1965 as the first Cambridge college exclusively for graduate students. The College consists of a group of houses in Silver Street along a tributary of the river, notably Newnham Grange and the Hermitage. In1966 Howell, Killick, Partridge and Amis were commissioned to design accommodation for 100 students, incorporating the existing buildings.

The garden of Darwin College at the rear of the two properties is connected by bridges to Little Island and Big Island. The Hermitage was occupied by a Hermit whose responsibility it was to maintain the Small Bridge, the forerunner of Lutyen's Silver Street Bridge. In 1396 the King (Henry VI) granted John Jaye, the hermit, for two years, certain customs on saleable articles passing along the bridges and causeway. This collection of tolls continued and in 1790 the city corporation leased the site of the Hermitage to Patrick Beales, a corn and coal merchant, who built a house 'Newnham Grange' on the site. In order to pay off his mortgage debts Beales arranged for his house to be sold in 1851. The sale documents describe "the Green-House, Shrubberies, Lawn, and Ornamental Garden, extending to the beautiful meandering Stream forming a branch of the River Cam, across which are Two Islands presenting altogether a most delightful Residence, suitable for a Genteel Family".

In 1884 Professor George Darwin, 2nd son of Charles Darwin, contacted the Beale family to enquire if he might rent the property; the reply was favourable. Mrs. Darwin noted "We found both islands lovely, the one just opposite the house simply a mass of blossom and nettles. Peonies, laburnum, lilacs, cherries, currants and gooseberries. It was much larger than I thought and so pretty...". The garden is dominated by a huge beech tree underplanted with snowdrops and aconites. The islands are connected by timber footbridges which were often repaired by the Darwins.

4.5 Cambridge, Corpus Christi College   OS449582

Corpus Christi College was founded in 1352 by two town guilds, Corpus Christi and St. Mary, and is situated between the churches of St. Bene't's and St. Mary's. Old Court was built around an irregular quadrangle and entered from Bene't Street. Loggan's map of 1688 shows Old Court with a rectangular lawn crossed by a path leading towards the Master's Lodge. The Master's Garden was to the south and comprised a walled garden enclosing a Bowling Green and four square plots for vegetables. Between the vegetable plots and the graveyard of St. Mary's Church were the Tennis Courts.

Custance's map of 1798 shows Old Court with a single lawn, not crossed by a path, and the Master's Garden simplified with the Bowling Green between 2 formal clumps of trees. In 1823 Wilkins built New Court with the College entrance along Trumpington Street. The 1st OS map of 1888 shows New Court, with a central lawn, leading to Old Court which now has a oval shaped lawn with an oval stone path within cobbles. The Fellows' Garden, to the north of the new chapel, had a central lawn surrounded by trees and shrubs. The Master's Lodge has been enlarged and the garden has changed from its earlier formality to a lawn with a path which winds amongst shrubberies and trees. The Tennis Courts have been removed.

Today the Fellows' Garden contains one of Cambridge's old mulberries. Old Court has climbing hydrangeas on its walls. New Court's fine lawn is enhanced by annual bedding below the ground floor windows and in window boxes.

4.6 Cambridge, Pembroke College   OS449581

Pembroke College was founded in 1346 by Mary, widow of Aymer de Valence, and daughter of Guy Count of Chatillon and St. Paul. David Loggan's etching of 1690 shows in more detail what is depicted on his map of 1688. The map suggests that Hobson's Conduit is taken around the south side of the College and then north through the College into Pembroke Street. Then to the east are orchards and a

Bowling green connected by a wide walk. The small gardens to the east of Wren's Chapel are more complex and can be seen clearer in the etching, although partially hidden by the Chapel. A dog is seen drinking water from the Conduit prior to the water disappearing under the road and passing through the College grounds. The gardens to the east of the Chapel contain formal layouts with narrow beds planted with low shrubs and flowers. There is a small mount surrounded by a low hedge and along the walls are fruit trees. Ivy Court is closed by a wall with a central gate which leads to the formal walk which runs along the north side of the far garden, overlooking an arboretum, a Bowling Green and finally an orchard. To the south was a field called Pembroke Piece. Custance's map of 1798 shows little change except that Ivy Court has more trees planted either side of the central path to the Bowling Green gate.

It has been claimed that Dr. Lancelot Andrewes who was master of the College at the beginning of the C17th had arranged for the construction of the water channel through the College grounds. It was known to pass beneath College buildings which were erected in 1633 and 1659. In 1753 Carter wrote of the Master's Lodge that "its chief beauty is the gardens and the waterworks contrived by the present master which supplies a beautiful and large bason in the middle of the garden and wherein he often diverts himself in a machine of his own contrivance, to go with the foot as he rides therein". Carter also refers to the Fellows' Garden, "There are besides several other gardens belonging to the apartments of particular fellows, in one of which is another, small and simple, yet well-contrived waterwork which is continually supplying a large cold bath with fresh water, the overplus of which runs through the second court and so into the King's Ditch". The oval to the east of the Chapel on Custance's map may be the 'bason' referred to by Carter.

By 1880 the Master's Lodge had been re-sited along the Pembroke Street frontage with its separate entrance court. To the east of the Lodge was a new sunken garden enclosed by a low wall overlooking the formal walk. The Bowling Green flanked by an orchard and an arboretum still remained, but a new walk with gates leading to Tennis Court Road had been laid out and the garden extended across Pembroke Piece. On the far lawn was the Observatory surrounded by planting, and the serpentine path was edged on the boundary side with more trees and shrubs. The new walk has plane trees to the south, and leads to a lily pond which was converted from a water tank originally intended for fire fighting during the Second World War. In 1933 a new Master's Lodge was built at the south-eastern end of this garden by M.Webb . Further alterations to this garden occurred in 1985 when again the Master's Lodge was re-sited to allow the building of a new range of student accommodation along the garden's south side.

Whilst one might imagine the presence of building contractors re-siting important buildings in various locations in a garden can only bring about the garden's destruction, Pembroke has a garden of much horticultural interest. The college has a legacy of asking Fellows to choose trees for planting; and the range of trees along the north side of the new walk mark tenth anniversaries of elections to Fellowships. The Rev. Meredith Dewey, a former Dean took much interest in the garden introducing new plantings and is remembered by his rock garden. The small pool in this garden is connected to the lily pond by an underground pipe which bypasses a mount upon which grew a mulberry supposedly planted by Spenser in 1560, when he was at the College. It died in 1977 and a root-cutting from the original now grows on the same mount. In spring there is a display of bulbs in rough grass beneath the trees and shrubs, and late autumn colchicums can be enjoyed in a wooded area recently planted on the site of the original orchard.

4.7 Cambridge, Downing College   OS453579

Sir George Downing, before his death in 1749, had arranged for a college to be established with his money. His extensive garden and park at Gamlingay had been abandoned (see Tour 22.7). Following delays resulting from litigation, building work commenced in 1807 to designs by Wilkins in the neo-Grecian style. The original east and west range of buildings enclosed a large grassed court crossed by paths. To the south a low wall enclosed the space, with views across the cricket ground towards the Catholic Church. To the west was the Fellows' Garden and to the east the Master's Garden, both dominated by cedars and evergreen oaks. To the north was a vista through a double avenue towards Downing Street.

In 1929 Sir Herbert Baker designed the northern range which enclosed the Great Court cutting off the view of the avenue, which was slowly being crowded by the Botanical Laboratory and the Geological Museum for the University. Howell, Killick, Partridge and Amis designed a new Senior Combination Room near the Hall, which led to a new appraisal of the grounds by Dame Sylvia Crowe in November 1968. The Fellows' Garden was to be improved by allowing the lawns to flow under the trees, and a break in the holly hedge and the inclusion of a ha-ha would give a diagonal view to the Catholic Church. The peripheral tree planting needed skilled attention. It was dense and tree planting for regeneration was proposed. Trees should be planted in the great court to complement the scale of the space and to provide a sense of enclosure. Simplicity was her key word, but Kenny Court could be improved with soft landscaping because of its intimate scale. The bicycle and car park areas should be organised and screened with pleached limes or high hedges.

In 1974 the elms in the boundary plantings died and a cedar, beeches and poplars succumbed in the following gales, but the rear of the properties along Lensfield Road are still screened from view. The Master's Garden has a fine Holm oak and Turkey oaks with a rose garden to the north. The Fellows' Garden did not carry out the idea of the ha-ha, but the copper beech and cedars are superb and lead the eye towards the thicker planting in the Glade. Pines have been established along the Tennis Court Road boundary, but will need more years to screen the buildings that dominate along the west side of that road.

TOUR 5
WEST CAMBRIDGE

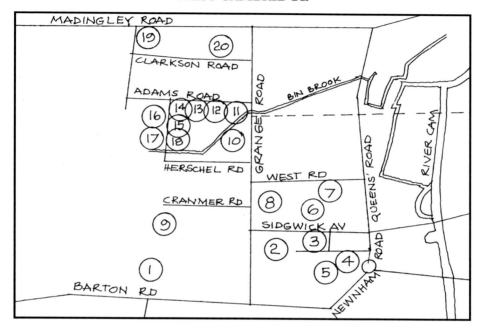

5.1 Cambridge, Wolfson College   OS437577

The College was founded by the University as 'University College' in June 1965. Following a substantial gift to the College by the Wolfson Foundation in 1972 the college name was altered. The site is along the Barton Road, and includes several existing houses and their gardens. In 1972 the first new buildings were designed by Ferrey and Mennin of York and accommodation was provided around Front, West and East Courts. The simple paving layout and planting retains existing mature trees and a row of seven mature cedars, originally along a low mound, have been protected at ground level from root compaction. The College is approached along a new drive bordered with hornbeams within a yew hedge. The Front Court is enclosed by wrought iron railings and gates, which have also been used to enclose the College's grounds along the Barton Road. A garden to the west of the Seminar Room has been planted to shield the impact of the car park. Originally a peat garden it is now backed by a yew hedge and planted with low growing conifers around an astrolabe in memory of the first President, John Sinclair Morrison.

To the east is Lee Court, with simple lawns enclosed by a timber pergola supporting roses and wisteria. The college now owns Norton House and its rear garden with mature cedar, willow and silver birch. Nearby is the President's Lodge with its private garden. To the north is the Lee Seng Tee Hall with plantings of hellebores, ivies, medlars and pulmonarias, and nearby are the Betty Wu Lee gardens with a mature cedar and contorted willow. These existing trees have been incorporated by Paul Edwards into a pleasing garden with willows and bamboos growing along a low wall between Chinese rocks. The garden contains a small octagonal metal bandstand. The College incorporates existing houses within its layout – Breedon House, Plommer House, Norton House- and also four houses along the Barton Road.

The largest of these houses is No 78 Barton Road which until recently was the home of Sir Vivian Fuchs. He established yew topiary in his garden in the shape of a very tall penguin with an egg in euonymus between its feet. This stands amongst tall Wellingtonias, three cedars and giant sycamores. To the rear of his house is a small formal kitchen garden consisting of six plots between brick paths enclosed by yew hedging. A jasmine arch is provided along the yew hedge.

No 74 Barton Road still retains it timber garage and shed in the front garden and the spring bulbs beneath the mature trees make a pleasant understorey. In the rear garden are two fine weeping limes and a shrub border, but with the removal of some of the garden fencing the trees, as at No 78, now become part of the College grounds. There is interesting planting along the Barton Road frontage, where the existing hawthorn hedge has been layered and behind are rows of newly planted yew and holly.

5.2 Cambridge, Newnham College   OS 578443

Lectures for women started at Cambridge in 1870, thanks to the efforts of Henry Sidgwick and his wife Eleanor. With funds raised from friends they built a Hall of residence, Old Hall, which was opened in 1875, under the care of Blanche Athena Clough who became the College's third Principal. The Hall was sited on land to the south of Newnham Walk and designed by Basil Champneys using crisp red bricks for the elevations. In 1880, two more acres were bought for North Hall, also by Champneys, to the north of Newnham Walk where a tennis court and fives court were provided. Other college buildings followed, and the Sidgwicks engaged the city fathers for three years to have the public footpath, which originally divided the college's accommodation, relocated as a road to the north (now Sidgwick Avenue lined with plane trees). This was accomplished at their financial expense in 1893.

Thus the garden was now overlooked by College accommodation with their backs to the new road. This stroke of genius allowed the garden to develop within its own framework. Fellows of the College had placed great emphasis on the need for women to have fresh air and exercise, coupled with the interest in gardening. This meant that no garden designer was given a free hand. The College's Garden Committee to this day exercises a firm control over garden matters.

James Blackhouse & Son of York proposed curved walks and the Mound for the telescope was provided in 1891 by Mary Boreham. Alfred Hoare Powell designed the sunken parterre in front of Kennedy and the semi-circular yew hedge at the end of the path from Clough. Gertrude Jekyll submitted plans in 1911, which included two hexagonal pavilions designed by Edwin Lutyens. He knew Mrs. Sidgwick well as he was related to her by marriage. The college hesitated, and by 1912 Mr. Watson of Edinburgh had provided plans which were accepted.

The Mound was to be enclosed by a seven-sided wall, and accessible from four paths. The west garden was to be an orchard and along the southern boundary a nut walk was proposed. The latter was actually proposed by Miss Jekyll. What exists today is partly a combination of ideas. The Mound now supports a sundial which is a memorial to Mrs. Sidgwick and a stone plaque with lettering carved by Eric Gill.

The planting of the garden is adventurous, tender plants clothe the walls and superb herbaceous borders flank the paths. But at the same time there is respect for the stages of this garden's history and its staff. This philosophy of continuity established during the Arts and Crafts movement marks Newnham's garden as separate from other colleges.

5.3 Cambridge, Ridley Hall   OS444578

Ridley Hall is a Theological College, training men and women for ordained ministry in the Church of England. It was founded in 1881, and the first range of buildings facing Ridley Road were designed by C.S. Luck with later additions by W. Wallace. The grounds were enclosed by a brick wall and yew hedge behind which a narrow band of trees and shrubs were planted. These still remain today. Behind the original range was a tennis court within large lawns. In 1912 a further residential block was built on land to the west. The tennis court was removed and an area in the large court was given over to the Principal's Garden. This garden is enclosed by large conifers and evergreens. The shrub planting against the buildings is simple but effective and *Acanthus mollis* grows with much vigour. Under the trees on the lawn are bulbs in the spring.

5.4 Cambridge, Plâs Dinas   OS445577

Plâs Dinas is situated along the south side of Malting Lane, Newnham with an ornamental verandah along its west façade. The garden layout is shown on Baker's map of Cambridge of 1830 and does not change for the next 50 years. The first OS map of 1888 shows its large garden divided into three areas by paths – a sunken garden to the west, with a lawn surrounded by flower borders, shrubberies and trees; an orchard to the south reached by a raised path; and a vinery against the house protected by shrubs which conceals the narrow vegetable garden to the east. A photograph taken of the house and garden in 1880 shows the house and verandah covered with climbers and the vinery along the south side of the house. There are flower borders along the north boundary wall, and low planting along the raised path to the orchard.

In 1864 the house was owned by Charles Foster; and from 1892 to 1936 the property was owned by the Hind family who at some time in the early C20th divided the property. The east garden is now divided into five private gardens. The Malting House garden is illustrated in *'Country Life'* 1915 and now consists of three small paved courtyard gardens connected by stone steps, and then continues behind the gardens of properties along Newnham Road. It is divided from the adjacent garden by a brick crinkle-crankle wall. Then come two small gardens rectangular in shape, divided by a mature rose hedge. Between these and Plâs Dinas is Frostlake Cottage, whose residents included Maurice Dodd, the economist, and Wittgenstein. This garden still contains the original vine now protected by part of the verandah relocated from the west façade of the house. In 1924 the orchard was sold for a building plot (see 5.5).

The west garden of Plâs Dinas still retains the raised path to the orchard and a sunken lawn is surrounded by shrubs and trees. Recent residents have planted sophoras and eucalyptus to remind them of the southern hemisphere, but have allowed the yew to increase in growth. The house is now called Little Newnham.

5.5 Cambridge, Church Rate Corner   OS445576

Church Rate Corner was built in 1924 by Baillie Scott for Marjorie Wilson Duckett in the orchard of Plâs Dinas (see 5.4). The House faces south and is surrounded by a garden on three sides which was also planned by Baillie Scott. To the east is the original orchard walk now lined with hazels, and underplanted with epimediums and pulmonarias. A narrow raised stone terrace along the south of the house is edged with lavender and small plots contain various herbs. A wide lawn runs parallel to the house with a wide herbaceous border beyond. This border is divided by an apple tree underplanted with cyclamen and spring bulbs. To the west of the lawn, Baillie Scott designed two formal areas which now are given over to bulbs. To the south-east is the original gardener's privy beneath a mature beech tree.

5.6 Cambridge, Sidgwick Avenue Site   OS443579

In May 1952 a competition for the layout for the Faculty of Arts along Sidgwick Avenue was won by Casson and Conder. This was the first post war comprehensive university plan, predating a plan for Sheffield University in 1954. On the site of Corpus Christi College's cricket ground and part of the Fellows' Garden, the architects envisaged a system of courtyard planning grouped around two focal areas: a raised and paved platform upon which the main building would be raised on piloti, and a sunken water square to give a sense of serenity and to echo the traditional riverside character of Cambridge. All buildings were to be linked by covered ways and paved walks, and changes of ground use to be delineated by changes of level, and/or texture and materials. Wheeled traffic was to be rigorously excluded from the central areas.

In campus planning, the spaces between buildings and their relationship are as important as the buildings themselves. Landscaping, treatment of levels, planting, verges, street furniture are of vital importance. Casson's concept was one of picturesque beauty; buildings beneath trees, lawns, a water walk with the tower of the University Library (1934) in the distance.

When the plan was implemented, parts were omitted here and there and slowly the overall concept was thinned down. The 'pilotis' were disliked by many but Lady Mitchell Hall, the Little Hall and the circular bicycle park are much admired. Today the site is three-quarters complete, the History and Law Faculty buildings strive to make bold statements on their separate sites without any reference to a sunken water square. The sites of houses along West Road have not been included in the plan and their rear gardens have not been incorporated into the landscape. It is over 40 years since the buildings were occupied and time for a new landscape appraisal.

5.7 Cambridge, Harvey Court   OS443581

Harvey Court, West Road, was designed by Sir Leslie Martin and Colin St. John Wilson for Gonville and Caius College in 1960. It stands on the site of Thorpe House, now demolished, which had an extensive garden to the south. Thorpe House was one of the earliest houses to be built along West Road. While other new houses along West Road were built for dons, Thorpe House's first residents were the Eaden Lilley family in 1883, who owned a shop in Market Street, Cambridge selling linen, carpets, general furnishings and bedding. The family stayed until 1923, when Mrs. Lilley moved to Ingleside, four houses further along West Road. The garden at Thorpe House was laid out with a series of serpentine paths between thick shrubberies planted with many conifers which gave privacy along the perimeter. There was an extensive conservatory along the south of the house, and at the far end of the garden a pond with wide sloping banks was established. There was no vegetable area or orchard within the garden, the whole given over for relaxation and pleasure.

In 1953 the house became an annex for Gonville and Caius College student accommodation. The siting of Harvey Court respects the mature planting and provides a view across the garden from the elevated court before one descends the wide flight of brick steps down into the garden.

Today a curved shrubbery leads towards the grassed banked Lilley's pond. There is a group of fine cedars and a Wellingtonia forming a dell, and nearby Judas trees are dwarfed by a blue cedar.

5.8 Cambridge, Selwyn College   OS440579

Selwyn College was founded in 1882 in memory of the first Bishop of New Zealand, George Augustus Selwyn. The site along Grange Road consisted originally of ridge and furrow meadows, hedgerows and footpaths in the shade of huge elms. The College was designed by Sir Arthur Blomfield who intended the central lawn in Old

Court to be level with the buildings around it. But a sunken lawn prevailed for 80 years, similar to the one still to be found at their sister College, Keble, Oxford.

The simple planting in Old Court, walls covered by Virginia creeper and gravel paths has only recently been altered. The gravel is now replaced by Yorkstone paving and a narrow bed at the foot of the walls is now widened and planted with shrubs. Along the north range wall, plants collected from New Zealand have been planted in memory of G. A. Selwyn; and either side of the Chapel are two myrtles. A vista through the railings and fine gates to north of the Chapel lead down into the Main Gardens where a circular walk amongst the boundary trees invites a further inspection.

Immediately inside this garden are two borders filled with rare trees and shrubs. A pair of incense cedars frame the view to the central beds planted in the late Victorian style with exotic half hardy plants. These form an exuberant centre piece where cannas, dahlias, and salvias dominate. Originally the garden contained a collection of 270 roses of which only 70 remain. A border of agapanthus and kniphofias has recently been established, and part of the edging of this border has revealed the original circular walk, lost for many years.

The Fellows' Garden to the south is protected by a thick shrubbery and contains interesting horse chestnut trees which have dwarfed the cement rockery beneath them. The shape of the lawn is identical to that shown on the 1927 OS map.

The Master's garden is enclosed by a beech hedge and contains a fine horse chestnut tree on the edge of the lawn which is edged by serpentine gravel paths. Around the lawn are mixed flower borders some extending to both sides of the paths. Plants on the terrace cascade down the retaining walls.

The garden grows a wide range of botanically interesting plants; wild collected iris from the Pyrenees and forsythia from Siberia. The white-flowering Prunus trees along Grange Road are a fine sight in April and present a tempting overture to the planting delights to be found elsewhere within the gardens.

5.9 Cambridge, Grange Road, No. 37 'Leckhampton'   OS436580

At the far end of a long cul-de-sac is a spacious brick Tudor villa of 1881 designed by W. C. Marshall. Later it became the home of Louis Clarke, who was Director of the Fitzwilliam Museum and one of its most generous benefactors.

The 10 acre garden lies to the south of the house and is planted in a William Robinson natural style. Originally the lawn was enclosed by conifer and deciduous trees, with a view through to a meadow beyond. A pool and temple on a mound were in the far distance, reached by paths around the edge of the meadow. By 1927 the space between the lawn and meadow was given over to a wider lawn with mounds either side, and a bank at the meadow's edge.

Today, a new hostel has been sited to the west of the house; and the main vista has been emphasised by a centrally mown grass path through the meadow which contains cowslips followed later by drifts of blue lupins. A later addition to the garden has been a formal rose garden to the west of the meadow. The lawn is dominated by a magnificent cedar.

5.10 Cambridge, Robinson College   OS439585

Cambridge has recently benefited from the generosity of David Robinson, a successful local business man. Funds were made available for a new maternity building at Addenbrooke's Hospital, and a new college bearing his name.

In 1974 Gillespie, Kidd and Coia, a firm of Glasgow architects, were appointed to design Robinson College on a site along Grange Road, which was crossed by the Bin Brook. four houses were demolished to make way for the main complex which kept the mature trees, lawns and the waterway which ran diagonally across the site.

At the same time Thorneycreek, a house along Herschel Road, was bought by the College and used for accommodation and offices during the construction of the new building. Thorneycreek was built in 1895 for Mr. Parker, Manager of St. Martins, now Barclays Bank in Benet Street. The garden of this large house stretched to the Bin Brook and a walnut tree planted in 1897 to commemorate Queen Victoria's Diamond Jubilee still grows along the edge of the brook.

In 1976 the site was cleared prior to new building work commencing. Following a detailed tree survey permission was given to fell over 100 trees, mainly prunus. In 1979 J.S. Bodfan Gruffyd was appointed Landscape Architect and submitted his plans which included an elevated causeway connecting the new buildings to the garden around Thorneycreek. In a letter to the Planning Officer he proposed "a wild woodland water garden across the middle of the site with a flood pond to buffer rising water levels and the connecting causeway – a park and informal woodland area with overtones of more sophisticated gardening beyond". This would be a formal hedge enclosing a silver and white garden with a weeping wellingtonia. This was different to Gillespie's idea of a natural garden incorporating the Bin Brook like the Dutch were promoting in the 1980s.

Luckily Robinson College has developed a sympathetic gardening philosophy of retaining original Victorian planting where appropriate. At Thorneycroft the hollies, aucubas, box and philadelphus were kept and the house sits comfortably on its terrace complemented by original plantings of clerodendrum, staphylea, hoheria and pink acacias.

The new College has shrubs bordering the path to the Porter's Lodge and since the removal of diseased elms along the Grange Road frontage and the yews which were obscuring John Piper's stained glass window in the Chapel, plantings of Silver Birch with evergreen shrubs along the base of the red brick walls now begin to look mature.

The west walls of the college are successfully planted with evergreen shrubs and climbers and soften the impact of the brick facade to the garden.

From 1975 the College acquired five adjacent properties and their gardens which backed on to the grounds. Each of these is connected to the main garden with subtlety. Even the inclusion of an exotic bicycle shed pleases the senses. Today the College own all but two sites bounded by Grange Road, Adams Road, Sylvester Road and Herschel Road, thus almost gardening the whole block.

5.11 Cambridge, Adams Road, No. 2   OS439585

This is Robinson College's latest acquisition, built in 1898 and formerly owned by Lord and Lady Kaldor from 1951, who gave hospitality to Hungarian refugees after the uprising of 1956. The house welcomed visitors who came to discuss economics, politics and philosophy. Kaldor became economic advisor to successive Labour Governments.

Their garden consisted of a terrace to the south and east of the house. To the south a flight of steps lead down to a gravel path flanked on both sides with herbaceous borders backed by espalier trained fruit trees and to the east is a lawn with perennial herbs growing along the north side. Towards the new building the remains of a Victorian fernery is now overshadowed by the Lawson cypresses.

5.12 Cambridge, Adams Road, No. 4   OS439585

This house was built in 1908 by Dr. Shillington-Scales, who pioneered X-ray techniques. In 1926 Brian Reddaway came, when young, to have his knee X-rayed in the adjoining garage. He and his wife later bought the house from his parents in 1952. He was subsequently Professor of Political Economy in the University from 1969 to 1980.

Their garden had a large lawn to the south enclosed by tall yew hedges with recesses and where openings were required, a curved arch was cut through and pairs of globes cut above the hedge. Today the hedges remain as does the important X-ray garage. A narrow herbaceous border lies along the west hedge and the opening originally led to the vegetable garden, now a car park. Immediately to the west of the house is a small rose parterre filled with *Rosa 'Trumpeter'*.

5.13 Cambridge, Adams Road, No. 5   OS439585

This house was built in 1902, and bought from Mr. P. A. Rottenberg by David Robinson in October 1975. It was occupied by the first six graduate students of the College in 1977.

Mr. Rottenberg was a passionate bulb collector of alliums and species tulips, and his *Narcissus bulbocodium* growing in large drifts was a fine sight in the early 1950s. To the south of his house is a large terrace leading to a wide lawn and spring bulbs occur everywhere, even in the rough grass beneath the spreading *Parrotia persica*. Towards the end of his garden were his vegetables. This area has been redesigned with roses and some specimen trees.

5.14 Cambridge, Adams Road, No. 6 OS430585

This house was built in the 1890s and was bought in 1950 by Sir George Thompson, later Master of Corpus Christi, and his sister Mrs. Joan Charnock, as a home for their mother Lady Thompson, widow of Sir J. J. Thompson, Master of Trinity and discoverer of the electron. Mrs. Charnock's husband is credited with his brother, for the introduction of football in Russia and the founding of Moscow Dynamo football team. The house was purchased by the College in 1986.

When Mrs. Charnock sold her house to the college she stipulated that her planting of Cyclamen hederifolium beneath a large copper beech tree should not be lost. Today one can see this fine display flowering though a carpet of ivy, protected by a low rail. The remainder of her garden is enclosed by a beech hedge.

5.15 Cambridge, Sylvester Road, No. 1 OS439585

This house was built in 1933 and was bought by the College in 1982 from Professor D. W. Sciana, who was sometime Fellow of Trinity and Churchill. From 1983 he became Professor of Astrophysics at the International School of Advanced Studies at Trieste.

His garden was surrounded by beech hedges and contained mulberry trees. Today the garden has been planted with silver birches and a circular bed edged with Euonymus is filled with deutzias, tree paeonies and roses. A new Graduate Centre has been built in his garden, designed by David Thurlow in 1990.

5.16 Cambridge, Sylvester Road, No. 3 OS439585

Owned by Robinson College since October 1991, 'Sellenger', 3, Sylvester Road is a small detached house whose last occupant from 1970 was Lady Barlow. She was a cousin of Gwen Raverat and the last surviving grandchild of Charles Darwin. She was born in 1885 at 'The Orchard' on Huntingdon Road, now New Hall.

While living at 'Sellenger' Nora Barlow, an amateur botanist, added plants to this garden using the existing framework with its Yorkstone paving. Arisarum, nigella, *Acer griseum*, rhamnus, passiflora have all survived and inside the gateway a clump of *Aquilegia vulgaris 'Nora Barlow'* (one of her plant legacies) remains. Recently the College gardeners have uncovered a raised paved area and steps along the southern shrub border opposite the garden door from the house. A collection of conifers to the west of the house are rather crowded but sheltered by a beech hedge, behind which was a large vegetable garden now treated as a wild flower garden with tall grass.

5.17 Cambridge, Sylvester Road, No. 4 OS437584

In 1974 David Robinson purchased 4, Sylvester Road from Canon J.W. Bowker, a University Lecturer in Divinity. The house had been built in 1930 for Dr. Rook who was a leading dermatologist at Addenbrooke's Hospital. In 1978 the house became the Warden's Lodge.

Between his garden and No 3, Sylvester Road is an ancient hedgerow and ditch which have been retained by the College. The terrace along the south of the house is planted with conifers at regular intervals, below which a lawn still retains evidence of field ridge and furrow. To the east of the lawn is a rose pergola with ropes swags supported by concrete posts and chains. The herbaceous planting to the south of the lawn includes a rare Persian buckthorn.

5.18 Cambridge, Needham Research Institute   OS437584

The Needham Research Institute is dedicated to research into the history of science and technology, principally of China and the whole of East Asia. The Institute was designed in the 1980s by Lyster, Grill & Harding and is situated in the late Sir Michael Postan's garden at the corner of Sylvester Road and Herschel Road.

The Institute is reached by paths passing through shrubs and trees, including contorted willow, magnolia, winter flowering cherry and laurel, and a stone sculpture enclosed by a low box hedge. A gravel path passes around a mature leaning Indian Bean tree. To the south of the Institute, a verandah overlooks a crowded landscape through which the Bin Brook flows, having passed beneath the building. Here viburnums, mahonias and bamboos are sheltered behind the mature trees along Herschel Road. The relationship of the verandah above the garden with the brook further below is most pleasing.

5.19 Cambridge, Wilberforce Road, No. 1   OS436591

Dr. Harold Youngman, a general practitioner, settled in Cambridge in 1929 and later became honorary anaesthetist at Addenbrooke's Hospital. His hobby was gardening and his passion was fruit trees. His small half acre garden was meticulously planned with every plant clearly labelled. He became recognised for his contributions to the displays by the Fruit Group at the RHS Shows. His intensely planted garden filled every available square inch of ground, so much so that each square seemed to have two or three fruiting plants at different levels. Figs and vines intermingled with roses and even the boundary wire fence supported gooseberries trained as espaliers.

5.20 Cambridge, Wolfson Court, Clarkson Road   OS437588

In 1969 Girton College obtained a three acre site for students in Clarkson Road, thereby reducing the journey into Cambridge by the 'elastic mile'. The first plan for Wolfson Court was by David Roberts and Geoffrey Clarke and the accommodation was laid out around a series of courtyards using specimen trees to give a separate identity to each court. A fine pergola supports a wisteria, and the sorbus, mulberry, lime and maple have grown well and begin to dominate the various courts.

In 1992 two further courts were added by Bland, Brown and Cole. These are not enclosed and have lawns edged with foliage plants. Throughout the site plants are well established and compliment the designers' intentions.

TOUR 6
NORTH WEST CAMBRIDGE

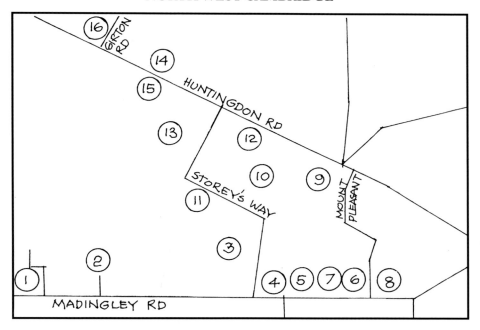

6.1 Cambridge, Conduit Head Road, 'De Stijl'   OS428595

Upon reflection, one wonders if Conduit Head Road was developed solely for pre-war houses designed in the International Modern Movement style. Here they were out of sight, out of the city and the local planners would not be flooded with complaints from the neighbours.

This Bauhaus-style single storey white house was built in the 1930s for Mrs. J. Whitt, a retired fashion journalist, who had spent most of her life in Victorian villas, cluttered with possessions. The full-length living room windows open onto a rectangular paved terrace with simple garden chairs. The lawns come to the edge of the house, where there is a simple edging filled with low growing plants. The lawn is mown up to the edge of the mixed tree and shrub boundary screen planting. The simplicity of the house is reflected by the minimalist simplicity of the garden.

6.2 Cambridge, The Observatory   OS433595

The first Observatory in Cambridge was built on top of the Great Gate at Trinity College in 1739. In 1821 a site of 6.5 acres was obtained where the meridian was not obstructed. The exact position of the building on the site had 'the tower of

Grantchester Church in the meridian to the south, which will determine the western end of the Observatory'.

The Observatory was designed by John Clamant Reed in 1822 in the Doric style with a portico and stars around the base of the drum of the dome. The grounds were laid out at great expense, and remained largely intact prior to the siting of the Royal Greenwich Observatory to the north of the Observatory in 1990.

The entrance from Madingley Road was through a gateway with cast-iron gates decorated with net and circle patterns, and stars hung from the granite piers. The long drive is planted with evergreen viburnums, hollies and yew, and leads to an oval lawn bordered by evergreen trees. To the east is the Director's garden with a fine Wellingtonia, surrounded by mature box, yew, phillyrea and other evergreen shrubs. The Observatory retains two palms either side of the portico and evergreen wall shrubs complement the Victorian atmosphere. Dotted in the grounds are buildings of various designs housing telescopes. A former staff house standing in its own private garden provides accommodation for visiting astronomers.

6.3 Cambridge, Churchill College   OS438592

Sir Winston Churchill was concerned about the lack of scientists and technologists produced by this country. In 1956 ideas for a memorial to him were considered, and by 1958 an outline scheme for a new Cambridge College was approved by the Senate. The requirements were for 540 students living in College, and 40 fellows with 20 flats for married members, a scale as yet not envisaged by the University. The site was a 42 acre sloping field adjoining the Madingley Road, a similar distance from the town centre as Fitzwilliam College but without the bicycle ride up Castle Hill. The assessors, who included Sir Basil Spence, Sir William Holford and Sir Leslie Martin, all eminent architects, made few stipulations but included a need for a suitable environment. Following a competition Richard Sheppard, Robson and Partners scheme was selected partly because of "the proposed campus, influenced by Butterfield's Keble, would penetrate the smaller residential units through continuous open cloisters".

The married quarters were built in 1959 and consist of a successful arrangement of flats on two storeys. The upper flats have two terraces and those on the ground floor have small gardens enclosed for privacy by high brick walls. The accommodation sits comfortably on the highest part of the site against the background of trees in the Observatory garden.

The next stage of building included accommodation for 236 students and the Master's Lodge, the central buildings – library, dining hall, common rooms and Porter's Lodge-which were occupied by 1965. Further cloisters have been built around the lecture hall and the tennis courts have been replaced by the Moller Centre.

The entrance to the college from Storey's Way is over rectangular pools. A covered way leads through the campus; the route provided is slightly above ground level so the green enclosed cloisters immediately become private to visitors, but few newly planted trees have grown above the three storey blocks. The perimeter planting scheme by Sheila Haywood is mainly lime, Oriental plane and silver willows, with several oaks within the grounds. Sir Winston Churchill planted a mulberry in 1959 which extends the range of specimen trees which have since been planted.

The planted bank along the Madingley Road frontage seems to have been left by the building contractor and has proved difficult to provide the dense privacy screen required. Perhaps it is needed as a backdrop to some of the pieces of modern sculpture the College displays. There are no vistas or avenues here such as those which enhance the display of sculpture at Anglesey Abbey.

6.4 Cambridge, Madingley Road, Pleasure Gardens   OS443592

By 1860 a site to the north of Madingley Road had been let out for 13 plots for professionals who resided in Cambridge and wished to create a larger garden, their city garden being cramped. Each plot was individually designed and included a summerhouse, ornamental glasshouses and a variety of walks amongst flower beds, trees and shrubberies. Most of the plots were 1/4 acre and water was laid on by St. John's College who owned the land, and collected an annual rent.

These gardens are similar to continental examples where larger gardens away from private residences were located outside the city walls or boundaries. One might compare these to beach hut ownership along the coastline.

By 1903 most of these pleasure gardens had been taken over for housing. One such example can be seen in 6.5.

6.5 Cambridge, Madingley Road, No. 12 'Elterholm'   OS443593

Elterholm, 12 Madingley Road, was designed in 1888 by Liverpool architects Grayson and Ould, for Mr. Thomas Thorneley, a fellow of Trinity Hall, who had married in 1885. The house lies well back from the road and is built over part of the Madingley Road pleasure gardens, and the adjacent Mount Pleasant Nursery. The house has exotic first floor half-timbered facades and is connected at the rear to accommodation over a garage.

The mature trees around the garden are Wellingtonias, cedars and pines to the west and oaks and a grove of mature beeches to the east. The clue that the present garden has been adapted from an earlier pleasure garden and the nursery is the mature yew and the old apple tree festooned with mistletoe on the south lawn. The house is covered with rampant vines and ivies.

Mr. Thorneley subsequently built No 10 Madingley Road which is situated closer to the road. This property was let to Helen Jonas in 1904. During his negotiations with the college, Mr. Thorneley mentions the gardens and being willing to compensate the tenants. Both properties are now student accommodation and the grounds are maintained by the St. John's College.

6.6 Cambridge, Lucy Cavendish College   OS444592

Lucy Cavendish was Britain's first college for mature women, and is located along Lady Margaret Road. It comprises a series of late C19th detached houses, running east to west (Torrisdale, Barrmore and Strathaird) originally built for married fellows. After acquiring these three houses in 1970 the college has joined the gardens together to form a large space, thickly wooded giving the impression of a garden around a country house in Scotland.

New college buildings are beginning to fill this space, but tucked away in the north-west corner of the grounds is a small Anglo-Saxon herb garden arranged by Dr. Jane Renfrew and Ms Debby Banham in1987 following their detailed research. The Anglo-Saxon texts referred to are Aelfric's '*Colloquy*' (Nominum herbarum) of AD 995 and Bald's '*Leechbook*' (a medical textbook) of AD 900-950. Today the garden contains 60 different species and is steadily increasing in numbers.

6.7 Cambridge, Madingley Road, No. 6   OS442592

Balliol Croft, 6 Madingley Road, was designed by J.J. Stevenson in 1886 for Professor Alfred Marshall, 'The Father of British Economics'. For several years it was the only house along Madingley Road and the site was chosen chiefly for its mature trees. With his professorship at Cambridge came £700 a year. His wife Mary Paley Marshall recorded in her book '*What I Remember*' that they "felt like rolling in wealth". The house had a study on the first floor and a balcony overlooking the garden.

Later a large revolving summer-house, 'the ark' was devised with special cogs and wheels by which it could be easily turned from inside. Marshall loved the lawn and trees, cared little for flowers, but he took a special interest in the vegetable garden. He wrote to his wife once: "I have always held that a kitchen garden at its best is more picturesque than a flower garden at its best. There is more depth and serenity and unconsciousness".

Today this secluded garden remains very much as it was when the house was built. Enclosed by dense tree planting the vegetable plot and fruit trees are still maintained. Climbers scramble up to the balcony and the lawn falls away from a gravel path to small island shrub beds. The house and garden now form part of Lucy Cavendish College.

6.8 Cambridge, Westminster College   OS444590

Originally the site consisted of a small nursery and a number of allotments which were let to St. John's College staff.

Westminster College, now a small United Reformed Church Theological College, stands at the north end of Queens' Road and was designed by H.T. Hare in 1899. He enclosed the site with high brick walls, broken at the entrance by impressive pillars, gates and railings. On the left hand pillar is a date of 1844 marking the foundation of the Presbyterian Church in London. In the wrought ironwork spanning the gateway is the motto of Scottish Presbyterianism. The forecourt has an obelisk which once supported ornamental lights which have now disappeared.

The formal pairs of yew hedges on either side of the entrance courtyard have now been replaced by a simpler planting. The wide grassed terrace is edged by shrub borders and the sundial stands in the centre path. To the west of the College the ground rises and is terraced towards The Bounds. Around this house are large specimens of copper beech, horse chestnuts, golden yews and holm oak which possibly were once within the nursery site.

6.9 Cambridge, New Hall College   OS443595

New Hall is Cambridge's third college for women founded in 1954 which now has new premises along Huntingdon Road designed by Chamberlin, Powell and Bonn in 1962

The site chosen was The Orchard, erected by George Darwin's youngest brother Horace in 1882. Once the home of Nora Barlow, Charles Darwin's last surviving grandchild, who with her sister Ruth gave the house and garden for the site of New Hall. Nora Barlow selected a lime-green and pink pom-pom aguilegia which is named after her (see 5.16). The garden around The Orchard was extensive. To the south was a flight of steps from the terrace with flower beds either side down to a large sunken lawn surrounded by clumps of shrubs and trees growing along a steep bank. In the centre of the lawn was a large stone vase.

Today the white domed hall and the library enclose Fountain Court which is at a level below the main access corridor. Here is a water landscape of canals, reflecting pools, and a central fountain. The planting is restrained; some water loving sedges are appropriate but the conifers seem intrusive.

Orchard Court is completely grassed. No paths cross the lawns which run to the walls of the buildings, now edged with shrubs. The yews, beech and sycamore are from the previous garden. In the Fellows' Garden an octagonal timber summerhouse, originally from The Grove garden next door, is shaded beneath yews and specimen trees. Near the dining hall is the stone urn from the Barlow's garden.

To the west, the college owns one half of the stables originally standing in the The Grove garden. The sundial on the stables has recently been repainted. Also in the grounds is the garden around No 69 Storeys Way, which has a vista from its south door across a croquet lawn surrounded by yew topiary and mixed herbaceous planting with shrubs. From the lawn a narrow path edged with viburnums leads down towards a semi-circle of clipped yew. Paths then diverge into an orchard where the trees are covered with mistletoe.

6.10 Cambridge, Fitzwilliam College   OS440596

Fitzwilliam College started as Fitzwilliam House in 1889, opposite the Fitzwilliam Museum along Trumpington Street. In 1958 the College moved to a new site along the Huntingdon Road, into accommodation designed by Denys Lasdun. The layout is one of a spiral commencing at the main entrance off Storey's Way, giving a spatial quality to the layout. This reaches its climax at the Chapel with fine views through the east window towards The Grove, a private house once owned by the Darwin family.

The Grove is a late Georgian house and was bought by Mrs. Charles Darwin after her husband's death in 1882. She described the garden as "being the very place for an old person, such nooks and corners for shelter and seats". Her daughter Henrietta added "It had old walls and spreading wych-elms which gave it charm and individuality".

Lasdun's Hall complex and north range no longer dominate the site, now that the land around The Grove is included within the college grounds. In 1989 Andrew Peters was asked to prepare plans to link the garden around The Grove to the rest of the College. This was achieved by retaining the Victorian garden around the house rather than letting lawns flow up to the walls. To the north are wide mixed borders filled with mediterranean plants, suitable for growing within the three storey walls of the court. Here purple sages, euphorbias, bergenias and olearias are thriving well.

The range to the west of the hall was re-landscaped in 1984, with shrubs and climbers in planters. The new Wilson Building stands within mature trees with views through to The Grove. Sadly, The Grove's stables and rear glasshouse are divided in half by a fence, and shared with New Hall. However a mature plane tree is now the focus of the garden and acts as a splendid screen when seen through the Chapel window.

6.11 Cambridge, Storey's Way, No. 48   OS435596

Baillie Scott designed the Roberts House in 1911. Subsequently he was commissioned to design a further four houses in Storey's Way

The garden to the street is bounded by a picket fence giving access to a central path which passes between topiary Irish yews. Either side, more topiary English yew hide the service access to the kitchen and to the east what was originally the bicycle room. To the south there were trellises over the bay windows supporting roses, and a pergola which has now been restored and then a "variety of effects full of mystery, surprises, and light and shade". Although the original layout of the garden remains, it has been recently replanted. The path passes through a formal square contained by yew hedges and surrounded by flower beds, then into a relaxed wilder area filled with spring bulbs and flowering shrubs leading to the shade of a vinery. The functional requirements for growing vegetables and fruit for the family are then accommodated and the garden path ends in a symmetrically planted orchard.

6.12 Cambridge, Huntingdon Road, 'Wychfield'   OS439596

Wychfield (named after the magnificent Wych-elm which grew near the house) was built in 1883-4 by Frank Darwin, University Reader in Botany at the turn of the century. Later when John Chivers, JP, lived here the grounds were used for garden parties for local Village Preacher's Association whose accounts recall the "beautiful gardens where croquet, lawn tennis and bowls were played". Their photographs show elegant ladies amongst numerous beds of standard roses.

Today the garden is incorporated within student accommodation which is owned by Trinity Hall. At the Huntingdon Road entrance, formerly a stable block, there is a green oasis leading to the centrepiece, a sunken garden with variegated foliage plants around a lawn enclosed by a yew hedge. A woodland walk has been established under mature trees between new buildings. In spring there is a circular bed of *Anemone blanda* flowering beneath shrubs roses. All this was executed in 1993 with skill by the garden designer, Andrew Peters. A further area is set aside for establishing bedding plants for the gardens at Wychfield and the College.

6.13 Cambridge, St. Giles Cemetery   OS435597

In 1856 this new cemetery was established under the name of St. Giles with St. Peter's cemetery, and is known today as Ascension Burial Ground.

The cemetery is reached along a narrow lane bordered with trees to the south of the Huntingdon Road. This ecumenical burial ground contains the graves of many famous Cambridge residents who lived in the parish: The Darwins and the philosophers Wittgenstein and G. E. Moore. The land around the Chapel of All Souls is divided into five plots which in total contain 1500 graves and memorials. The cemetery is bounded by conifers and contains Irish and English yews, Scots pines and various cypresses. In 1856 the cemetery was placed amongst open fields and today it is hidden behind detached houses and their large gardens.

6.14 Cambridge, National Institute of Agricultural Botany   OS433604

In 1921 King George V and Queen Mary opened the Institute which consisted of an open ended court facing Huntingdon Road. Later in the 1960s more buildings were planned along Howes Place.

Behind the boundary hawthorn hedge is a formal arrangement of pleached lime trees, enclosing two lawns either side of the small path which leads to the oval gravel entrance court. Beech hedges complement this simple design. The pleached limes form further avenues either side of the Institute. That along Howes Place has a double avenue set on narrow grass verges. The arrangement is enhanced by one Judas tree on a lawn, and carefully chosen low shrubs at the base of the walls. Would that more organisations exercised such restraint in their planting.

6.15 Cambridge, Huntingdon Road, No. 197   OS433603

In 1938 Dr. Hilary Taylor, Fellow of Clare College, built a detached residence in the Neo-Georgian style and laid out a garden on the edge of the glacial moraine, which marks the limit of the Gipping Glaciation. This well drained site is divided by gravel and heavy yellow clay. Taylor asked his colleague Professor Nevill Willmer, also a Fellow of Clare, to advise on the layout of the garden on a flat field.

Willmer's concept of garden design had been illustrated in Clare Fellows' garden; that of surprise and colour harmony. In Taylor's garden he set about planning a series of rooms at different levels. Immediately to the south of the house is a lawn bounded by raised semi-circular flower beds, planted to display dahlias and backed by yew hedges. These screen but give access to a sunken rose garden, also enclosed by tall beech hedges. The main vista is terminated by topiary yew.

His second principle of colour harmony is expressed by gradations of colour in both flower gardens. The dahlia blooms shade from pinks at either ends through reds to bronze and yellow in the centre. The garden has been well maintained without losing Willmer's original design intentions.

6.16 Girton College   OS425610

No other Cambridge College can compare with Girton's grounds of 46 acres. The main buildings were designed by Alfred Waterhouse, and other members of his family, and stand back secluded from the Huntingdon Road by mature trees along the boundary. In 1873, a 16 acre site belonging to John Dennis was obtained and slowly the new planting began to provide privacy and to keep out the cold east winds. The entrance lodge was built and Orchard Drive was laid out to the north of Emily Davies Court. Tennis courts were laid out, a Home Garden for vegetables was located in the eastern corner and the Honeysuckle Walk was in place by 1884. Miss Davies' co-founder was Barbara Leigh Smith Bodichon who had met Gertrude Jekyll in 1872 while on holiday in Switzerland.

In 1885 Elizabeth Walsh became Mistress of the College and was responsible for establishing the Pond, the Yew Walk, the Home Garden, The Fellows' Garden and the Old Orchard. In 1886 a further 17 acres had been acquired by the College and the Home garden continued to produce vegetables for the College for the next sixty years.

In 1921 Jane Swindale was appointed as the first Garden Steward to oversee seven gardeners and 46 acres. The same year she wrote to Gertrude Jekyll thanking her for her planting plans for Cloister Court with drifts of silvers, greys, blues and soft pinks. In 1923 another design by Jekyll was presented for Emily Davies Court using drifts of stachys, bergenia, paeonies and mallows. In 1933 Chrystabel Proctor took over the garden and concentrated on the 14 acres of vegetables and fruit, producing gargantuan quantities of produce and with equal energy improved the garden so that by 1940 it had become one of the sights of Cambridge.

After the Second World War the vegetables slowly disappeared, flowering shrubs replaced herbaceous borders and specimen trees were planted under the care of William Stringer, the head gardener. He improved the apple collection in the Orchard, and the College won awards at the Royal Horticultural Society's Late Fruit Shows in London between 1960 and 1980.

In 1992 Penelope Hobhouse, an Old Girtonian, designed a green theatre for the Fellows' Garden which used yews for the theatre wings against a backdrop of trees. The auditorium is a semi-circular lawn edged with shrubs and scented flowers for summer performances.

TOUR 7
NORTH EAST CAMBRIDGE

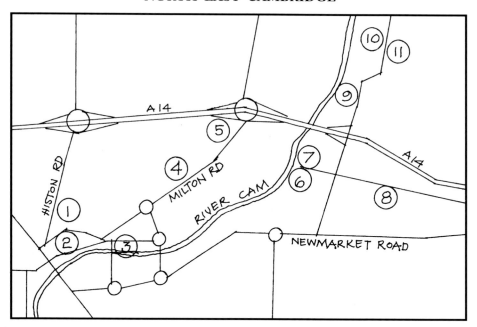

7.1 Cambridge, Histon Road Cemetery   OS444596

John Claudius Loudon laid out the Histon Road Cemetery in 1842. The lodge and chapel were designed by his favourite architect, E. B. Lamb. Lamb had intended an Italianate chapel, but in the end it had to be Gothic in a white brick.

The design of the cemetery is recorded at length in *'The Gardener's Magazine'* 1843 where Loudon was writing about the principles of Landscape Gardening applied to Public Cemeteries. "For £600 the grounds were to be enclosed by a holly hedge planted on the top of a broad bank of soil. The trees to be planted should occupy as little room as possible i.e. cypresses because they were narrow and were connected with places of internment by classical association. Other trees should be evergreens of dark shades of green as being more solemn than light shades of that colour. That no flowers, flowering shrubs or deciduous trees be planted. Trees were to be planted along the walks at regular intervals, Taurian pines because that species has a dark and solemn air. Cedars of Lebanon and Irish yews were also permitted."

The 2,120 hollies were obtained for £10 12s 0d, the 14 Cedars of Lebanon in pots cost 2s 6d each and the 76 Irish yews amounted to £5 14s 0d.

Today the original planned landscape has been lost mainly because of the removal of the Mortuary Chapel from its central location.

7.2 Cambridge, Alexandra Gardens   OS447595

Alexandra Gardens lie to the north-east of Castle Hill and were created when the Victorian Brickworks were closed down in 1887. In 1891 and 1892 an epidemic of diphtheria in the New Chesterton area held up the purchase of land, but in 1904 Chesterton Rural District Council bought the land for £425 and it was agreed this land in Carlyle Road should be laid out as a public recreation ground.

In 1905, 17 new trees replaced dead trees along the road frontage, and new boundary fences were erected around the area of the brickfields. The site was levelled, turfed, then new plane trees and Italian poplars planted.

The grounds were formally opened in April 1907, following the approval of regulations for playing bowls and lawn tennis in the recreation ground.

The site slopes towards the river and, except for the replacement of tennis courts with children's play equipment, the layout has remained unchanged. An avenue of lime trees along the northern boundary encloses the grounds and the plane trees now mature, serve to remind the visitor of the garden's age.

7.3 Cambridge, Chesterton Road, No. 80   OS455595

80 Chesterton Road was not developed until after 1887. In 1891 Frederick Deene Prior, a brewer, built his house and stayed until 1898 when a succession of Church missionaries and rectors occupied the premises up to the end of the First World War.

In 1916 the Rev. Charles Macan Rice, Chaplain of King's College, was resident and received from Miss Gertrude Jekyll planting plans for the rear garden to the south of the property. These plans were only recently discovered when a parcel of documents was handed to the Surrey Record Office. The detailed plans indicate a central path with narrow lawn to one side and wide herbaceous borders within the wide plot. The borders were to be planted with roses, spireas and lupins along the walls and santolinas, dicentras, pinks and stachys along the front edges. The Rev. Rice has written on his plan "where someday we shall have an arbour for garden seat as in your former plan".

The garden has been shortened by an Anderson shelter and the provision for a garage and parking spaces. A mature silver birch next door provides extensive shelter over the garden.

7.5 Cambridge, Stott Gardens, No. 21   OS463607

Here amongst the housing developments of north Cambridge is a small oriental water garden recently designed by the owner in 1998 for minimal maintenance. The garden has a central crescent shaped pond surrounded by gravel and a series of stepping stones arranged in a circle. Apart from a clump of grasses in one corner and a waterlily on the pond no other plants are used. The design succeeds because of the harmonious relationship of the pond to the perimeter fences and is restful to look at from the house. Ornamental cranes and a stone lantern are placed to encourage the eye to focus on the garden's simplicity.

7.6 Cambridge, Science Park   OS467618

Between 1970 and 1980 Trinity College developed a site, which they had owned since 1443, along the Northern Cambridge By-Pass to the west of the A10, devoted to small industries based on hi-tech electronic and industrial research within the university.

In the centre of the site is a lake with lawns and trees creating a park-like setting. Although the individual sites have access to a central ring road, each office is designed without regard to its neighbour, similar to American industrial park layouts but with English plot divisions. Each building stands in its own landscaped space but there is no sense of being in a large parkland setting as car parking layouts tend to predominate. Those buildings located on the outer side of the ring road are unable to enjoy views of the central landscape.

7.7 Fen Ditton Hall   OS483603

Fen Ditton Hall was built c.1630 in red brick by Thomas Willys with Dutch gables. It overlooked a small park to the south which has now lost its central avenue and boundary planting.

Originally the garden lay to the south-east of the hall with a walled orchard to the north and further walled enclosures to the east. Today the garden extends into the orchard, where the remaining area is planted with pleached limes relating to a restored medieval timber warehouse which is covered with climbing roses. The enclosures to the east are now a grass field, and a housing plot.

7.8 Fen Ditton, The Old Stables   OS083604

In 1973 the present owners converted the C16th stables which originally belonged to the adjacent Rectory, and laid out a garden on the site of the Rectory's formal kitchen garden. With innovative skill the garden has been developed with herbaceous borders around the perimeter and clumps of shrubs and trees in the centre of the lawn. The garden contains rare plants which according to the reference books should never grow on chalk (the garden lies at the west end of Fleam Dyke). There is a seaside garden with gravel dunes and grasses, a grotto, a neat vegetable garden with a display of garden tools and a shuttlecock birdscarer. To the west in the adjoining paddock are two fine specimen Black Poplars.

7.9 Fen Ditton, Hardwicke House   OS497597

Situated on an exposed site to the east of the village, this two acre plantsman's garden is protected by high formal hedges from the cold east winds.

The garden has been developed during the last 30 years, and is divided into four areas each connected by a narrow path which runs parallel to the south of the house. An enclosed garden grows abutilons and plants available in this country before 1650; formal herbaceous borders edged with box; a rose garden underplanted with cranesbills with Turkish plants scrambling over timber structures and silver birch cross avenues underplanted with bulbs in long grass. Plants are tightly planted and spill over the paths. The garden contains the National Collection of Aquilegias.

7.10 Horningsea, Abbots Way, No. 15   OS492624

A plantswoman's garden of 1 acre, to the west of the village, on the flood bank of the River Cam, which overlooks the willow-lined river and its adjoining water meadows. Along the flood bank in the garden is a spring and natural pond which are both planted with a large range of unusual plants. The garden has recently been extended along the edge of the water meadow and a long timber pergola supports an extensive range of clematis. To either side of the path beneath the pergola are borders well planted: a collection of Solomon seal species are worthy of inspection. The garden grows a wide range of trees suitable for the smaller garden.

7.11 Horningsea, The Lodge   OS498636

The Lodge, originally thatched, is shown on the Enclosure Map of 1810, and was enlarged in 1840 by the addition of two rooms.

Before the turn of the century, the grounds around the Lodge comprised a lawn to the south edged with conifers and a central path leading to the first of three adjacent orchards. The present owners have established a specialist plant nursery within the grounds. They have developed the three acre garden without destroying the mature existing plantings of willow and old native trees. A large pond is planted with an extensive range of water-loving plants suitable for fenland gardens. The island beds demonstrate the need for Cambridgeshire gardeners to grow drought resistant plants in an area of low rainfall.

7.12 Horningsea, Eye Hall   OS499636

Eye Hall consists of a house and farm buildings. The north range was built in the C16th and the south wing added in the early C19th.

The sale particulars of 1885 mention pleasure grounds, an extensive productive kitchen garden with greenhouse and orchard. There still exist remnants of enclosed parkland probably of an early C19th date, with a ha-ha and a small lake. The Victorian kitchen garden can be recognised today by its perimeter yew hedge. There is a short avenue of chestnut trees lining the drive to the hall.

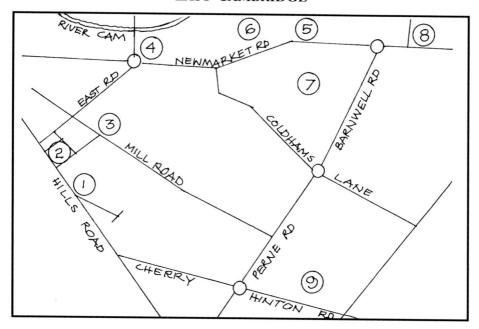

8.1 Cambridge, Highsett

OS458574

In 1957 Eric Lyons proposed a 15-storey block of bachelor flats along Hills Road which was accepted by the local planning authority but was not erected, hence the name 'Highsett'. The site chosen was that of Eastbourn Villa in a Victorian 'Dell' garden. To the rear of the house the garden opens out onto a large lawn, a pool and island with grottoes. These are set amongst mature trees enclosed by a grassy bank, with a walk at high level with bridges crossing paths beneath. The garden continued with shady walks through tree lined paths separating large lawns, which stretched almost to Tenison Avenue.

In 1958, Stage 1 comprised a three-storey courtyard with a simple lawn and raised pond. Stages 2 and 3 were completed by 1964 and provided terraced housing arranged around two sides of the exotic garden which had been saved by the 1st Stage. Everywhere there is interesting planting of shrubs, trees and wall climbers surrounding small lawns between the terraces. The car parking is divided by beech hedges and privacy to terraces is achieved with low hedges suggesting rear gardens.

The landscape planting was designed by Ivor Cunningham. The central exotic 'Dell' garden is still to be admired with ivy covered banks under the shade of mature beeches, limes and acacias. Perhaps the two evergreen oaks have now grown too close to the courtyard housing.

8.2 Cambridge, Harvey Road, No. 6   OS456577

In 1882 large semi-detached houses were built along Harvey Road by the Victorian architect R.R. Rowe. These houses became the homes to which newly married dons aspired to bring their wives when they were first allowed to marry. Among the first of these academic wives to reside in 6 Harvey Road was Florence Ada Keynes, wife of John Neville Keynes and mother of John Maynard Keynes.

The rear garden of 6 Harvey Road was extended by the Keynes family who gradually acquired a strip of land which lay between their garden and the rear villa gardens along St. Paul's Road. The OS map of 1888 shows this strip of land extending between other properties with access from No. 6 and had a path with several trees planted along its boundary. Today this extra strip of garden has been reduced by garages and temporary school buildings, but the fruit trees still remain and the acanthus and daylilies by the paths soften the boundary fences. A number of stone fragments were found in the garden which were collected by Mrs. Keynes from the Augustinian Priory at Barnwell.

8.3 Cambridge, Mill Road Cemetery   OS4463582

Once the home of the University Cricket Ground, this Cemetery is approached along an avenue of pleached lime trees from Mill Road. In 1844 the playing field of 9 acres was purchased by the Cambridge Parish Burial Ground Committee for £2,146 from the estate of the Rev. R J Geldart to provide additional burial grounds for 13 parishes in the city. Each parish was allotted a portion of land and the boundaries marked by stones, some of which are still visible, set into the perimeter wall.

The cemetery was consecrated by the Bishop of Ely in November 1848. In 1858 a chapel designed by Sir George Gilbert Scott was completed in the centre of the cemetery, but was demolished in 1954 due to its unsafe condition. Trees planted in 1850 like the wide spreading pine and the yews have reached their maturity. Today many seedlings of ash, sycamore and elderberry have been removed which would have destroyed the Victorian planting.

In 1996 Cambridge City Council Landscape Design Group produced a report for the future of the cemetery. It had become run down due to shortage of resources, subsidence and vandalism. Using the University of York Cemetery Research Group's evaluation methodology, their report used criteria "to examine the landscape, ecological, historical, leisure and educational value, and the sensitivity in relation to visits by the bereaved to address these problems and conflicts and to look for opportunities to utilise the cemetery for the local people in a way which safeguards its essential character". The City Council's proposals are eagerly awaited.

Robert Sayle, d. 1883, whose departmental store is in St. Andrew's Street, Cambridge, is buried along the western boundary beyond the custodian's lodge, now a private residence. Would that a C21st business man, similar to Mr. Sayle, could endow the cemetery with funds to save it.

8.4 Cambridge, Abbey House   OS461589

Abbey House was built in the late C16th and C17th to the south-west of the site of Barnwell Priory which had been dissolved in 1550. The garden boundary wall running to the north-east is probably part of the precinct wall of the priory. In 1922 Arthur Askam, son of a Cambridge landlord, kept the garden in a good condition, and held country dancing for children on the lawns. The drive, originally from Newmarket Road, has been sold and the entrance is now via Abbey Road. Towards the end of his life Askam let the grass grow tall and kept goats to maintain the lawns. In the garden are numerous wrought stones, presumably from the Priory. They include, incorporated in two rustic arches, parts of C12th mouldings and a C13th stone base used as a capital. Elsewhere various moulded dressings are built into the wall and flanking the entrance gateway are two medieval carved heads. Today there are drifts of spring bulbs beneath the trees, which frame views of the Church of St. Andrew the Less, and the Cellarer's Chequer which is all that remains of the Priory.

8.5 Cambridge, Station House, Barnwell Junction   OS472596

Prior to Beeching axing the Mildenhall branch line, Barnwell Junction had its Station Master who tended the platform gardens and maintained the orchard to the north. The branch line was kept open for shunting of oil for central heating requirements, and the garden either side of the track is now gated. Keeping all the existing station buildings, the booking office, sack store, half-timbered waiting room and the platforms, the present owners have created a garden on both sides of the track since the mid 1950s. Only the plate layer's cabin has been removed. To the west of the track is a terraced garden with conifers and herbaceous plants backed by a line of silver birch trees. Along the main platform a new brick pergola has been built and a timber pergola, covered with hops and clematis, leads to a formal herb garden with raised beds. To the north of the station is the remains of an orchard which is now the resting place of Montana, a Pulman carriage built in 1923, which was behind the Golden Arrow on its regular journeys to France.

8.6 Cambridge, Stourbridge Common   OS470598

Sterebriggefeld and Sterebriggegren appear on a field map of Cambridge dated c.1300. Stourbridge Common's claim to fame is Stourbridge Fair which began in 1211, grew to be the largest medieval fair in Europe and lasted until it was abolished by the Secretary of State in 1934.

King John granted a charter to the town's leper hospital to hold a market on a large piece of common land on the south side of the the river, where navigable access for heavy goods was possible. Regular trading and entertaining fairs were held and traders brought shellfish, iron, timber and livestock by barges. There were puppet shows, rope dancers, wrestling and a theatre in 1797. The fair ran for three weeks always in August and September after the harvest.

Daniel Defoe wrote about the fair in 1728, describing the large cornfield which extended for about half a mile. He lists goods bought and sold in bulk – hops and wool (£100,000 worth in one year); wholesalers transacting business in their pocket books; and other traders: goldsmiths, milliners, mercers, pewterers, and ironmongers were sited amongst brandy shops, taverns and eating houses all in tents or booths. This great event was followed by an important horse fair.

Florence Keynes, as Mayor of Cambridge, officiated at its final year. She recalled "The first proclamation was made on Barnwell Bridge to the bewilderment of motorists from Newmarket who were held up by the Police. The second took place on the common in the presence of a couple of women with babies in their arms, and a puzzled youth in charge of an ice-cream barrow bearing the legend 'Stop me and Buy one'. This was the end".

Today the common is used for grazing horses and cattle.

8.7 Cambridge, Coldham's Common   OS475585

Coldham's Green is shown on the 1300 Field Map of Cambridge and was designated a Green Common by 1700. Between 1665-6 outbreaks of plague afflicted the local inhabitants. In the plague's final year Parliament gave permission to use Coldham's Common for permanent pest houses to isolate victims. As the need had passed, these dwellings were never built and in 1703, temporary ones were removed.

The common covers 98 acres and is bounded by Coldham's Brook. Its Gatehouse remains today along Coldham's Lane. In the C19th the Common was divided by a rifle range. But with the coming of the Cambridge to Newmarket railway line across the Common,the rifle range was relocated to the north but retained its 800 yard range from the butts and made use of a small pavilion. A further miniature rifle range was established to the south of the railway line. By 1944 Stourbridge Grove was developed for housing within an old field boundary along the southern boundary of the Common.

22 acres are set aside for sport, which include 13 football pitches and a floodlit sports area. In March 1972 the common was the venue for the 59th International Cross Country Championships. A children's play area has been located along the Coldhams Lane frontage which often appears to be flooded after heavy rain. Recently an open air Bathing Pool along the northern boundary has been improved by making it an all-year round facility and is now the Abbey Swimming Pool .

8.8 Cambridge, Newmarket Road Cemetery   OS483594

This cemetery to the east of the city was laid out in 1905 and now is owned by the City Council. The grid layout of paths was later extended eastwards over allotment gardens. In the centre of the cemetery is the site of a Special Services Plot, established by the Council in 1940, where 47 men and women had been buried. In 1942 the Air Ministry suggested this plot might be extended for the burials of Royal Air Force, Dominions and Allied Forces personnel. The Council agreed and 731 airmen were buried together with three members of the Women's Auxiliary Air Force.

This cemetery is enclosed by clipped yew hedging and is planted within its boundary with several trees. The layout is planned on similar lines to War Grave cemeteries throughout the World. A white pavilion stands at the east boundary between two silver birches looking towards a Lutyens Stone of dedication, raised on three stone steps, which was dedicated in 1951. Around this stone are rows of headstones (replacing the wooden crosses erected during the War) with narrow beds growing small herbaceous plants. The maintenance of the plots is undertaken by the Imperial War Graves Commission

8.9 Cherry Hinton Hall   OS482565

Cherry Hinton Hall was built in 1834 for John Okes, a surgeon at Addenbrooke's Hospital. The Hall stood in a 35 acre park, and was surrounded by lawns, flower parterres, shrubberies and fernery, kitchen garden and two orchards. The sale particulars of 1870 list a fine collection of trees; Ailanthus, walnut, maple, elm, ash, pine and birch. The Hall remained in private ownership until 1937 when the City Council acquired it from Trinity Hall. The park was remodelled in 1963, much needed tree surgery carried out, and a wild fowl collection introduced. In 1983 a parterre garden was laid out to the south of the Hall, the lake improved and children's play facilities provided. The kitchen garden has become a Plant Propagation Centre providing over 200,000 seasonal bedding plants for the city and other councils. The gardens contain the National Collection of Hardy Geranium and Bergenia cultivars. Each year the Cambridge Folk Festival is held in the grounds and attracts 10,000 fans from all over the world.

TOUR 9
SOUTH CAMBRIDGE

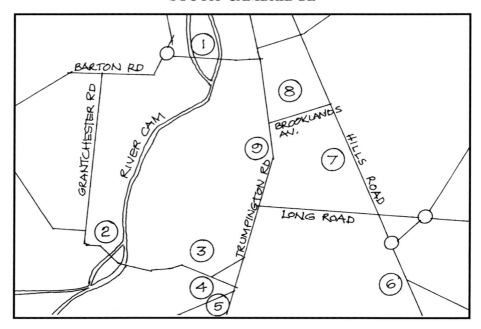

9.1 Cambridge, Coe Fen/Sheep's Green   OS446578

These are both low-lying meadows prone to flooding by the River Cam, which prevented the expansion of Cambridge in medieval times. They are as the name Sheep's Green suggests grazing lands. The grazing is controlled by an officer, still known as The Pinder, who lets the land between April and October. In 1815 proposals to enclose Coe Fen failed and in the mid 1800s proposals to bring the new railway line to Cambridge across these lands also failed.

By 1877 the land consisted of some 35 acres and although a new road and bridge was proposed to connect Trumpington Road to Newnham in 1912, the site has hardly changed in size for over 100 years.

During the late C19th part of the river was used by men and boys for nude bathing. This stretch of the Cam was preferred because of the levels of sewage deposited into the river at Magdalene Bridge and Barnwell Pool. Women passing were expected to lower their parasols over their eyes.

This common land originally formed part of a continuous belt around Cambridge. By maintaining the Commons system the city has been enhanced, allowing the countryside to come into the centre of Cambridge, whilst Newnham expanded to the west. The poplars and willows complement the rural scene of animals grazing in damp meadows.

9.2 Grantchester, The Old Vicarage   OS435553

There has been a Vicarage on this site since 1380. The present building was built 300 years ago and incorporated parts of an earlier house. Since 1780 the house has no longer been used as a Vicarage.

In 1850 Samuel Page Widnall, the son of a successful Grantchester nurseryman and florist, acquired the property and ornamented his garden in the Gothic manner. His sundial in the shape of an open book, and the island he created in the River Cam at the end of the garden still remain. A Swiss cottage, a bathing house and a conservatory have disappeared; a pigeon-cote still stood in Brooke's time, while the fountain lost its ornamentation in the 1920s. His most striking creation was a 'sham ruin' which was built of clunch in the style of a medieval oratory.

Rupert Brooke rented three rooms of the house in 1910 and wrote to his friends that "the garden is the great glory, there is a soft lawn with a sun dial and tangled antique flowers abundantly: and a sham ruin . . . and no drains".

After Brooke's death his mother bought the house in 1916 and as a memorial to her son, gave it to Dudley Ward his great friend and grandfather of the present owner. Her wish was that the garden be kept much as it was in her son's time. During the 1920s and 1930s Ward entertained Maynard Keynes, the Strachey family, the Oliviers and the Cornfords in the garden.

In 1979 the house was bought by Lord and Lady Archer who have carefully maintained the garden with advice from Professor Willmer. Weeping willows have been planted near the Ruin and a small pond with an island has been created to the north of the lawn.

9.3 Trumpington, Anstey Hall   OS444549

Anstey Hall is a late C17th house built for Anthony Thompson, which was doubled in size in 1909.

In 1695 Thompson laid out a large garden to the south, the surrounding brick walls partly surviving until 1980. To the south were pleasure grounds overlooking a meadow and pasture land. Adjoining the field was an orchard and two productive gardens planted with trained and standard fruit trees. Nearby was a well stocked dovecotee. Following the additions to the property, the south garden was simply laid out with lawns edged with low retaining walls and paths around a small circular pond; the meadow became a small park with specimen trees. In 1837 the sale particulars described the northern approach via a circular avenue of elms interspersed with shrubbery and enclosed by a lofty wall. In 1941 the Hall was requisitioned by the Government and is now no longer a private residence.

9.4 Trumpington Hall OS443553

In 1675 Sir Francis Pemberton, Lord Chief Justice of England, bought the estate and a Tudor mansion from the Pytcher family. The Hall was built in 1710.

The Hall is approached from the east by a long avenue, via a lodge dominated by a fine *Phillyrea latifolia,* and through extensive parkland established in the 1820s, when the hall was repaired. The drive turns and enters a large segmental-ended forecourt with wrought-iron gates flanked by tall brick piers supporting urns. To the north are stables, behind which is a large kitchen garden enclosed by walls, some of which are crinkle-crankle built before 1830. To the west are views across parkland to Grantchester Meadows. Nearer the hall are formal rose beds and at the end of the lawns are three fish ponds which have been formally canalised. To the north are uninterrupted views of Cambridge's college skyline.

9.5 Trumpington, Allen Court OS446546

Along the Hauxton Road, just beyond the cemetery, are 6 white-washed bungalows for retired clergy designed by Lister and Grillet. They are grouped around a paved court and connected by concrete blockwalls, also white-washed, with square openings of irregular Mexican pattern. Each residence has a small garden shielded from view by its white wall. In the centre of the court is a single Judas tree which is covered in spring with pink flowers along the branches, before the leaves appear. This is pruned to grow as high as the roofs of the bungalows.

9.6 Cambridge, The Bell School of Languages OS469551

In September 1955 The Bell School of Languages was opened by Lord Tedder, Chancellor of the University. Summer students had asked the Board of Extra-Mural Studies why the University did not teach English to foreign students. F.E. Bell was the prime mover to fill this gap although Davies's School of English was established in Cambridge 2 years earlier.

The garden around the school covered about 25 acres with south facing views across fields to the Gog Magog Hills. Originally 6 acres were set aside for establishing plants for the garden, and greenhouses were built for growing foliage plants for indoor use in the school buildings. There are large areas of naturalised bulbs in the spring. The garden contains mature trees and a profusion of shrubs for foliage colour. The herbaceous borders and roses add to the effect of a small country house standing in a small park.

9.7 Cambridge, Homerton College OS462562

The first range of buildings erected in 1876 by Giles & Gough were for Cavendish College. Homerton College moved in from London in 1894 and today is a training college for teachers. Situated along Hills Road, the college stands in 25 acres of grounds behind mature trees, including cut-leaved beech. This original planting then continues into the site with purple beech, phillyrea and catalpa. The grandiose range of buildings overlook a large lawn enclosed by a row of smaller trees and shrubs with a path through long grass. Along the south side of the buildings is a terrace with two recesses, one planted in memory of a disabled student and the other a gardener. Joan Salter, an enthusiastic head gardener, ran an extensive market garden with the help of students from 1935 and pigs were kept until 1980. Her memorial garden is filled with large-leaved purple and yellow shrubs growing over paving and through gravel. The wheelchair student's garden is filled with Mediterranean and grey leaved shrubs arranged around a sundial.

To the south of the site is a fine lime tree avenue which then turns along an old field boundary; the College is obliged to maintain this avenue for ever. Nearby is the remains of an orchard established by Joan Salter, and along the western boundary a planting of hornbeams and North American conifers screen the playing fields from the railway line.

A new library has recently been built in the south corner of the grounds, which also provides car parking spaces for visitors. The new planting around the building is dominated by a specimen Caucasian wing nut.

Immediately to the north of the college new development is in progress and hopefully a *Juglans ailanthifolia* will be spared by the contractors. Then further north, but within the College grounds, is Trumpington House which has a collection of hollies, a fine purple beech, cedar, evergreen oak and large yews around the front lawn. To the rear is a fallen mulberry, a Wellingtonia and the remains of a small orchard. The Victorian house has vertical metal rods to the eaves to support climbing plants. Along the north drive is a boundary brick wall supported by metal buttresses with climbers and shrubs planted by Joan Salter.

9.8 Cambridge University Botanic Garden OS456572

The original site of the 1762 Botanic Garden was along Downing Street at the junction of Free School Lane. The present Garden along Trumpington Road is laid out on 40 acres obtained in 1831 and was opened in 1846. From its beginning the Botanic Garden has provided facilities for research, education and amenity. The original plan of the Garden is based on an idea of the first curator, A. Murray. The layout consists of a serpentine perimeter walk by Professor John Stevens Henslow, either side of a main walk, which leads from the entrance by Hobson's Conduit on Trumpington Road to a circular fountain, designed by David Mellor in the mid 1970s.

The systematic beds are arranged according to De Candole's classification and are divided by low hedges. Henslow sited the first rock garden and the glasshouse range c.1830 along the north boundary. The original bog and water garden was redesigned in 1882; and a year later the first ornamental bamboo collection in the country was planted. Cory Lodge, the Director's house was designed in 1924 by M.H. Baillie Scott.

After the Second World War the eastern half of the Garden, formerly allotments, was developed for research purposes. A winter garden established in the 1950s has been superseded by a larger layout in 1976. The Pinetum of the 1960s replaced earlier planting and the informal lake and water gardens were improved and extended at the same time. The range of cedar glasshouses of 1888-91 were rebuilt to the same design in 1934-3. Recently one section has been redesigned and was replanted in 1988-89 to demonstrate the range of plants, ferns, cycads and orchids from America, Australia, Africa and Asia.

During the 1950s an Ecological Area was established with a mound of outcrops of carboniferous limestone for native species that grow on limestone hills in western, central and northern Britain. Nearby are beds of wetland plants that can be seen at the nature reserve of Wicken Fen. There is also a demonstration of the natural variation in a single native British species, the Juniper, planted from 1970 onwards. Other areas include native species to be found on the Breckland; rare species protected by law; plants with different pollination mechanisms, and variations within wild species. The Garden holds National Collections of tulips, alchemillas, bergenias, ribes, saxifrages, species geraniums and fritillarias, butcher's broom, and woody honeysuckles. A scented garden was built in 1960; and in the 1990s a grass maze and a garden which will receive only rainwater have been planted. Today the Botanic Garden grows 8,600 plant species. The garden can be enjoyed for both its C19th or C20th planting.

9.12 Cambridge, Latham Road, No. 15 'Whitsunden'   OS449568

Whitsunden was designed in 1912 by Arnold Mitchell in the Edwardian Arts and Crafts style for H.W. Lewin, a civil engineer. Latham Road was laid out to a deliberate plan imposing restraints and guidelines, which still retain its rural character.

The garden layout today is the result of the late Dr. John Procope's sensitive handling of the spaces around the house. The south terrace overlooks an octagonal lawn surrounded by borders which provide a late summer display of exotics. Diagonal paths lead to a narrow Bulb Walk and a Wild Garden tightly packed with evergreen trees and shrubs through which wind serpentine paths. The White Walk leads one past glimpses to the Venus Garden, a Secret Garden and a small wild flower meadow each enclosed with hedges. To the west of the house is a sunken Dutch Garden with a rectangular pool surrounded with circular brick columns also enclosed with hedges. Opposite the front door is a secret alcove within two parallel hedges with a garden seat. The whole garden layout has been created with assured confidence.

TOUR 10
BARTON

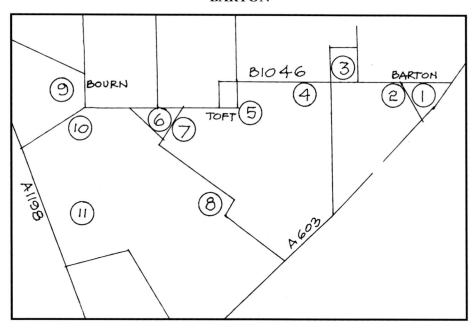

10.1 Barton, Burwash Manor   OS408556

The early C17th manor house is surrounded by a water filled moat and is approached from the church to the west and by a drive from the Barton Road to the north.

To the south is a small, rectangular forecourt enclosed by a C17th brick wall and to the west was a larger, enclosed rectangular garden with sheds in the corners against the walls. In the small park bordered by lime trees there are views through the remains of fine pollarded trees. There has been recent tree replanting in the park. Walnuts and willows grow alongside the moat. The adjacent farm buildings have been restored and are now occupied as handicraft shops.

10.2 Barton, The Seven Houses   OS404559

In 1939 Elliott Howes, a retired banker, designed 5 houses for his sisters around a courtyard and laid out a formal garden with yew hedges and box topiary on the central axis of the layout. As only one sister wished to live here, he gave the group of houses and garden to the Gardeners' Royal Benevolent Society in 1967.

The Society built a further 2 houses in 1970 without destroying the original garden layout. The courtyard remains and garden sheds have been cleverly arranged either side of the covered gateway. A magnolia has been planted in the courtyard in memory of the first custodian. Around each house is a small garden tended by the occupant. The site is sheltered from westerly winds by a beech hedge and clumps of larch and poplar. The south garden retains old fruit trees whilst a gap in the hedge leads the eye across a field to a group of poplars.

The Gardeners' Royal Benevolent Society was founded in 1839 for professional gardeners who became homeless on retirement. At first, only head gardeners were eligible if they had paid a subscription during their employment. Today, 580 beneficiaries are cared for by the Society. Some reside in their own homes.

10.3 Comberton Maze   OS381562

The former turf maze, known as 'Mazles' was circular, 50ft in diameter, and an important part of the villagers' Easter Fair. Following the re-cutting every third year the workers were given a feast for their labours. The curves of the maze were separated by trenches marked with pebbles. By 1846 it was enclosed in the school playground with the stipulation that it was to be preserved. An early example of conservation?

The site of the maze was formerly the village green, adjacent to land owned by Barron Britten who married Martha Sparrow of Hilton in 1654. She is thought to have been the sister of William, who is believed to have created the Hilton labyrinth in 1660. It has been suggested that the 'Mazles' was cut some time after 1660 as a copy of the Hilton maze. By 1897 the Comberton Maze was in a bad condition and was restored in 1908 under the auspices of the Cambridge Antiquarian Society. Its foundations were visible in 1925 but three years later it was buried under tarmac. It was the last turf maze to be destroyed in England.

10.4 Comberton Village College   OS376560

This is an impressive Village College set in attractive grounds to the west of the village. Designed by the County Architect, R.H.Crompton, it was opened in January 1960 and dedicated by the Bishop of Ely, Dr. Noel Hudson.

Today the buildings are fronted by lawns with mixed deciduous trees. A line of cherry trees is set within raised beds for summer bedding plants. Island beds of mixed conifers add interest and variety. To the west of the grounds is a line of poplar trees, the original boundary planting around Village Colleges. To celebrate the College's 25th anniversary a statue of a figure with outstretched arms by Lee Grandjean, was placed in front of the college.

10.5 Toft Manor   OS347564

The house, of flint with stone dressings and built as a Parsonage in 1845 by Samuel Whitfield Dawkes, was clearly inspired by the early work of Pugin.

The Manor stands in 2 acres of gardens with extensive views across open meadows to the south. The drive and garage arrangement have been altered recently to provide a further dwelling. Sadly, the pleasure ground walk related to the Manor is lost.

10.6 Kingston, Moat Farm House   OS338550

This C15th timber framed house is set in 2.5 acres with 1.5 acres of paddock. The garden comprises many specimen trees, shrubs, a vegetable garden and flower beds. It is surrounded on three sides by a partially dried moat with a footbridge. The garden layout sympathetically respects the historic site. Roses and clematis, favourites of the present owner, abound.

10.7 Kingston, The Old Rectory   OS347554

The house, a late C13th building, originally with an open hall, lies east of the church on the former village green in grounds of some 3 acres.

A 1 acre meadow to the east contains a thatched coach house/stable, and two ponds fed by a stream. The upper circular pond is probably a horse pond connected by a decayed brick bridge to the lower pond which is rectangular and may be a medieval fish pond. The front garden to the south and the north garden retain their Victorian layout. The south garden, with its circular carriage drive and box edging, includes fine trees – beech, ash, Irish yews and two *Pinus nigra*. The north garden was the kitchen garden (dated c.1882) comprising three box-edged beds, but is now grassed over. The northern boundary is an 8ft brick wall and an old espalier pear still remains. To the east is a tennis lawn of Victorian origin.

10.8 Great Eversden, The Manor House   OS360537

The present C17th moated Manor House, remodelled in the 18th century, stands on the site of an earlier house recorded along with a drawbridge in 1382.

There are 3 acres of gardens approached through a short lime tree avenue over an outer moat, then over a bridge of the inner moat. Around the Manor are flower, rose and vegetable gardens in rectangular divisions within the moated area.

10.9 Bourn Hall   OS325563

Bourn Hall, built in 1602, is set in a 22 acre park to the west of the village with an access drive from Ermine Street.

It sits on an elevated position with views of the surrounding countryside. The site was chosen by Picot de Cambridge, the first Norman Sheriff of the shire, for the location of his castle at 'Brune' in the C11th. The castle was of the ringway and bailey type with two enclosures, each constructed as a raised embankment within a ditch. These remains can still be seen in the park to the south of the Hall. A garden of the early C17th was laid out in a formal style. In 1871 the estate was sold and the sale particulars detail a C19th formal revivalist garden. The raised walk along the top of the ringway has yew hedging. Humphry Repton and his son John Adey Repton carried out improvements at Bourn Hall in 1817-19 for George John Sackville-West, great-grandfather of Vita Sackville-West. Alterations to the approach drive, diverting it into a graceful curve past Victorian and C17th stable blocks, were made between 1826 and 1886.

10.10 Bourn, Fox House

Fox House was originally the site of the kitchen garden and orchard serving Bourn Hall. It is situated to the south of the Hall and south of Fox Road, and now comprises 5 acres. Access from the Hall was via Bandyleg Walk. Since the Countryside Stewardship Educational Access Scheme was established in 1996, the orchard and woodland have been restored together with the old kitchen garden's peach wall, stream, pond and sluices. There are now rare breeds of domestic animals, laid hedgerows and coppicing and other environmental features to be discovered.

10.11 Kingston Wood Manor

OS328538

Although the present house on the site dates from the late C15th and sits within a complex moat of earlier date, the present gardens are entirely the creation of Sir Alexander and Lady Reid between 1964 and 1992.

They are approached through a newly planted avenue of plane trees. Three new bridges cross the moat in addition to the existing 18th century brick bridge. One in the Japanese style was designed by Heather Hughes. Within the moat are a formal herb garden, a circular rose garden, topiary chess pieces in yew, an herbaceous border and wild flower garden. The moat is treated as a bog garden. To the east of the old farm buildings is a vegetable garden and an ornamental lake with a recent plantation of poplars beyond.

TOUR 11
MADINGLEY

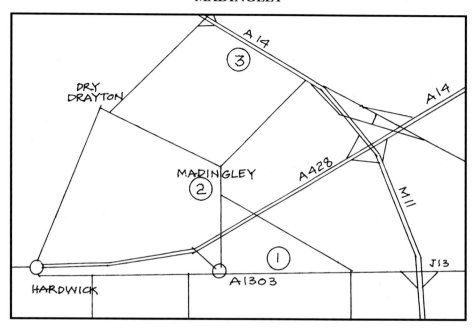

11.1 American Cemetery   OS405595

This 30 acre cemetery was laid out on the site of a temporary cemetery established in 1944 on land donated by the University of Cambridge. It was selected as the only American Second World War cemetery in the British Isles.

The cemetery is situated on a hill to the west of Cambridge with a north facing slope from which, on a clear day, Ely Cathedral can be seen, 14 miles away. The cemetery is framed by woodland to the south and west. Before the Chapel is a long reflecting pool bordered with polyanthus roses edged with box. A line of double flowering pink hawthorn trees acts as a screen to the sloping cemetery where 3,912 gravestones are arranged in seven curved plots. Each is enclosed by box hedging. Beech, oak, tulip trees, sweetgums and Indian bean trees complement the design. The architects for the cemetery were Perry, Shaw, Hepburn and Dean from Boston and the landscape architects were the Olmsted Brothers from Brookline, Massachusetts. The cemetery was dedicated on 16th July 1956.

11.2 Madingley Hall   OS392604

This impressive building, sitting on a rise in the landscape, dates from the C16th with C18th and C20th extensions. The formal gardens and pleasure grounds extend to 20 acres and there are 2 acres of walled garden. In the C18th 'Capability' Brown advised on the park and garden layout. He planted cedars and created a serpentine lake with a sham bridge at the lodge and gates. He also removed the original village high street to create 'The View' to the east from the Hall. Through a handsome Gothic archway the courtyard is planted with an extensive range of shrubs and wall climbers, well maintained. To the south of this courtyard is a walled garden at a higher level, visually connected by a claire-voie along the retaining wall. A thatched summer house and hazel allée were added to the walled garden in 1849. In 1920 a terrace topiary garden was added east of the Hall. To the north-west a stone sundial stands in an enclosure of yew hedging, and nearby is the north croquet lawn with a stone-edged pool.

The sloping area to the north is now successfully managed as a wild flower meadow. Recent improvements include the positioning of a statue of the Prince Regent at the upper fish pond in 1956, and the development of the walled garden with rose pergola and sunken rock garden in 1990. The game larder, ice house, lake and ha-ha have been recently restored. The grounds are enclosed to north and west by an extensive Park with fine clumps of trees and medieval ridge and furrow.

Madingley Hall is the University of Cambridge Board of Continuing Education.

11.3 Cambridge City Crematorium   OS399626

The Cambridgeshire and Counties Crematorium was built in 1938, to the designs of the architect J. Percival Chaplin of Norwich. It is situated to the west of the A14 in pastoral surroundings on the Huntingdon Road, four miles from the centre of Cambridge.

The site is over 4 acres and is approached by a tree-lined semi-circular drive. To the rear of the new chapel is an extensive lawn with a large rose garden leading into a woodland area planted with dedicated trees. A footbridge leads across a stream to a small summer house. The stream feeds a large pond surrounded by bullrushes. To the west is a formal garden with two pergolas supporting climbing roses, and two small ponds. The original layout has proved too small and is now being extended.

TOUR 12
MILTON (CAMBRIDGE)

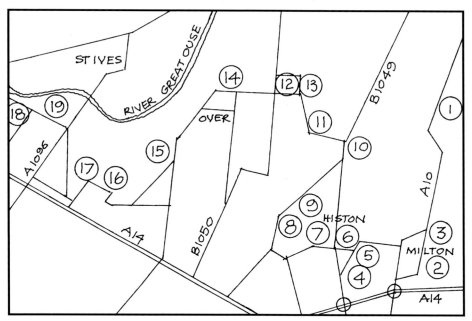

12.1 Waterbeach, Denny Abbey Garden remains   OS492685

Prior to 1170 this monastic site was occupied by a small community of Benedictine monks. It was transferred to the Knights Templar who made use of the site until the order was suppressed in 1308. It was then taken over by a house of the Franciscan Order of Minoresses, established by the widowed Countess of Pembroke who held it until the Dissolution. The present building is an C18th house which incorporated part of the C12th cruciform church.

The site is surrounded by 15 acres of earthworks, including the remains of fishponds and some unusual rectangular ditched plots which were probably once gardens tended by individual monks. The 1880 OS Map shows an extensive moat partly edged with trees and a small walled garden divided into four by cross paths. This belonged to the farmhouse there.

12.2 Milton, The Country Park   OS480623

Formerly on farmland, north of the A14 Cambridge Northern Bypass, this new park owes much of its present appearance to the extraction of sand and gravel for roads and house building between 1930 and 1960. About 1800 years ago, clay was removed in small quantities by Romano British potters. In 1993 the Park was opened and is maintained by South Cambridgeshire District Council. There are two lakes connected by canals which are surrounded by a network of paths over 2 miles long.

The mixture of woodland, grass and water area within the Park ensures that there is always a wide variety of wildlife present.

12.3 Milton Hall   OS483630

In 1794, Samuel Knight completed a new house to designs by Wilkins on the site of a house which had been built by his father north of the church.

Samuel Knight, a man of style, met Humphry Repton while at Trinity College, Cambridge. The new house was set in a park which was laid out in 1789 to designs of Humphry Repton, producing a vista east from the house surrounded by plantations, with a lake to the south-east. Repton noted in the Accounts Book that he advised 'en ami' only charging expenses. Samuel contributed an essay to Repton's *'Variety'*. In 1794-5, to enlarge his grounds to the west, Samuel had the Cambridge-Ely turnpike diverted away from the west front of his house. Today the park landscape and the Repton proposals have been lost. The estate passed to the Baumgartners in 1835 and was sold at the end of C19th. It was bought in 1948 by Eastern Electricity for use as a regional headquarters and in 1983 by Sinclair Research Ltd. One of the two lodges remains but is in a dilapidated state.

12.4 Impington Village College   OS447633

Impington Village College was opened in 1939. It was designed by Walter Gropius and Maxwell Fry and described by Sir Nicholas Pevsner as "One of the best buildings of its date in England, if not the best. Equally successful in its grouping and its setting among the trees of the Impington Hall Estate...". Because of the economic depression of 1931 the scheme had been put into abeyance. However, the Chivers family with determined generosity offered additional land and a capital sum of £6,000. Impington Hall was to have provided a Warden's House, and other college facilities. Henry Moore agreed to provide a major sculpture for the front of the college, and Graham Sutherland designed a mural for the wall at the south end of the promenade, but no fees were forthcoming. The college however owns the designs for both works of art. The college has frequently been extended from the 1950s.

12.5 Impington Hall   OS447632

John Pepys, great-grandfather of Samuel Pepys, built a substantial red-brick mansion in 1579. It was later remodelled c.1724 and remained in the Pepys family until 1805.

The Hall stood in a park of 85 acres to the south of the village church. By 1661 the Hall had a formal garden and in 1770 there were canals. A small ornamental lake in front of the house and the avenue to the south still survived in 1872. In 1774 the Rev. W Cole wrote "At a small distance from the Church, and south of it, stands a very elegant seat, belonging to Mr. Pepys, adorned with beautiful gardens and canals about it". The OS Map of 1887 indicates a canal to the south of the hall with lake and fish ponds; then on the axis of the canal a double avenue leading into the park. To the north-east there was a walled kitchen garden with glasshouse and rustic summer houses. The sale particulars of 1921 includes photographs of a topiary parterre. The parkland was offered in 1930 by the Chivers family to be used for the building of a village college. The hall has been demolished and the site has been developed for housing.

12.6 Histon Unwins Seeds Trial Grounds   OS443635

Along the north side of Impington Lane are the trial grounds of Unwins Seeds Ltd. These cover 6 acres where 4,500 varieties of annuals, biennials, perennials and vegetables from seed are assessed. Many new and experimental strains are on show each year. The company uses the trials to determine the garden worthiness of new varieties and monitors the trueness to type of strains it already lists.

Whilst his brother stuck to more traditional farming, William Unwin started to grow stocks, asters, shasta daisies and sweet peas for the London Flower Market at Covent Garden. Around 1902, he and a colleague, Professor Biffen, a geneticist, noticed an attractive frilled sweet pea flowering in one of his fields along Impington Lane. Biffen was able to instruct William how to propagate this flower, which soon became a must amongst a rapidly growing circle of sweet pea fanciers. This proved to be a hardy and disease resistant variety. He named it after his eldest child, Gladys Unwin, and because of its success he realised that more profit could be made in mail order seed sales than in blooms. Later he extended his plant-breeding work and raised the pea Onward and the tomato The Amateur.

In 1912 the Daily Mail organised a Sweet Pea competition with a first prize of £1,000 which attracted 35,000 entries. All the main prizes and the silver medals awarded to 63 runners-up were won by William Unwin's customers. His son Charles gave the first broadcast talk on Sweet Peas from the Savoy Studios, London in 1923 and in 1979 he was presented with a silver salver commemorating 70 years service to the Horticultural Seed Trade. He had bred over 250 Sweet Pea varieties which were introduced into cultivation by the family firm. Charles's favourite is a salmon pink named after the family friend Frances Perry.

12.7 Histon Manor   OS436639

The lay-out of the grounds around the Manor house appear remarkably similar to those shown on the OS map of 1887 despite many changes of ownership. The property is approached via the hexagonal lodge at the entrance drive from where the visitor would have seen the extension arm of the moat which was the site of an earlier house abandoned in the late medieval period.

To the west side of the house is a formal garden with a central ornamental pond. There are many yews trimmed to differing shapes and sizes. Two conical clipped yews, the height of the house, are depicted on the south front in a Relham painting c.1810 and still dominate a photograph taken a century later when Mr. Ambrose Harding was the owner. A noted zoologist he kept a private zoo, the brick and thatched snake-house being part of it.

Beyond the formal grounds is a small park where the moat with its fine weeping ash tree is situated, with woodland beyond. Along the north boundary wall is a red brick arched gateway with a footpath leading to the church.

12.8 Oakington, Meadow House   OS146647

Alan Bloom, renowned plantsman and nurseryman, started his first nursery on a 6 acre site at Meadow House. Although Alan was born at Victoria House, High Street, Over in 1906, his father wanted to devote time to growing flowers and moved in 1922 to an 1860 property set back from the road with no neighbours. His father planted shelter hedges of laurel and after 1934 Alan Bloom concentrated on alpines and perennials.

By 1936 15 acres were in full production growing perennials and alpines for the wholesale trade. New varieties bearing the prefix 'Oakington' were raised and can still be obtained today. His 1938 catalogue listed 1,870 items and the nursery increased to 38 acres, employing 36 full-time staff. He was growing 100,000 each of the named delphiniums and phlox and had increased quantities of herbaceous plants. The outbreak of war saw the demise of the nursery near the RAF bomber station, and Alan left Oakington in 1941. The property was vacated in 1947 and is now a council depot.

12.9 Westwick Hall   OS421651

Westwick Hall with its cast iron verandah with tented roof was built in 1855 on the site of a C17th house.

The hall is approached by a lime and chestnut lined drive underplanted with snowdrops, and overlooks a small park to the south and west. A corn windmill in the park in 1880 is now demolished. To the north is an enclosed garden, but the late C16th dovecote was demolished after 1905. Behind this is an extensive walled garden and a row of estate terraced cottages each with its own garden. An abandoned railway cuts through the park and the stream has been diverted to run adjacent to the railway line.

12.10 Cottenham Village College   OS451670

The College was designed by the County Architect R.H.Compton and opened in November 1963 by the Queen Mother.

The College is approached along a tree lined drive with shrubs and flowers. An island bed at the entrance is thickly planted with deciduous and evergreen trees and provides a backdrop for a wild life pond containing water lilies. The College is designed with a large promenade in the centre of the plan with views out towards the playing fields.

12.11 Rampton, Manor Farm   OS427680

This medieval Manor Farm, entirely rebuilt in the early C17th, is situated to the east of the village green.

An 1819 Relhan drawing indicates elegant poplars and evergreen shrubs within the narrow front garden. A map of 1825 shows six garden plots (possibly vegetables) to the east of the house laid out formally bounded by a narrow hedge on two sides. A pond runs along the whole of the north boundary. The sale particulars of 1976 lists "an unspoiled front garden with mature yews and fine yuccas and ash tree. Then a large moat pond with willow tree and adjoining well all in a large open paddock".

12.12 Willingham, Church Street, No. 60a   OS406704

Gardens lie to the north and south of an enlarged and remodelled post-war house with integral conservatory. During the last fifteen years the gardens have been laid out for visual pleasure, shelter and warmth but mainly for gardening. The north garden is contained within a picket fence and comprises a curvilinear box edged parterre around shrubs and flowering crab trees. To the south, completely hidden from the street the garden is divided by trimmed privet hedges. Raised beds walled in dry bricks, small lawns, round pools, a chunky pergola, and timber arbour provide settings for fragrant plants to grow in the various compartments.

12.13 Willingham, Rampton End, No. 4   OS 408701

This was a fine example of the long medieval garden plots which made up so much of this village. Originally 100 yards long by 40 feet wide the garden, like other plots in the village, was used to grow cut flowers, these were sent every evening to Covent Garden Flower Market in London, until Beeching axed the local railway line to Cambridge in the late 1960s. Here the garden was laid out to include a series of spaces with a Mediterranean garden to the south of the house, a clipped holly 'carousel', a vegetable garden and in the distance an orchard. The length is to be reduced to allow a residential development covering adjacent similar sized gardens.

12.14 Over, Thomas Robinson's Garden   OS378708

The homestead and garden of Mr. Thomas Robinson, a wealthy farmer in the 1770s, is shown in detail on a map dated 1797 which was surveyed by Thomas Lovell, Clerk to Mr. Jenkinson.

Mr. Robinson's garden was laid out in the form of an enclosed parterre to the west of the farm house. An enclosure with fencing further to the west of the parterre is named the 'Garden'. The map delicately depicts trees, ponds, roads, gates, farmyard outbuildings with elegant accuracy. The site is to the east of the village along Wants Lane which today is called Meadow Lane. All that remains today of Mr. Robinson's house and garden is a section of wall and gateway almost lost in a modern housing estate without a parterre in sight.

12.15 Swavesey Village College   OS362682

The seventh village college to be created, it is on a 16 acre site to the west of the village and was opened in 1958 by the Vice-Chancellor of Cambridge University, Lord Adrian.

John Gale, the first Warden, recalled the care taken over the grounds. "Swavesey to me" he wrote, "will always be beautiful: the daffodils behind the car park, George Smart's Queen Elizabeth roses, the sight of skaters on the top field when it was flooded and frozen, the flowers in the Common Room, the posters in the entrance (I wonder how many people knew that the Lowry in the Red Hall was an original)". Today the gardens in front of the College are filled with trees, shrubs and bush roses.

12.16 Fen Drayton House   OS338685

A Victorian house stood in large grounds between Coote's Lane and Daintree's Road. The 1880 OS map shows the house surrounded by mixed planting of trees and shrubs with the entrance drive to the east.

There was a conservatory on the south-west corner of the house. North of the house was a walled kitchen garden with glasshouses, standing at the edge of a small park to the west with perimeter shelter belt and path. To the east was an orchard. By 1924 various improvements to the grounds had taken place, a windpump in the park and a gasometer had been added, but the layout in the kitchen garden had been simplified. Today the house stands in its garden amongst a mixture of lilacs, yews, and other shrubs, all surrounded by a new housing estate. A village hall and a new primary school and old people's bungalow complex subtly called 'The Plantation' have somewhat changed the original concept of a house with its pleasure grounds and mini park.

12.17 Fenstanton, Manor House   OS318688

Although the majority of houses in Chequers Street are C17th timber framed, a brick house, now painted, with shaped gables at each end and a porch was the home of Lancelot (Capability) Brown when he obtained the manor from the Earl of Northampton in 1768. It is thought that Brown received the manor in payment for his work improving the gardens at Castle Ashby. He died in 1783 and there is a monument to him and his wife Bridget in the church.

The front garden of the house is of interest, but hardly a Brown landscape. Two topiary holly bushes frame the gate and bulge over the low brick wall, behind which a privet hedge just appears. Either side of the front porch are lawns with a magnolia and jasmine to the right and a cotoneaster and jasmine to the left.

12.18 Hemingford Abbots Park   OS278708

Hemingford Park was designed in 1842 by Decimus Burton (Palm House, Kew, 1845). The Georgian house stands in the centre of a well wooded park of 70 acres with lake and fish pond, to the south-west of the village. The south drive commences at a picturesque thatched lodge and then is flanked by rose beds and a giant yew when it sweeps opposite the front door. The north drive is from the High Street and passes through an avenue of lime trees. There are clumps of trees and larger plantations within the park, and one of the ponds has a small island reached by a rustic bridge.

The 1920 sale particulars list a rose garden with a sundial on a marble column with rose beds edged with dwarf box. "A double tennis lawn is shaded by oak and cedar trees, whilst beyond is long grass and a long rose bed. At the end of the terrace is a beautiful rock garden with small pools. Beyond are flower beds, rambler arches, roses, wilderness walks and shrubberies sheltering the house from the cold winds. The grounds are carpeted in season with primroses and daffodils. There is also a partly walled kitchen garden with central water tank edged with clinker and planted with plenty of wall and espalier fruit trees. There is a large lean-to vinery and smaller glass house".

12.19 Hemingford Grey, The Manor   OS287707

This Norman house built by Payne de Hemingford in 1130 is probably the oldest continuously inhabited house in England. It is situated along the south bank of the River Ouse and for 53 years was the home of Lucy Boston, artist and author of the classic set of children's books set in Green Knowe.

Lucy Boston bought the house in 1937 and set about laying out the garden, later creating topiary coronation and chess pieces. She planted nearly three hundred roses, of which some two hundred remain, which are now considered to be of historical importance. These have all been recently identified and labelled. The garden is liable to flood and depressions in the ground indicate the earlier presence of a double moat, sections of which remain as pools. Borders are filled with scented flowering shrubs and there is a fine collection of Dyke medal winning irises many dating to the 1950's. A jewel in a fenland landscape.

TOUR 13
FULBOURN

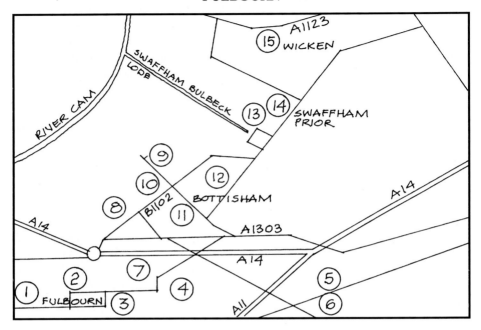

13.1 Fulbourn Hospital   OS550565

In September 1856, the Earl of Hardwicke laid the foundation stone of the new Pauper Lunatic Asylum, which was to stand on a chalk knoll in 55 acres on the edge of the Fens. Kendall's design was considered too costly and consultations were held with the Commissioners in Lunacy in London. In 1855 George Fowler Jones of York, and Samuel Hill, the medical supervisor of the West Riding Asylum drew up a design which won approval for work to begin which consisted of a long range of buildings which can be seen from the road.

To the south, formal parterres on a terrace were repeated either side of the main entrance. Both parterres were enclosed by hedges, each with a summerhouse overlooking the drive, and a bowling green in the field beyond. In 1859 the greater number of patients were agricultural labourers, who were set to work developing the grounds and setting up a farm. A border wall for fruit trees, 700 yards long, was made along the north and east boundary of the site.

The field to the south was divided into large petal shapes and each petal cultivated with a different crop. The sweeping curves of the design dwarf the scale of the Hospital with its formal parterres. The vegetables and crops fed the patients, but the field was ploughed up in 1917 "at the insistence of the War Agricultural Committee".

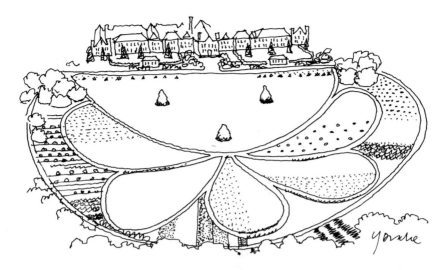

Fulbourn Hospital Grounds 1927 – from an aerial photograph

Today the hospital has been enlarged and the terrace remains but without its formal Victorian parterre and the petals in the field have been replaced by a hedged enclosure, sports pitches, extensive lawns and specimen trees dotted within the site. In 1992 permission was given to develop part of the grounds for a supermarket which has now been built.

13.2 Fulbourn Pumping Station   OS513565

The old pumping station at Fulbourn is well known for its somewhat 'religious' appearance, and fine garden. It was designed by Charles Hawksley, who specialised in gas and waterworks from Shanghai to Buenos Aires.

It was opened in 1891 and its roof accommodated the two 15 h.p. steam driven beam engines which extracted water from a shallow elliptical well in the chalk. Hawksley required an outside container for water and the garden soon possessed a pond to cool condensed steam from the engines, the water then being fed back into the station to produce more steam, thus preventing a build-up of chalk scale on the boilers. Originally the entrance to the garden was via a drive from the west, which passed the large pond which also had a central island. The pond had a continuous stone edging and evergreen shrubs were established close to the pond. Many conifers were planted and form the perimeter planting around the garden.

Today the premises are the offices of Erdas UK Ltd. A new entrance has been made along Cow Lane in line with the flight of steps which lead to the building. The garden is well maintained, the lawns and herbaceous border, mature trees, limes, yews and Scots pine are growing well behind the privet boundary hedge.

13.3 Fulbourn Manor House   OS521563

The manor house has been in the Townley family since 1788 and has been occupied by them almost continually since that date. It was largely rebuilt in 1910 by Dudley Newman, incorporating part of the original house.

The grounds extend to a park to the east of the manor, and there is a flint wall along the village street around the property. The entrance gate piers are brick with stone finials in the form of eagles with heraldic cartouches between their talons. These came from Beaupré Hall, Outwell near Wisbech. In the entrance court is a stone statue of William of Orange facing the house. The plinth of the statue is inscribed with a quotation from D. Hume's *'History of Great Britain'*. To the east of the house is an extensive lawn leading to a ha-ha giving long views across the park. A stone wall extends from the house along the north side of the lawn with a long herbaceous border. Arched metal supports for climbers provide shade along the border over a seating terrace.

The walled kitchen garden has been developed for housing but the earlier Tudor stone and half timbered Old Manor still overlooks the edge of the park. The whole is reminiscent of a medieval French country estate prior to Le Nôtre stamping his formality on the tree planting.

13.4 Great Wilbraham, Wilbraham Temple   OS553579

During the middle ages the manor was owned by the Knights Templar. This late C16th house has been extended and re-faced in the C19th. Originally the entrance drive came from the north passing over the stream to the east of the park which was extended in the late 1700s to 25 acres.

The entrance today is from Temple End to the west. The gardens around the house have recently been developed with improvements to the area around the carp pond, a new garden to the south with circular yew hedge, and a timber and brick pergola in the west garden. There are extensive shrub and herbaceous borders either side of the lawn to the west of the house. A terrace has been added to the east and south of the house. which is generously planted. The park has been reinstated with a recent planting of over 1000 trees and two new ha-has improve the edge of the park as it meets the garden. The east park is planted with narcissus giving a fine display in the spring. This view across rising ground is backed by the Wilderness and the Star and Garter Woods.

13.5 Six Mile Bottom, Swynford Paddocks   OS580575

Swynford Paddocks, formerly The Lodge, is now a hotel. In 1813 the property was owned by Colonel George Leigh and his wife Augusta, who was Lord Byron's half sister.

Byron was a frequent visitor to the house and wrote many of his works at the foot of a fine beech tree which was near the entrance door. The sale particulars of 1917 list the winding carriage drive from the Entrance Lodge, the wealth of timber and ornamental deciduous trees in the pleasure grounds, shady gravel walks, and lawns comprising 54 acres. There was a walled kitchen and fruit garden with mushroom house, fruit store and second vegetable garden. The house was adorned with a tiled paved verandah.

Until 1976, it was the Newmarket home of Lord and Lady Halifax when they attended race meetings. The walled garden is now a car park, and is divided by a road lined with chestnut trees. It is also the site of the grave of the race horse Brigadier Gerard, winner of many races in the 1970s, including the 2000 Guineas, and the King George and Queen Elizabeth Stakes. The entrance porch is surrounded by immaculately clipped pyracantha, and a small garden has been planted to the south of the hotel.

13.6 Little Wilbraham, Six Mile Bottom Hall   OS581571

This large irregular house built in the late C19th in the style of Norman Shaw, was rebuilt in 1901. It stands in the western corner of a small wooded park which is bounded by the Cambridge-Newmarket railway line and the A11.

The surrounding estate consisted of 6,643 acres. The first OS map indicates walnuts, white thorns and firs in the park which was laid out at the same date as the hall. There is a birch walk in the park and a well stocked kitchen garden to the south of the hall.

13.7 Little Wilbraham, The Old Rectory   OS546586

This is a red brick house built in the late C18th, where Charles Lamb is believed to have stayed.

There is a formal gravelled entrance court with lime trees leading to the house. There is a garden to both the east and south of the house. That to the south was the kitchen garden, and some old fruit trees still remain. Along the north wall is a glasshouse and the other walls are part crinkle-crankle. The garden to the east overlooks the small park falling away to the Little Wilbraham River, with a river walk and avenue of poplar trees.. There are mature specimen trees and shrubs (including phillyrea) with herbaceous plants nearer the house. In the spring there is an impressive display of daffodils, aconites and snowdrops, the whole being sympathetically maintained.

13.8 Stow-cum-Quy Hall   OS515611

The present hall, built on the site of the old manor house, was remodelled in 1870 by William White, a pupil of Sir Gilbert Scott. The south front was given Dutch gabling for the new owner Clement Francis, a Cambridge solicitor.

The formal gardens were laid out with a pond and ha-ha. These were later incorporated with the island in Quy Water as it meanders towards Lode. The park originally 20 acres, was extended to 150 acres and all village houses in the larger park were removed. A long elm avenue was planted half a mile in length towards the south lodge through the park. The avenue terminates at a cast iron bridge obtained from St. John's College in 1853 when the Bin Brook was diverted. The original walled kitchen garden has been given over to lawns leading up to the river.

13.9 Lode, Lode Road, No. 21   OS535626

A small 0.25 acre garden, designed by the present owner, to the north of a 15th century thatched cottage.

Here the head gardener of Anglesey Abbey has created his own garden with mysteriously winding paths which conceal the boundaries. In early spring his collection of snowdrops appear before the bold groupings of herbaceous plants push through the soil. The shrubs are carefully chosen with several cut-leaved and variegated elders, which act as backdrops to the other plants. Needless to record that the lawn and grass paths are immaculate. Interesting miniature gunnera, hosta and rheum are to be found growing in pots under the shade of the thatched roof.

13.10 Lode, Anglesey Abbey   OS529622

The remains of an early C13th Augustian priory which was converted into a house in 1600, lies south of Bottisham Lode. Before the grounds were acquired by the 1st Lord Fairhaven in 1926, the garden consisted of specimen trees around the house, an enclosed formal garden and an orchard, all possibly by the Rev. John Hailstone, Vicar of Bottisham who altered the house in 1861. Some boundary shelter belts had been planted in 1860 visually enclosing a larger area of land. Upon his arrival Lord Fairhaven set about laying out a grand landscape over some 100 acres with his gardeners. No overall plan was agreed at the start of the planting.

As time progressed, schemes for other areas followed: the completion of avenues, vistas, hedged enclosures and walks. Luckily Lord Fairhaven was able to collect fine garden ornaments, statues, urns, columns and vases during the 1930 depression. These he located to enhance the walks and terminate the vistas he had planted earlier. His plans incorporated hedged herbaceous borders, a hyacinth garden, a dahlia garden, island shrub beds, and arboretums of conifers and deciduous trees; sometimes with the help of his friend Major Vernon Daniels.

Upon Lord Fairhaven's death in 1966, the house and garden were accepted by the National Trust, who with the help of his head gardener Mr. Noel Ayres and his son Richard, have continued to maintain and expand this garden during the last 70 years. The garden lost several hundred elms in the 1970s and other trees in following gales, with the result that the avenues have been replanted and now are beginning to look mature. Recently a winter walk has been planted, in memory of the 1st Lord Fairhaven, along the eastern boundary which will enable the public to visit the garden throughout the year. The location of the visitor's entrance has never been satisfactorily solved, entering a garden and experiencing the layout in reverse has not been improved by a recent planting of giant redwoods near the tea rooms. There are extensive collections of philadelphus and galanthus in the garden.

13.11 Bottisham Village College   OS542609

The College was designed by S.E.Unwin and opened in 1937 by Oliver Stanley, MP, President of the Board of Education.

Marked by a row of poplar trees the College was laid out specifically without boundary walls. Early in the 1930s, Mr. Noel Newman, a Bottisham farmer met Henry Morris strolling across his arable fields. A covey of partridges skimmed over a thorn hedge and Morris thought this could be the place for his main classroom block. Nearby were growing a ragged clump of willows, possibly the site for a carefully tended lawn with an herbaceous border, for was not the setting of a school almost as important as its book, teachers and buildings.

Mr. Ted Norton was the College's first gardener whose efforts in the magnificent herbaceous border drew appreciative comments from visitors who used to tour the county to see the 'famous' village colleges. Before he retired in 1952, Mr. Norton grew vegetables for the College kitchens, and older boys helped with the pigs, which were kept for bacon. He also encouraged the pupils to keep bees in the grounds. Villagers came from afar to purchase his surplus vegetables; even Henry Morris bought his vegetables every Saturday morning from the College.

13.12 Bottisham Hall   OS551615

The Elizabethan manor house stood within the moat which lies just west of the Hall and probably had its own formal garden around it. By the mid C18th a small rectangular park of some 40 acres had been laid out to the north-west and south-east, associated with long avenues. Between 1770 and 1790 the park was enlarged and the Bottisham to Swaffham road was diverted around it.

After the Hall was rebuilt on its present site in 1797 by the Rev. George Jenyns the park was extended again to its present size, drives laid out, new belts planted and copses established. The grounds around the Hall can be explored by following a circular route which passes through clumps of conifers and shrubberies. A further circular path to the north of the service buildings encompasses a large walled kitchen garden. Either side of this path are drifts of spring flowers and yew and box which provide evergreen avenues. Within the kitchen garden are old fruit trees and figs growing against the walls, where there is evidence of hothouse flues.

The moated site is now well wooded, but the existence of a magnificent plane tree amongst the other trees suggests there was a garden around the manor house. In the park towards the site of the deserted medieval village, Angerhale, is a large field maple of considerable age. Near the sheep pens is a corn mill, and to the west of the hall is a concrete squash court, a reminder of the sporting interests of airmen during the Second World War.

13.13 Swaffham Bulbeck, The Abbey   OS559635

The Abbey is situated to the northern end of the village and comprises an C18th house built over a Medieval undercroft, believed to date from c.1300. It is the only surviving building of the Benedictine Nunnery founded in the C12th by Isabel the Bolebec.

The Abbey is surrounded by numerous earthworks within the grounds of 7 acres. The undulating field is treated as a large wild flower meadow, and there is recent shrub planting to the north which encloses a small lawn. A vegetable garden is tucked away from sight to the right of the entrance gateway. The Abbey stands on slightly raised ground with outstanding views to the surrounding countryside and across the fen.

13.14 Swaffham Prior House   OS564638

Dr. John Allix, Dean of Gloucester and later of Ely, had Swaffham Prior House built in 1750.

Until the early C19th before the house was altered, the garden was a rectangle of 10 acres of which the 80 yard long ha-ha still remains. Between 1814 and 1834 a small park of 45 acres was laid out to the west of the house, which still survives with little alteration. A further enlargement to the park occurred in 1880 when the road to the south-east of the house was diverted to its present line. It was at this time that the elaborate water garden to the south was created including a cascade, woodland pool and small lake all linked to an underground reservoir and pumping system. An avenue of trees was planted at the same date aligned on the newly built Swaffham Prior railway station to the north. The park is approached from two drives, each with its entrance lodge. The layout of original paths across the lawns has been simplified, but the large walled kitchen garden is well used. There has been recent planting in the park and the whole is well maintained.

13.15 Wicken Fen, Wicken Fen Cottage   OS564705

A simple thatched and tiled cottage stands to the left of Lode Lane which is the access drive to Wicken Fen, now owned by the National Trust. By looking over the garden hedge one can admire this simple, unpretentious garden filled with jumbles of foxgloves, hollyhocks, yarrows and white daisies. Amongst these grow a few roses and butcher's broom (the previous owners were Mr. & Mrs. R. Butcher). A small area is set aside for fruit and vegetables, and not surprisingly several nettles as the cottage is so close to such a fine Nature Reserve.

TOUR 14
CHIPPENHAM

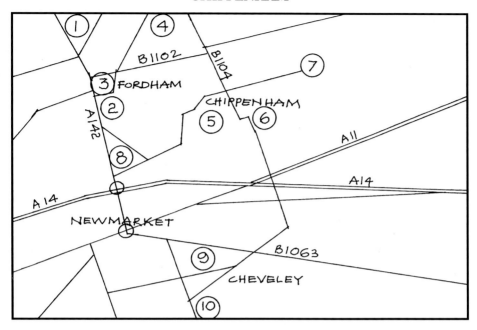

14.1 Soham, Netherhall Manor OS600726

This is a 1 acre walled garden around a recently restored manor house with a courtyard to the east. The garden includes part of a larger orchard to the west, which is now developed for housing. Along the perimeter wall grow many herbaceous plants distributed by keen gardeners to their friends in the 1960s, before many Garden Societies were established. Several rarities have been nurtured by the owner for many years and have been saved from extinction. In spring there are displays of Crown Imperials, Victorian hyacinths, and old primroses. Later in May, florists ranunculus and tulips (rose, bizarre, bybloemen) can be admired, the latter growing where the potatoes were harvested the previous year. In August, the formal beds are planted with Victorian pelargoniums, calceolarias, fuchsias and heliotropes.

14.2 Fordham Abbey OS630697

The C13th Gilbertine priory which once stood on the site has totally vanished and Fordham Abbey today is a Georgian mansion built in 1790. The Abbey is surrounded by a 4 acre garden with lawns, mature trees, and an orchard with wild flowers. There is a walled kitchen garden to the south of the Abbey, and to the east a bridge over a tributary of the River Snail and an C18th dovecotee with pyramidal roof and lantern, which has recently been restored. Between the river and the road is a narrow park of 50 acres which was established in the C19th in which grow a number of conifers, and a Wellingtonia avenue which is unusual in the east of the County.

14.3 Fordham, Shrubland House   OS626706

In 1864 George Townsend had established himself as a nurseryman in Fordham, and by 1875 he had extensive nurseries and a seed growing establishment. In 1883 with his brother John and son George they owned over 300 acres of nursery land to the west of Market Street.

Their house, 'Shrublands', was built in 1893 and was surrounded by gardens containing a wealth of trees which were available at his nursery. The yew and holly hedges with their topiary still remain beneath the cedars, Wellingtonia, cut leafed beech, silver lime and weeping ash. The nursery area is now reduced to 40 acres and behind the rear garden of Shrublands House is Townsend Wood 2.5 acres of mixed deciduous and conifer wood managed by the Woodland Trust.

14.4 Isleham Hall   OS637744

Isleham Hall is a C16th house, associated with the Bernard and Peyton families, now divided into separate buildings. The 1849 sale particulars state that it is a capital mansion known as 'Great Barnards Hall'.

It had a walled kitchen garden and orchard and paddocks and 420 acres of rich arable and pasture land. It is approached from West Street by a private road. Today the original entrance from West Street is lined with pollarded sycamore trees. The hall is protected from winds by a *Cupressus leylandii* hedge which is lowered to afford views to the fields beyond. The small orchard still remains. There is no rear garden as such but a small park to the east.

14.5 Chippenham Park   OS664694

In 1696 Edward Russell, Lord Orford, acquired Chippenham Park and between 1702 and 1712 he laid out a park of some 350 acres, enclosing the land and cutting off the southern half of the village street. It is thought that a formal garden was laid out to the south of the house before the park was enclosed, and a lime avenue running east from the house dates from that period.

By the end of the C18th John Tharp had acquired the property and asked William Emes to provide a plan for landscaping the rather flat park. Emes includes a tapering lake with its south end backed by woodland. Also at this time the formal gardens were destroyed. There are canal-like stretches of water in Ash Wood which have recently been cleared and contain water once again. Over 1,000 trees were planted in the 1790s by Tharp, including two lines of lime trees to the south of the park representing the formations of the British and French fleets at the Battle of La Hogue.

There are fine South Lodges and a triumphal arch Gateway c.1745 with a further avenue running south through farmland to the east of Newmarket which has been cut across by a railway line and a dual carriageway by-pass. To the north are a pair of Neo-Classical Lodges c.1794 by James Wyatt. Behind the stable block is a restored 18th century dovecotee and to the west an extensive walled kitchen garden with an herbaceous border along its southern wall. An area to the south of the walled garden has recently been planted with a wide range of trees and shrubs.

14.6 Chippenham Lodge   OS669698

Originally built in 1840 , and known as The Cottage, then later changed to the Manor House, Chippenham Lodge stands to the east of the village in extensive grounds and small park with a race horse breeding establishment.

The Lodge which has been extended several times is approached by a drive lined with beech and chestnut trees. The gardens comprise herbaceous borders and fine shrubs and in spring there are a mass of bulbs. To the south-east are views across the ha-ha to the grounds beyond. There is a kitchen garden to the south which is partly walled with extensive glasshouses.

14.7 Chippenham, Badlingham Manor   OS678709

Originally known as Badlingham Hall, this C16th farmhouse was a grange of Sibton Abbey in Suffolk. Badlingham Manor is situated within a rectangular moated site with access across a brick bridge from the west. The moat is 50 feet wide and a considerable part of the River Kennett runs through it, the level being maintained by small weirs. A wall running north from the manor is covered with roses. The garden to the east contained two fish ponds which were later canalised. There is a mixed collection of deciduous trees.

14.8 Snailwell, The Old Rectory   OS643675

Originally an early C18th rectory, including within the plan two separate medieval buildings the Old Rectory is flanked by two storey wings.

To the north the rectory overlooks a wide lawn studded with a few young trees, towards the village church and the spring of the River Snail rising in a pool. To the south the garden rises gently to grazed pastures with a ha-ha. Here there are herbaceous and shrub borders either side of the rectory and the whole is dominated by a mature beech. To the south west is a walled garden with overgrown evergreen oaks and yews – a wilderness – with meandering paths. This garden was possibly the late C17th garden associated with the manor house which stood immediately to the west of the Old Rectory.

14.9 Cheveley Park   OS672608

In 1681 Jan Siberechts painted a view of Cheveley Park and the garden enclosures around the house when Lord Dover owned the estate. To either side of the main entrance court are two enclosed gardens, one for flowers, the other for vegetables and fruit, both arranged formally. There is a further enclosed garden with four grass plats divided by paths with clipped trees around the walls. Some gardeners can be seen tending the grass. A wide grass terrace to the east of this enclosure gave fine views over the park. To the other side of the house is the stable yard with a large circular brick-walled pool with a flight of steps down to the water. In 1775 a map for the Rt. Hon. Marquis of Granby by Thomas Warren shows the extent of the park with two rides lined with trees. Also shown are Castle Hill with a moat to the north-east and clumps of trees nearer the house.

By 1864 the property was owned by the Duke of Rutland and the park consisted of 300 acres enclosed by a brick wall. Portions of the house were demolished, until in 1883 only a part was remaining for use as a shooting box and the main terrace was all that remained of the formal gardens.

In 1896 the park and house were bought by Col H. L. B. McCalmont who rebuilt the house and kept the terrace overlooking the park. McCalmont had inherited £4 million from his great uncle and spent vast sums on the new house, enlarged the park to 700 acres, laid out a jumping course within the park and owned several racehorses. The house was demolished in 1920 and today the park is divided into paddocks for racehorses. Part of the original park wall still remains along the east and south boundary. A tight clump of trees marks the location of Castle Hill.

14.10 Kirtling Tower   OS 686574

A huge turreted brick gate-tower and house was built in 1530 for the 1st Lord North, and was situated within the moated site once owned by King Harold. The house itself was enlarged in 1578. In 1801 the 9th Lord North demolished the house but the gate-tower remains today, and now forms part of a house which was built in the mid C19th by J.A. Hansom.

Lord North's son Roger accompanied Queen Elizabeth in 1578 on her progression from Greenwich to Norfolk to avoid the plague. On the return journey the Queen stayed at Kirtling Tower set amongst orchards, gardens and outer courts. A banqueting house and a 'standing' in the park for the hunting were built for her day's visit which cost him £762 4s 2d.

The moat is the largest surviving one in Cambridgeshire and encloses a rectangular area which has been levelled, although the land slopes rapidly away to the north-east. Owing to this slope the moat only contains water in the north and east sides, the south side has been filled in. Outside the moat to the west is a bank which ends in a mound at the north corner.

During the 1930s the gardens around the Tower consisted of clipped yew hedges with views towards the moat. There was a walled kitchen garden and an avenue to the south through fields. The present owners are developing the gardens in the walled garden to the south of the Tower.

TOUR 15
BALSHAM

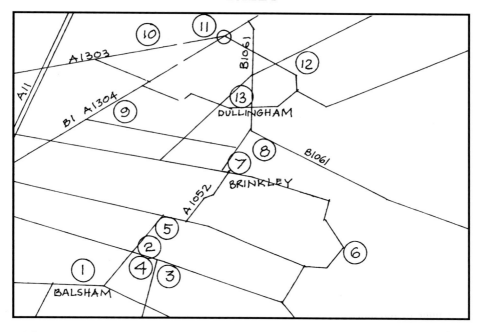

15.1 Balsham Manor   OS585508

Balsham Manor is a small early C17th house which was enlarged in the later C18th and C19th. The gardens cover some 4 acres to the north of the house, and a further 7 acres of paddock contain mature trees.

In spring the gardens are full of flowering bulbs around a small lake and in a wild flower meadow. There is a fine view from the conservatory across a wide lawn edged with herbaceous plants and shrubs to the lake, with mature oaks in the distant paddocks. In 1993 a music maze was planted. Now known as the Balsham Maze, it is curvilinear in outline and laid out to represent, from the air, a treble clef and two French horns. These are picked out with golden yew whilst the remainder of the hedges (approximately 100 yards long) are in English yew. The paths between the hedges are nearly half a mile long and are all grass except a raised paved terrace in the centre of the treble clef. For those lucky enough to find the French horns, they will be rewarded by further planting delights.

15.2 West Wratting Hall   OS 608523

The manor of West Wratting was acquired in the early C19th by Harry Frost (d.1831), who enlarged the existing C18th farmhouse adjoining the church and who probably laid out the simple park around it. The property remained in the hands of the family until the 1930s. Edward Purkis Frost, Harry's grandson, was a pioneer of aeroplane building. In the late C19th he built a steam flying machine and in 1908 became the President of the British Aeronautical Society.

The park to the east of the hall was often used by Edward to test his flying machines. In recent years the park has been greatly reduced in size and the grounds around the Hall now comprise only some 8 acres. The entrance drive is edged with lavender and around the hall are lawns, shrubberies and flower beds with a view across the ha-ha to the parkland beyond.

15.3 West Wratting Park   OS610516

In the early C18th Sir John Jacob leased land here from Peterhouse and built himself a house called West Wratting Park. This is a red-brick mansion c.1730 that still stands.

Its adjacent 120 acre park overlooking rolling country was presumably created at the same time, although it was probably altered by later occupiers, perhaps in the late C18th when the house was extended. The mansion is approached by a picturesque drive which continues round to the large walled kitchen garden. West Wratting was once used as a preparatory school so it is not surprising that the 1935 sale particulars mention tennis courts, cricket field and a 9 hole golf course. There is a fine walk along the park side of the mansion which continues east along the edge of the boundary planting, giving fine views across the park.

15.4 West Wratting, Padlock Croft   OS605516

Padlock Croft garden lies above the 350 foot contour line. Here are displayed an extensive range of alpine plants including the National Collection of Campanulas, 176 species and 123 cultivars. Around the glasshouses re-used cold water tanks are used to grow the rarer alpines. The owners have planned a garden to grow plants which require good drainage and have incorporated a screed mount in a tight layout together with a potager with raised beds for vegetables.

15.5 Weston Colville Hall   OS613529

Weston Colville Hall was built in 1720 to the west of the village. A map, dated 1828 shows John Hall's property with the garden which consisted of an orchard, main garden and the kitchen close bounded to the south by a moat. John Hall remodelled the building which later became a farmhouse. Today the road has been moved further away from the hall and the drive is dominated with giant redwoods, pines and conifers and a series of unusually rotund clipped yews. There are gardens to the side and rear which now are mainly lawn. A paddock which is partly walled lies to the south of the hall.

15.6 Carlton Lopham's Hall Garden remains OS646522

This is the site of the manor house of Carlton Parva, successively known as Barbedor's and Lopham's and lies to the south east of the village church.

In its present form it consists of an oval area, surrounded by a wide and deep moat. There are two modern breaks in the circuit, one allowed access to the C17th farm house in the centre, the other is where a long length of the moat has been filled. The farm house derives from a C15th house where Sir Thomas Fynderne sometimes dwelt. In his son's time it included a chapel and parlour and was surrounded by gardens and a park of probably 78 acres. Outside the moat and to the south is a round flat-topped mound. This was thought to have been a barbican, but it seems to fulfill no defensive purpose and may have been part of some garden scheme and carried a gazebo or summer house.

15.7 Brinkley Hall OS630550

William Frost purchased the estate c.1800 and built Brinkley Hall incorporating parts of a smaller house.

It is likely that Frost created the park that lies north of the Hall. The hall is now approached by a short chestnut tree avenue. Just past the village church a further drive approaches the property from the south. To the west of the house is a wide lawn with flower beds and herbaceous borders leading to the avenue. Wrought iron gates lead to the walled kitchen garden with standard and walled fruit trees with a layout divided by gravelled paths and box hedges. The 1886 OS map shows a range of glasshouses, plant houses, potting sheds, an apple store and tool shed. There was an Ice House near the north boundary of the park.

15.8 Burrough Green Hall OS636555

Burrough Green Hall was built c.1575 and is situated to the north of the village church, west of the green.

Standing originally in a deer park with a Saxon moated site in Park Wood, the hall was once the seventh largest house in the county. It is now greatly reduced in size. The main front of the hall faces onto a walled forecourt now with lawns and a gateway with brick piers which led to an enclosed kitchen garden. There is an ornamental duck pond with surrounding shrubbery on the west side of the hall

15.9 Burrough Green, Windmill Folly OS580580

To the south of the A1304 on Bungalow Hill, near an old windmill stands a remarkable Sino-Gothic house. It consists of three sweeping pagoda-like roofs over flint walls with pointed windows which are repeated on its two side wings. It was constructed by the owner of the windmill during the C19th

The folly stands within a grass field with a view to the surrounding landscape, through a gap in the boundary hedge. There is a range of deciduous trees to the north of the folly.

15.10 Stetchworth, Egerton House   OS607613

In 1891 Lord Ellesmere built Egerton House with stables for 80 horses as the most up to date stud in the country. The estate comprised 120 acres of arable land which was converted to grass with serpentine tree plantations dividing the various paddocks. This created an entirely new landscape around the house which was later sold to the Earl of Harewood in 1925, as his horse racing base at Newmarket.

The grounds are approached via a lodge drive through a paddock landscape in which sits the fine house, surrounded by mature trees planted by members of the Royal Family. The lawns sweep away from the house through shrubberies to a small ha-ha. There are herbaceous borders to the north of the house and an oval pool. Behind the house is an extensive walled kitchen garden and a large stable courtyard with 2 further plots for cultivating produce.

15.11 Stetchworth, The July Racecourse   OS610620

This historic landscape for racing horses is included here as it was designed for pleasure. In 1605 James I "did hunt hare with his own hands in the fields of Fordham". He took his lunch close to the King's Park which adjoined the village. Hunting, hawking and horse racing continued for 3 days during the King's visits to Newmarket.

In 1619 serious steps were taken to improve sport around the town, and a new warren or chase was extended to a circuit of ten miles but in 1654 all meetings and horse races were forbidden by Oliver Cromwell. After the Restoration Charles II visited Newmarket and soon horse racing became fashionable.

By 1666 the Round Course to the west of the Devil's Ditch had been laid out over a distance of 3 miles and 6 furlongs finishing at the Rowley Mile Stand (in Suffolk) on The Heath. The Bunbury Mile, now the July Course, runs parallel to the west of Devil's Ditch and existed in 1787 for matches between two famous horses. The Beacon Course was laid out commencing at the Cambridge Road further to the west and was 4 miles and 1 furlong long. Its start is marked by a post in a field at the top of Four Mile Hill, but the course has been shortened by the recent construction of the A11. A plan of Newmarket Heath in1787 shows an extension of the Beacon Course to Six Mile Bottom.

By the 1750s The Jockey Club was set up in Newmarket and became the governing body of the sport and from 1808 bought land around the town in order to preserve the Heath for racing and its associated activities. Devil's Ditch, overlooking and to the east of the July Course, has the distinction of being the only part of the Heath from which the Jockey Club could not warn off people if they offended against the rules of racing.

15.12 Stetchworth Park   OS642592

Stetchworth Park lies to the west of the Devil's Ditch. The present house was built by Richard Eaton in 1796 and in the early 1800s the park, ponds and garden were laid out.

The park is approached from a Regency thatched lodge and the drive passes along the edge of the park and then via the pleasure grounds to the house. In 1876 the sale particulars record two ornamental sheets of water with overhanging willows, birch and ash, two fruit and vegetable gardens each enclosed by lofty brick walls. The park consisted of 40 acres and the gravelled drive was flanked with flowering and other shrubs. A domed game lodge is sited as an eye-catcher on the north boundary of the park. The walled garden in the pleasure grounds has been removed, but the walled garden to the east of the stables was extended when the Earl of Ellesmere bought the property in1883. More trees were planted in the park at the end of the 19th century and the boundary park planting still remains.

15.13 Dullingham House   OS625582

Dullingham House was built in 1749 for Christopher Jeaffresson. The house stands in a triangular shaped park gently sloping to the south. The pleasure grounds to the north are early 18th century. In September 1799 Humphry Repton was called in to landscape the grounds. Repton's Red Book of 1802 proposed replacing the walled forecourt with a lawn and trees, and laying the road-side stream in brick culverts under this lawn. Both these proposals were carried out so that Dullingham is a good example of Repton's work. To the north of the house are wide lawns and herbaceous borders against extensive walls. The walls are broken by a claire-voie with a vista to the park, across an octagonal banked bowling green surrounded by yews. The garden has been improved by the present owners with extensive new planting and timber garden structures. Today the park is sub-divided into paddocks. The entrance gates no longer lead to the house and the adjacent stable block and extensive walled kitchen gardens have been developed into individual houses with private gardens.

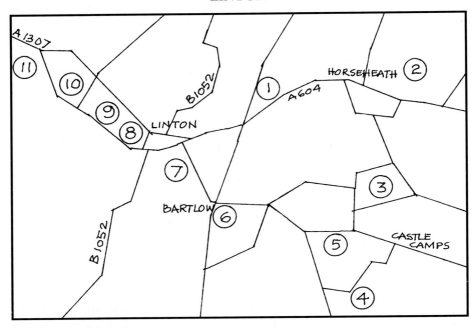

16.1 Horseheath Lodge   OS593478

In 1803 the Horseheath Estate passed to Stanlake Batson, son of Henry Batson, who built this large gault brick house between 1815 and 1825 to the west of the parish, on a former heath and park. He incorporated red bricks from Horseheath Hall for the foundations, cellars and garden walls for the new house called The Lodge.

The Batsons were keen sportsmen and interested in horse racing. They had a private training ground at The Lodge called the Gallop, now used for Point-to-Point races. Here Lucetta was bred by Mr. Stanlake Batson, and in 1829 the horse was sold for 1,800 sovereigns. His horse 'Plenipotentiary' won the Derby Stakes in 1834. The Lodge is situated in a small fold in the landscape through which flows a tributary of the River Granta. The grounds are enclosed by boundary planting with specimen trees in the long, narrow park. To the north of the Lodge is a walled kitchen garden and stables. There are plantations of conifers and deciduous trees to the south east of the Lodge.

16.2 Horseheath Hall Garden remains   OS624473

In 1663 William, 3rd Lord Alington, built a new house to designs by Roger Pratt on the hilltop east of the village and within an old deer park. John Evelyn described the Hall in his diary as "standing in a park with a sweet prospect and a stately avenue", referring to the elm tree avenue which extended for over a mile. The hall was on a grand scale with a 500 foot frontage, the most imposing in the county of that date.

The house was surrounded by a garden comprising elaborate walled compartments, the foundations for which have recently been recorded during earth-moving work. In 1700 the Hall was sold to John Bromley, a Barbados sugar importer, and his grandson Henry employed William Kent to design the interior of the Hall and the gardens. This involved the removal of the walled gardens and their replacement by landscaped pleasure grounds which included the small Acre Pond.

In 1747 the estate comprised 880 acres, which slowly reduced in size to pay for Henry's gambling debts. Henry's son Thomas, 2nd Lord Montford, continued his father's improvements. An orangery was built in 1762 at a cost of £1,300, and contained 150 orange trees at one guinea each. This stood between the hall and Acre Pond to the north, which was well stocked with fish and had two boathouses and a punt for duck shooting. The gardens and grounds were well stocked with statuary. South of the hall was a smaller Garden Pond adjacent to the wilderness, edged by a ha-ha. Either side of the hall were cedars. There was a menagerie which housed monkeys.

Because of further gambling debts the estate was put up for sale in 1775. Items in the sale included orange, lemon and myrtle trees, exotic plants in pots, aloes, roses plus a variety of foreign birds in cages. A series of further sales were held, a stone bridge, vases, statuary, and other outdoor artefacts were dispersed including three pairs of wrought iron gates which can still be found in the county; at Trinity and St. John's Colleges in Cambridge and at Glebe House, Cheveley. No one came forward to purchase the hall, so in 1777 it was demolished. Today the site of the hall is a slightly raised grassed area with cedar trees, and ducks once more enjoy Acre Pond.

16.3 Shudy Camps, Park House   OS624447

Park House is a 9 bay, red brick house built c.1702 for the Dayrell family standing in a large park.

In June 1763 Richard Woods was asked to make improvements to the garden behind the house and to take in the first lane and lay it to lawn. It is possible that Woods was responsible for the small pond with perimeter planting, a length of ha-ha and another pond with an island in a belt of trees to the south of the house. Accounts and letters show Sir Marmaduke Dayrell paid £100 to Richard Woods, his garden designer. There is a balustraded terrace to the west of the house leading to a lawn edged by a ha-ha. The orangery to the north is now used as a swimming pool. The elevated position of the house allows extensive views over the park, grazing meadows and the countryside beyond.

16.4 Shudy Camps, Mr. Ford's Topiary   OS620439

To the west of the public footpath from Shudy Camps to Camps Hall where it crosses

Mr Ford's topiary, Shudy Camps

the road between Bartlow and Castle Camps is Mr. Charles Ford's roadside topiary. After the Second World War Mr. Ford patiently waited every morning for the bus to take him to work in Saffron Walden. For more than 5 years he trimmed the hawthorn hedge with his penknife into the topiary that remains today. Framing the topiary are two fir trees planted on the road verge, but most of the field boundary hedge has been removed leaving only the length of Mr. Ford's topiary. Since his death, Mr. Ford's son and grandson have maintained the topiary to this day.

16.5 Castle Camps, Castle Farm   OS625425

This castle, the largest medieval fortress in the county, was built by Aubrey de Vere, Earl of Oxford, shortly after 1068. Nearby is the site of a motte and bailey with a deserted medieval village to the north.

A Buck engraving of 1730 shows a multi-gabled house with its C15th brick tower and a walled garden to the west. Thomas Sutton of the London Charterhouse lived here at the same date. Charterhouse became owners and built much of what is standing today. The garden wall to the north east is largely C16th or C17th. In 1919 the sale particulars record the walled-in garden and small orchard. Today some fruit trees remain and there is evidence of an earlier terrace leading to a lower lawn with evergreen shrubs and topiary yews which leads to the garden gate giving access to the nearby church.

16.6 Bartlow Park   OS586451

Bartlow Park is a neo-Georgian house designed by Claud Phillimore east of the site of a large Victorian house which burnt down in 1947.

The garden around the new house has been created by the present owners over the last 30 years with the help of John Codrington and incorporates the Victorian terraces and flights of steps that lead down towards the River Granta. There is an island in the river with plantings of acers which are used throughout the garden for autumn colour.

There are fine views towards the small park to the south-east. To the south of the river a path leads to the large walled kitchen garden, which still retains the central glasshouse and its basement boiler which is connected by a track in an underground tunnel for coke deliveries from a side driveway. There is also a long peach house in the kitchen garden adjacent to water troughs. Within the south boundary of the park stands one Romano-British tumulus. The other 3 tumuli are nearby, to the south of the disused railway line.

16.7 Linton, Barham Hall   OS575460

In 1560 John Millicent built the medieval farmhouse called Barham Hall on the site of the convent of the Crutched Friars, which was dissolved in 1539.

A Relhan watercolour shows a much reduced hall in the early 19th century with a large circular drive in front. The garden walls around the north garden still stand. These date from the late C17th with dentil brick cornices to the copings. The gate piers are C18th with ball finials to the caps.

16.8 Linton Village College   OS556469

Linton Village College was opened in 1937 by The Earl of Feversham, Parliamentary Secretary to the Ministry of Agriculture and Fisheries.

'The Architect's Journal' of October 1937 shows a site plan of the college indicating sports pitches in front, a grassed entrance court and at the rear a paved court leading to gardens. The entrance drive was planted with flowering cherry trees and to the north a row of Lombardy poplars was planted in March 1938. Today the poplars have been removed and replaced by conifers.

16.9 Little Linton, Garden remains   OS555475

To the north-west of the village in a broad bend of the River Granta, is a complex site comprising a double moat, moat and farmhouse.

The double moat surrounds a small rectangular island on which stood a summerhouse but only the foundations remain today. Some 17 ancient yew trees strategically planted on the banks provide the clue that this was once a garden. The adjacent moat served as a fishpond. The garden existed in 1771-2 when the whole site was described as 'summer house, boathouse, land, orchard and fishpond'. By the late C19th the garden was abandoned and has become overgrown.

16.10 Hildersham Hall   OS541485

Situated to the south of the village, Hildersham Hall is a Regency stuccoed villa designed in 1807 by Edward Lapidge which incorporates a former farmhouse in the wing (Nether Hall manor house).

The hall was built for Thomas Fassett, who designed and laid out the park in 1810, which contains a large lake, described by W.T. Pike in 1912 as "a picturesque sheet of ornamental water". From the hall, a portico facing west overlooks the park of

70 acres and the drive from the Lodge lined with beech trees. In 1920 the sale particulars record woodland walks, flowerbeds, clumps of rhododendrons, an orchard and kitchen garden. The estate was bought in the 1930s by a nephew of Cecil Rhodes whose sisters lived there into the 1970s. The plantations and lake remain, but the by-pass to the east of Little Abington intrudes on the park.

16.11 Great Abington Hall   OS526485

The original medieval manor house of the Earls of Oxford has long since disappeared. In 1712 a house was built for Maximillian Western, the son of a wealthy London ironmonger.

This was incorporated into the present late C18th hall which still retains its iron verandah along the south front. Western did much rebuilding and having built new stables to the north west of the hall, started to lay out an ornamental canal on a stretch of the River Granta that flowed through his land.

Later the park around the house was laid out by Humphry Repton in 1803 for John Mortlock, the Cambridge banker. Unfortunately the whereabouts of the Red Book for Abington Hall is unknown. The park is approached by two long drives, which converge on a lime avenue widening into a broad sweep at the entrance to the hall. Behind the stable block was a productive walled garden with box-edged paths, espalier and walled fruit trees, lean-to plant houses and 7 heated pits with stoke holes. There is an attractive view across the park to the village church. After the Second World War the property was sold to the British Welding Research Association and the house is now converted into flats and offices.

TOUR 17
HINXTON

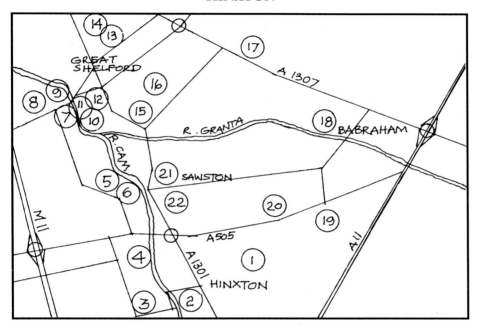

17.1 Hinxton Grange

OS503465

This house built in 1835 has a fluted Greek Doric portico and a tented canopy to the south verandah.

It stands on an elevated position and is approached by a long shady drive through an avenue of beech trees, its entrance lodge no longer existing. At the end of the avenue the drive passes through a small park with clumps of trees and some boundary planting. The pleasure gardens around the house consist of extensive lawns with an Italian formal garden and conservatory. There were two vineries, a forcing house, and a lean-to fruit house in the walled kitchen garden to the east. Today this is partly used by the farm owners for storage of machines.

17.2 Hinxton Hall

OS498448

Hinxton Hall is a three storey red brick house built between 1748 and 1756 for John Bromwell Jones, and is flanked by late C18th wings. It replaces an earlier C18th house on the same site. Until the middle of the C20th the hall stood within a park, which was established between 1833 and 1886 when the existing village street layout was altered.

The sale particulars of 1900 record the two carriage drives with the principal one having a pretty lodge at the entrance. The mansion was surrounded by pleasure grounds and gardens, with a large well timbered park in which was a sheet of water. There were two walled kitchen gardens, a vinery and glass houses. Extending towards the park were wide stretching lawns, decorated with flower beds and intersected by broad gravel paths. The grounds were adorned by magnificent ornamental trees and shrubs, charmingly laid out and inexpensive to maintain. In 1953 the Hall and park was sold to Tube Investments Ltd who built extensive office accommodation in the grounds. Now it is the home of Genome Research Ltd.

17.3 Ickleton Caldrees Manor   OS493438

This long rambling manor house faces the road behind pillared wrought-iron gates. In the early C19th Percy Charles Wyndham MP converted a C17th farm house into a gentleman's residence and laid out pleasure grounds and a park to the north of the house. Later, members of the Herbert family enlarged both the house and the park, diverting a stream to make ornamental ponds, one with a circular island. A high flint and brick wall forms the boundary to the east and north, behind which is an extensive woodland area of conifers and deciduous trees with paths through. The small pond still remains and the herbaceous borders and conservatory are to the north of the house.

17.4 Duxford Mill   OS484473

This old water mill and miller's house is mentioned in the Domesday Survey and was often visited during the Protectorate by Oliver Cromwell. The mill was worked from 1307 until 1937. In 1946 the house and the mill were sold and later converted into a private house. The garden, which consists of 9 acres, was laid out along the River Cam in 1948, and took 20 years to complete. Originally 2,000 roses were planted to give a constant display, and to produce cut blooms; and some roses were bred here. Vistas take advantage of the river, mill pools, statues and a Regency temple together with a mausoleum removed from Hinxton Hall in 1869. The garden contains a large collection of trees, in which birches and maples predominate.

17.5 Whittlesford, The Guildhall   OS473484

This half-timbered Guildhall was built in the early C16th by a village guild, a kind of local religious friendly society. Following the Reformation the parish obtained possession, using it as a workhouse, poorhouse, and schoolroom. Later it was converted into several cottages. In 1966 the parish sold the building as a single private residence and it was renovated in 1972. Although there is little land to the north of the property, the present owners have planted a small knot garden. The surrounding walls are covered with fig trees, which provide a suitable backdrop enhancing the medieval atmosphere of the garden.

17.6 Whittlesford, The Lawn OS475483

The extensive 'green' alongside the Duxford Road originated as a small landscaped park or 'lawn' attached to a modest country house erected in about 1785 by Ebenezer Hollick. Hollick went bankrupt in 1825 and the house was abandoned and then demolished in 1858. Its lawn survived and in 1957 was purchased by the parish council as a village open space. South Cambridgeshire Rural District Council subsequently erected council houses on two sides so that, with its fine C18th trees and extensive grassed areas, it appears to be and functions as a village green.

17.7 Little Shelford Hall OS455516

In 1851 Robert Gregory Wale pulled down most of the existing house on the site then known as The Lodge. He built a new house on the same site in the Gothic style with his architect W. J. Donthorn. Much of that building was burnt down in 1928. The north wing and part of the 19th century stabling survive and have been converted into private houses.

Between 1775 and 1845 a family mausoleum, designed by William Wilkins, stood west of the house in Camping Close. The House stands at the north end of a small park adjoining the Whittlesford Road and is bounded by a stream partly canalised, which joins the River Cam near Shelford Mill. The park is enclosed by a wall along the road boundary, and was laid out with a belt planting almost dividing it in two separate areas. Today the more southern area has been developed for housing.

17.8 Little Shelford, Priesthouse OS454517

In 1858 the old rectory in Little Shelford was demolished and a new brick house in the Gothic style built on the same site by J.E. Law. The rectory was sold in 1962 and in 1980 the house was renamed Priesthouse. It is the home of Cambridge Fine Art. In 1914 Fanny Wale wrote in her *'A Record of Shelford Parva'* that it was built for the Rev. J.E. Law who was a natural scientist. His telescope is still on top of the summer house (thatched) and the garden remains as he planned it. The lawns are perfectly kept. A belt of trees shuts off the churchyard and near the gate is a remarkably thick well cut box hedge. Hot houses and kitchen garden are on the north side of the house, also a fowl run. There are many box and yew trees clipped to varying shapes.

17.9 Little Shelford Manor House OS455519

A new house was built here soon after 1600 by Sir Tobias Palavicino, son of Horatio, of Babraham Hall, who added a moat or refurbished an existing one. In 1745 William Finch replaced this house by the present brick one, added a small park to the west, planted avenues on both sides of the house and created a formal garden. These gardens were swept away and what remains to the north and south of the house, extending to the banks of the River Cam, are largely of C19th origin and include kitchen and flower gardens with lawns and cedars.

17.10 Great Shelford, Kings Mill House   OS458516

This Regency country residence was built about 1825 with a frontage along Kings Mill Lane.

Hidden behind a screen of trees and a hedge, the house overlooks open meadows to the west. To the east is a walled garden with a lawn flanked by shrubs and a yew walk. To one side is a vegetable garden. Beyond the main lawn is a further lawn with several trees and shrubs which terminates with a long brick wall extending the whole width of the garden. Beyond this is a view towards the fish ponds and water gardens. The site was the inspiration for Philippa Pearce's children's classic *'Tom's Midnight Garden'* written over 40 years ago.

17.11 Great Shelford, The Grange   OS459518

This two storey house to the south of Church Street, built in the C16th and C17th, then remodelled in 1890, was the home of a Mr. Church, a friend of the celebrated Cambridge antiquary William Cole, who used the paddock as a small deer park. The house has a south facing garden with extensive lawns with fine trees, including a mature copper beech. Luckily the new housing development to the north east of the house does not obscure the view across the paddock.

17.12 Great Shelford, Southernwood   OS465518

In 1906 George Macaulay came with his family to live at Southernwood. With him came his daughter Rose, then aged 25.

The house was built between 1888 and 1903 and had a garden leading down to the river which she described in one of her early novels *'The Secret River'*. Today there are two large weeping willows guarding the entrance drive, part of the ground to the left of the drive has been sold, but the castellated entrance can be seen behind well clipped hedges and shrubs. A hawthorn hedge backed by mature beech trees separates the garden from the adjoining recreation ground The lawns and small orchard remain but the land bordering the river has been developed for housing. Before 1914 Rupert Brooke, as an undergraduate, was a frequent visitor for Sunday lunch or for boating on the river with Rose.

17.13 Great Shelford, Nine Wells House   OS466538

A Victorian house set among trees along Granham's Road to the north of the village overlooking the Cambridge to London railway line, gives no clues of its horticultural importance at the turn of the century.

It is well known that dons and parsons were concerned with the first steps in the rise of the old simple flags to the present glories of the bearded irises. Sir Michael Foster (1836-1907) was an eminent Professor of Physiology at Cambridge University and also Secretary of the Royal Society. 'Huddled in a little garden' in Shelford, on difficult Cambridge soil. Foster grew over 200 irises collected from all over the world.

His notebooks covering his observations from 1878 to 1902, accompanied by his lucid drawings, still exist. He was the first to publish descriptions of some of the species iris.

After collecting more eastern irises he became interested in crossing species to form hybrids. His records were made available to William Rickatson Dykes who wrote a monograph 'The Genus Iris' in 1913. Amos Perry, the north London nurseryman, marketed some of Sir Michael's iris. Foster was known for his quotation "Horticulture is a pious occupation" giving as his reason "The gods rejoice when they see a good man struggling with adversity". He was among the first to receive the Victoria Medal of Honour from the RHS.

Many good Eremurus Shelford hybrids (Foxtail Lilies) were also raised by Sir Michael Foster at Ninewells.

17.14 Great Shelford, Nine Wells Springs   OS462542

Thomas Hobson (c.1544-1631) was jointly responsible with Dr. Andrew Perne for bringing fresh water to the typhoid-ridden city. In 1574 Perne identified a series of springs in the chalk near the northern end of the parish, and proposed digging a channel the three miles to Cambridge. Thirty years later, in 1610, Hobson put up the larger part of the funds towards realising the project.

The channel can still be traced, from Long Road to Trumpington Road. Until 1856 the channel terminated in Market Place at an hexagonal stone fountain called 'Hobson's Conduit'. This structure now stands at the junction of Lensfield Road and Trumpington Road in Cambridge. At Nine Wells, an Obelisk is situated on a high point in the south-east corner of the wooded area which together with the land surrounding the chalk springs is scheduled as a Site of Scientific Interest. The Obelisk is enclosed by iron railings; the first side states: "The supply of water to Cambridge from the adjacent springs was first suggested in 1574 by Andrew Perne, Master of Peterhouse. The design was revived by James Montague, Master of Sidney Sussex and in 1610 carried into effect at the joint expense of the University and Town".

17.15 Stapleford House   OS469517

On 18th May 1848, Richard Headley of Stapleford House, near Cambridge, won every prize at the popular tulip show held by the Cambridge Florists' Society in the concert room of the Lion Hotel. Mr. Headley had been slowly amassing other prizes between 1831 and 1843. From the Society's Minute Books his name appears repeatedly as winner for Auriculas, Polyanthus, Pansies, Ranunculus, Carnations, Dahlias, Pinks, Roses and Tulips. It is obvious that his skill at growing Tulips – flamed bizarres, flamed byblomens, flamed roses, feathered bizarre, feathered byblomens, and feathered roses – was appreciated far and wide. In 1836 at the Society's Auricula Show, the Rev. J.S. Henslow, Professor of Botany, commented on "the improvement of 'weeds' to their beautiful appearance and splendid colours as exhibited that day".

Today Stapleford House has a garden of conifers and mixed deciduous trees with box hedges. The present gardener often comes across bases of old greenhouses in the garden, which is now reduced in size by the modern houses either side.

17.16 Stapleford, Middlefield · OS480529

Middlefield, once called Mount Blow, looks southwards down a gentle slope over a stretch of Cambridgeshire farm lands. The house was designed by Sir Edwin Lutyens between 1908 and 1909 for the legal scholar Henry Bond. It is red brick, neo-Georgian with big hipped roofs and tall chimneys.

Lutyens promised Miss Gertrude Jekyll, in a note, that the garden was ready for her attention but there is no evidence that she prepared any planting plans. It seems likely that Lutyens indicated the layout of radiating allées on the garden front. The main vista has double herbaceous borders backed by hedges. The whole garden has been extensively restored and elaborated during the 1990s. Middlefield is one of four Edwardian mansions built in extensive gardens on rising ground known since the C13th as Foxhill.

17.17 Stapleford, Wandlebury · OS494534

Wandlebury is the best preserved Iron Age defensive work in Cambridgeshire. The raised bank encloses an area 900ft in diameter. It remained relatively untouched until the middle of the C18th when Lord Godolphin built a stableblock and handsome Racing Lodge in the south-west part of the the enclosure. He landscaped the grounds within a high wall establishing a circular drive amongst newly planted trees, with a kitchen garden and orchard to the west. By 1800 after some years of neglect, the estate was being cared for again. More trees were planted, and a large forcing machine worked by horses raised water from the well, 201ft deep which supplied water for domestic use and also fed a fish pond near the centre of the Ring.

The Godolphins, now Duke and Duchess of Leeds, left Wandlebury in 1893 and the sale particulars record the grounds with shady lawns, box hedges, rose arches, a sculptured stone pump, a grand old yew hedge – a mere 18ft high and 8ft thick – rose gardens with an old mulberry tree in the centre, and a sundial on a stone pedestal. Two entrance lodges, Keeper's Lodge, Gardener's Cottage, kennels, stabling and fitted fruit store are also listed.

The Estate was bought in 1904 by Mr & Mrs. H.W.S. Gray who carried out improvements to the gardens. In the summer of 1933 18,000 people (including Mr. and Mrs. Stanley Baldwin) assembled on July 26th to enjoy ten hours of fun at a fantastic fete at Wandlebury. An aerial photograph of 1949 shows the house and layout of the garden prior to the death of Lady Gray. Their son Terence Gray presented the house and garden within the Ring to the Cambridge Preservation Society in 1954, who then purchased the remaining 96 acres of the estate.

The Society noted that the expenditure to restore the house would be excessive and reluctantly decided upon demolition. The felling of the mulberry tree aroused local passionate protest. Today the mansion has disappeared and the central garden is more like a park which is often grazed by sheep. Only the circular entrance-lodges and stableblock remain, and within the archway is the grave of the Duke's horse The Godolphin Arab, which died in 1753 aged 29. Traces of the garden layout can be seen from the terrace lawn on which stands the sundial with its engraving of a dolphin and a ducal crown.

17.18 Babraham Hall   OS507503

Sir Horatio Palavicino, a wealthy Italian, became the owner of Babraham Hall during the reign of Elizabeth I. He showed great business acumen and was a spymaster for Elizabeth I, Lord Burghley and the Earl of Leicester. With his wealth he purchased Babraham in 1589 from Robert Taylor, who had built one of the finest Gothic houses in the county within a large park.

It is possible that Palavicino laid out elaborate gardens around the hall as a letter records a fine mansion surrounded by formal gardens. Palavicino died in 1600. His widow married Sir Oliver Cromwell, uncle of the future Lord Protector. In 1632 the estate was sold to Richard and Thomas Bennet, and their cousin Hugh May, a well known architect, supervised the construction of an extensive new watercourse for irrigation of the water-meadows in the 1650s. The half-mile canal running parallel to the house was probably part of this scheme.

The present hall was designed by Philip Hardwicke and built between 1833-7 for the Adeane family. To the south of the hall are two stone-edged beds in the large lawn. In the drought these show parch marks of scrollwork parterres. There is a rockery along the river frontage, which was a children's garden with a raised walk through alternating yews and box to a stone building (now in ruins). Along the River Granta is a pleached lime walk, and to the other side of the canal is a wide avenue of limes, planted 100 years ago, leading towards Sawston.

The village church lies to the west of the Hall and is surrounded by a yew hedge. A gateway in the red brick wall leads to the Petticoat Garden in which stands an elegant summerhouse. From this small garden a path leads to the first of three walled kitchen gardens which open onto the canalised river. To the north-west of the hall were extensive pleasure grounds. In 1948 the estate was sold to the Agricultural Research Council, now The Babraham Institute. Several new research buildings and houses have since been erected in the pleasure grounds and park.

17.19 Pampisford Hall   OS510485

Pampisford Hall stands within formal gardens, pleasure grounds, arboretum and a park planted from 1820–1870 by William Parker Hammond senior with an exceptional collection of conifers. After 1840 Robert Marnock (1800–1899) provided plans for the grounds at Pampisford Hall. Marnock had designed the Sheffield Botanic garden and became its first curator in 1834. In 1840, together with Decimus

Burton he successfully submitted plans for the layout of the Royal Botanic Society's gardens in the Inner Circle of Regent's Park and became curator there from 1841 to 1869.

Both Kelly's Directory of 1879 and the Gardener's Chronicle of 1884 have extensive descriptions of the gardens listing "the magnificent collection of conifers and the planting carried out in a grand conception and with good taste". The Parker Hammonds imported 1,000 exotic trees and shrubs for their grounds which soon became famous as containing one of the largest collections of conifers in the country. All the more amazing as the soil is chalk.

After some years of neglect and the loss of many trees in gales, the garden is undergoing restoration with enthusiasm. The Trust and the owner would be interested to hear if Marnock's plans for this garden still survive.

17.20 Pampisford, Old Vicarage   OS498483

Built in 1880 of brick with flint dressings, the Old Vicarage is situated to the south of the village church.

There is a fine cedar forming the centrepiece of the front garden. To the east of the house are shrubs and herbaceous borders, with island beds planted to flower each year in July. There are mature trees along the boundaries and to the south an extensive kitchen garden. A small Victorian style conservatory is planted with rare plants.

17.21 Sawston Hall   OS488491

Sawston Hall was inherited in 1502 by Lady Isabella Nevill who married William Huddleston of Millom Castle, Cumberland, and it remained in the Huddleston family. The earlier moated house was burnt down in 1553 by members of the Lady Jane Grey faction after Mary Tudor had spent a night in the house. The present house was built between 1557 and 1584 around a courtyard. Mary Tudor granted Huddleston stone from Cambridge Castle to build a better house.

At this time elaborate gardens were laid out around the Hall. Evidence of their design was shown as parch marks on the lawns in an aerial photograph which revealed geometric planted compartments separated by straight paths on a grand scale, with a raised terrace walk aligned to the north front of the Hall. Today there is a more simplified layout with formal lawns, a picturesque moat, yew hedges, specimen trees and woodland walks. The lawns are cleverly mown in circular patterns. The hall is now a school of languages.

17.22 Sawston Village College   OS483497

Sawston, the first Cambridgeshire Village College, was built in 1930 It was designed by the architect H.H. Dunn in a neo-Georgian style with hipped roofs and chimneys. The symmetrical plan encloses an open courtyard to the east with a central fountain. Originally on a site of 4 acres, the college grounds later increased to 26 acres. The boundary is planted with a shoulder height *Cupressus leylandii* hedge backed by spindly lime trees. The limes form an avenue along the entrance drive, and are underplanted with iris beds.

TOUR 18
HARSTON

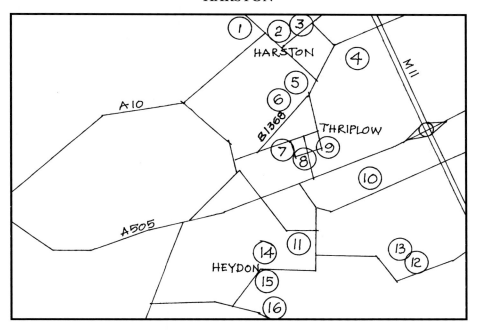

18.1 Harston, Manor House   OS418509

Access to this early C19 house is from the village street, near the church, through a pillared gateway and a drive lined with mature trees.

The extensive west garden has lawns with a pair of sunken flower beds along the River Cam walk and a perimeter path with large specimens of clipped box. There are oblique views to a mill. The main view from the house is across an elegant footbridge which leads to a large circular island with perimeter trees and lawn, the site of a medieval manor house.

18.2 Harston House   OS423507

This walled garden and its early C18th house can be seen from the A10. It has literary associations because the author Graham Greene stayed here as a small boy in his summer holidays at his uncle's home.

He recalled a special walk shaded by thick laurel bushes, beyond it an orchard, and a pond with an island in the middle. His imagination took him on long overseas journeys, and perhaps the orchard and pond became the inspiration for locations in Africa, India and the American West. Today the giant redwoods have become a local landmark, although one has been struck by lightening. Box hedges to the south lead to a rose garden around a sundial, shaded by a tall Gingko. The path to the west of the house continues across a stream into woodland with narrow cross paths edged with box. Beyond is the site of an old tennis court enclosed by tall trees. To the east is a vegetable garden with a rose tunnel leading to an orchard.

18.3 Harston, Park House   OS426513

Standing back from the A10 in the centre of the village, Park House was built by the Hurrell family in 1854 as The Park.

The long road frontage is marked by a fretwork stone wall with stone piers at the drive and the footpath entrances. To the southern side of the house are mature trees, including giant redwoods of similar stature to those at Harston House. Trees now block the view from the house across the road to the mini-park opposite, as yet not a housing estate. A Victorian garden layout on the 1888 OS Map included a pond, summerhouse, fountain, conservatory, and glasshouses at random in a walled garden with an orchard, some of which still remain.

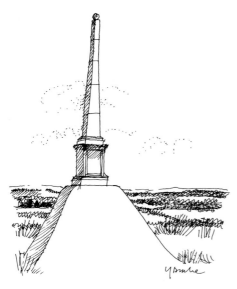

18.4 Harston Obelisk   OS443507

Visible from the M11 and the Kings Cross Railway Line, Harston Obelisk is raised on a pyramidal mount on St. Margaret's Mount overlooking the River Cam valley. The obelisk was erected to the memory of George Wale, Conservator of the River Cam, Justice of the Peace and Deputy Lieutenant of the County, who died in 1739, by his friend James Church. The obelisk was made by the Cambridge mason and sculptor Charles Bottomley. Why is the new mobile telephone tower placed so insensitively close to this historic monument?

Harston – The Obelisk

18.5 Newton, Manor House   OS4454911

The Manor House was rebuilt in the 1850s amid a C17th great barn and brewhouse. There are two parks around the house. Each has a different history. The smaller one to the north surrounds the site of the medieval manor house. It was probably created in the early C18th by William Hurrell, a prosperous local farmer, who acquired the house and land here in 1718. Hurrell removed houses from the south side of the village to make this park. The larger park to the south of the brook dates from the mid

C19th when the house was rebuilt. This park is of a simple form with only boundary plantations, scattered trees and a sinuous drive.

18.6 Newton Hall   OS443485

Newton Hall is linked to Newton Manor House by the Hoffer Brook. The garden was created in the C18th by a member of the Pemberton family who acquired the land in the 1760s. The Pembertons built a new house there and by the late C19th had created formal beds immediately south of the house with lawns beyond and with small wooded pleasure grounds to east and west. The estate was purchased in 1908 by Sir Charles Waldstein (later Walston), who rebuilt the hall in a neo-Queen Anne style. Now only the perimeter planting and a few isolated trees remain.

18.7 Thriplow, Manor House   OS438465

The Manor is approached through a wide gateway in the middle of a long brick and clunch wall which encloses the formal garden. This wall may date from 1678-96 when the property was held by Sir Christopher Hatton of Longstanton who built the brick wall around the formal garden which is mainly laid to lawn today, and left vases which bear his coat of arms. The lawns are surrounded by herbaceous borders and mature trees. The rear garden has a southerly aspect and there are vegetable gardens, with fruit cages and a greenhouse. To the east and south is a moat which marks the site of the medieval manor house. It is now an orchard and open woodland. The whole garden comprises 10 acres and has an extensive display of spring bulbs.

18.8 Thriplow House   OS439461

Situated within 10 acres of mature wood and parkland on the southern edge of the village, Thriplow House was built between 1858 and 1863 for the Ellis family who were local landowners. The gardens to the south retain many of the original Victorian features including extensive lawns with specimen trees – copper beech and spreading golden yews. Although the house is now subdivided into flats, the drive still winds through yew trees; the solid brick entrance gate piers remain. There is a Victorian lodge with a separate garden.

18.9 Thriplow Bury   OS435462

Thriplow Bury is a Georgian red brick house with a facade which fronts an earlier timber-framed house. The gardens are approached via a lodge and drive bordered with lime trees. In 1884 there were two lawns with shrubberies, a walled kitchen garden, orchard, pond and dovecote. An early 19th century plan proposed the removal of the garden in favour of an extensive landscape design and provided excellent shelter for plants. The old three-sided moat is lined with trees.

18.10 Duxford Grange   OS454443

Duxford Grange is a late Victorian, painted brick house to the west of the village of Duxford. It is situated in open, rolling chalk fields, with little tree cover or woodland.

The short drives are bordered with alternating beech and yew on raised banks and the garden is laid out formally around a central large lawn. There are fine views to the south through the wrought iron boundary fence. The walled garden lies behind the Grange with herbaceous borders and there is a walk through the Home Plantation. In recent years the beeches have suffered through drought.

18.11 Chrishall Grange   OS443427

This William and Mary Manor House lies in open rolling countryside and is hidden by extensive tree planting. The gardens are approached by a drive from the north. To the east perimeter plantations enclose rectangular fields leading to Chrishall Grange Plantation. The central plantation is an extensive conifer avenue and the estate boundary to the south east is planted with alternating Scots pines and beech trees. The gardens and grounds that surround the Grange consist of lawns and herbaceous borders, with trees and shrubs. The rose gardens, herb and kitchen gardens are partially walled. A walnut tree avenue is shown on a map of 1886.

18.12 Ickleton, Old Grange   OS462419

The Old Grange was built between 1618 and 1685 and nestles at the foot of a hill 2 miles west of Ickleton village. The Grange was re-fronted in the C18th and is surrounded by stables and barns, and reached by a straight drive. Owned by the Wyndham family, who lived at Caldrees Manor in the village, the complex of buildings is centred on a simple geometric setting of lush grazing meadows bounded by old flint walls. In 1803 the garden around the Grange included a large pond and extensive orchard, and little has changed since that date.

18.13 Ickleton, New Grange   OS462424

This large, red brick house, set high on a hill, overlooking the Old Grange, was built between 1885 and 1901 for G.W.Bowen, whose father, Sir George, was the first Governor of Queensland.

The drive to the east passes through mature beech trees, from a lodge designed by the London architect, Hubert Christian Corlette. The New Grange stands amongst mature trees contemporary with the house, with fine views from the south terrace over the beech hedge. The terraces have a balustrade with stone diaper pattern and brick piers supporting climbing roses. The lawns are studded with specimen trees and Scots pine dominate the garden and boundary planting. The boundary hedge along the roadside to the estate is of clipped lilac.

18.14 Heydon House   OS433410

Approached by a sweeping carriage drive from the east, Heydon House is a fine C17th house, standing to the north of the road behind mature trees and shrubs.

The house was built for Sir Peter Soame, Lord Mayor of London and is surrounded by an extensive brick wall and claire-voie overlooking the road and field to the south. The 7 acre garden consists of lawns bounded by shrubberies, originally dotted with rose beds and intersected by a gravel path. The trees of the pleasure gardens frame a view across a lawn to a formal lake, previously a three-sided moat. There is a view to the north towards woodland (High Park). The walled kitchen garden to the west contained espalier and other fruit trees. The outbuildings included a game larder, and a range of apple and potato stores.

18.15 Heydon Place (Rectory) OS432399

This large, brick Regency House has extensive grounds looking towards the church to the north. The garden is to the north and east of the house, with lawns and shrubberies leading to a fruit tree lined formal walk running along the southern boundary of the field overlooked by Heydon House. To the south of this walk is a small field used for grazing with several trees. Immediately south of the house is an extensive orchard.

18.16 Great Chishill Hall OS429385

The mid-19th century Hall is built of gault brick, with red brick and flint in the rear elevations and stands to the south-east of the village. The semi-circular drive to the north-east passes through fine deciduous trees. This garden is enclosed by flint walls and ornamental wrought iron railings with a claire-voie in the centre, and includes a lawn bordered by small island flower beds; a walled kitchen garden; and a formal orchard with crossing paths and two small outbuildings. There are fine views of woodlands in Essex from the garden.

TOUR 19
MELBOURN

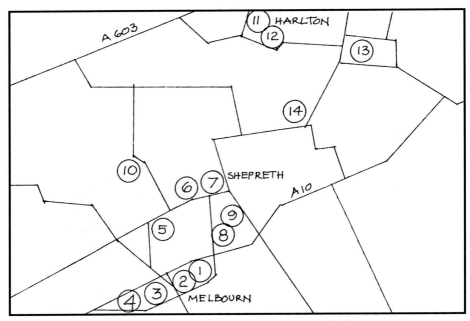

19.1 Melbourn Village College   OS385452

Melbourn Village College was designed on a 15 acre site by the County Architect, R.H. Compton. It was opened in 1959 by Sir David Eccles, Minister of Education.

The grounds consist of stately plane trees, an approach avenue of flowering cherry trees, island beds of pink and red floribunda roses, shrubs and mixed plantings of deciduous trees. These were maintained by Ernie Smith from 1969 to 1972. Past staff and pupils recall "my first impression was of space, all that grass, the trees, the shrubs and the rose beds. On the horizon was our groundsman Ernie Smith, whose bending figure described a perfect inverted L, terminating in the largest wellington boots I have ever seen". Today some of the original planting has been lost to extensions for existing buildings.

19.2 Melbourn, Glebe House   OS383448

This 1964 stuccoed brick house stands on the site of an ancient Vicarage. An 1834 map by Cocket & Nash, Royston surveyors, shows watercourses, gates, garden layout with two lawns to the south, a pond and orchard. The present house has a walled garden with central lawn surrounded by roses and a lawn with fruit trees enclosed by a fence.

19.3 Melbourn Lodge   OS382446

This 1830 brick house stands within 2 acres of grounds laid out in 1968, with a gravel drive around a central lawn. The garden has an extensive range of ground cover plants and shrubs designed and planted so that it can be maintained by the owner with only nine hours work each week during the season. The irregular site has provided many cross views, which have been planted with small collections of conifers, irises, clematis and old shrub roses which all grow well on the chalk.

19.4 Melbourn Bury   OS375444

The mid-19th century castellated house on the site of the medieval manor of Melbourn Bury, stands in 5 acres of garden with a small ornamental lake with island, feeding one of the sources of the River Cam. There is a large wall-backed herbaceous border and rose garden, and extensive lawns with mature beech trees.

19.5 Meldreth, Bury Farm   OS378467

The existing late Georgian house, on the site of a C12th moated manor house, is set in 2.5 acres of grounds on the edge of the river Meld.

The site is divided into a series of formal gardens with a long yew avenue terminating in a box hedge circle. There are plantsman's borders, white borders, a red border and a pergola supporting roses and vines underplanted with spring bulbs. Today the moat is still bordered by ancient chestnuts.

19.6 Shepreth, The Crossing House   OS389478

This internationally renowned garden was started around the level crossing house and later extended along half a mile of the Kings Cross to Cambridge railway line. Doug and Margaret Fuller moved to the house in 1959 and found that the previous owner had kept pigs on the triangular site, which they cleared. Because the site was flat, the Fullers decided to create raised beds with sleepers and these allowed plants to survive that would otherwise have been impossible to grow.

Plants were exchanged with John and Faith Raven at Docwra's Manor and by the mid-1960s plants being given by Lord De Ramsey, Valerie Finnis, Tony Venison and Albert Pike, among many. In 1974 the garden was first opened by Margaret, and 1000 visitors were recorded. Doug has a collection of auriculas, pelargoniums and rare bulbs which he tends in his three greenhouses. Margaret is now collecting more hammamelis, hepaticas and hellebores. Recently they were given an award by the National Garden Scheme for opening their garden, every day, for 21 years.

19.7 Shepreth, Docwra's Manor   OS393479

A botanist's garden of distinction made in the 1960s and 70s by John Raven who wrote the New Naturalist series volume 'Mountain Flowers' with Dr. Max Walters (1965). Since John Raven's death in 1979, the garden has been maintained by Faith Raven, who contributed the photographs to her husband's 'A Botanist's Garden'. They moved to Docwra's Manor in 1954 and the 2.5 acre garden has been divided, using buildings, hedges and walls, to create themed areas such as the paved courtyard with pool, walled garden and main lawn with temple, a semi-wild garden and a winter garden, all filled with plants from friends, nurseries and trips abroad. The dry Cambridgeshire climate suits plants from the Mediterranean. Originally John Raven intended to group plants botanically but there is now a more relaxed approach to planting.

19.8 Shepreth, Nun's Manor   OS394470

Nun's Manor is a 16th century farmhouse built on fast-draining chalk. It is recognised by a neat vegetable garden situated immediately on the garden side of the roadside ditch. The 2 acre garden is divided into separate gardens. The access gravel drive is bordered with lavenders and rock roses. A pond with summer house is adjacent to a twin herbaceous border. A croquet lawn gives access to a walk planted with oak, beech, wild cherry and field maple around the edge of a field.

19.9 Shepreth, Tyrells Hall   OS396477

Tyrells Hall, an C18th house, remodelled in the early C19th is situated in the centre of its own timbered parkland and was originally approached by a carriage drive from the A10 to the south.

From 1759 until the 20th century it was owned by the Woodham family, who laid out the park following enclosure in 1823. They also added ornamental buildings to the park including an elaborate cottage at the entrance which has now been turned into a thatched motel. Sale documents of 1953 list fishponds, trout stream, heated greenhouse and peach wall, walled kitchen garden, small orchard and informal Italian garden. The layout is today simplified but many original features not mentioned in the sale document survive – medieval moats, flint mock miniature castle tower, Victorian bath house and timber summer house. The boundary planting around the 30 acre park conceals the village dwellings on two sides.

19.10 Orwell, Malton Farm   OS373484

Today the site of this garden is a tranquil oasis with uninterrupted views across meadows and cornfields. This is exactly what was intended by Lady Margaret Beaufort, mother of Henry VII and founder of Christ's College, Cambridge, who left it to the scholars there that they might escape the 'ague-ridden darkness' of Cambridge and take refuge in the refurbished farmhouse at Malton.

A few mature trees remain but early maps show two rectangular moated areas fed from the river Cam to the east, that were probably orchards. There is a large weeping ash in the centre of an undulating lawn which slopes down to the river. An 18th century framed and boarded pigeon house stands on the opposite side of the road.

19.11 Harlton Garden remains   OS385530

A complex arrangement of moated enclosures, ponds and watercourses suggests that there may have been gardens here in medieval times. The central moated site appears to have been a C16th or C17th house surrounded by gardens and ponds while the moat to the south may have been the site of a medieval manor house. A further moat to the north surrounds a small island, and streams to either side filled two fishponds.

19.12 Harlton, High Street, No. 83   OS388524

This third of an acre garden has achieved fame for the use of colour in the overall design. Of special interest are half-moon flower beds which run along one boundary of the garden. Each bay is individually planted for single colour groupings. The furthest from the house contains mauve flowers and purple foliage. Elsewhere the garden is arranged to include terraces with containers for alpines, a small pool and rock garden, and an octagonal greenhouse containing rare alpines.

19.13 Haslingfield Hall   OS405523

Sir Thomas Wendy, physician to Henry VIII, built Haslingfield Hall in 1555. Queen Elizabeth I left here for her famous address to the University in 1564 and her image on a white charger is now the village emblem.

The Hall was situated within a three-sided moat and surrounded by a small park, the whole bounded by a brick wall. By 1815 all but the east end of the house was demolished. The C17th brick bridge over the moat and a pigeon house survive, both shown on R. Relhan's painting of 1814. The park was 21 acres in 1810, had already been reduced in size, and is still being encroached upon today. The original garden contained an extensive orchard, pleasure garden, a terrace and a rusticated brick gateway. A later painting by Relhan shows the nearby church and part of the park wall.

19.14 Barrington Hall   OS396500

This white brick Hall opposite the village church conceals a 17th century core. Richard Stacy, brick contractor to William III built a hall for his son-in-law Thomas Bendyshe, but much was destroyed. In 1920 the house was remodelled by W.J. Keiffer and H.S. Fleming for Captain Bendyshe, a collateral descendant of Lord Nelson.

The grounds are approached through a pillared gateway and the drive soon reaches the Hall. The dense and mature planting contrives to obscure the hall from the road, even though it can be glimpsed from the green. A lodge, specimen trees, herbaceous borders are sympathetically maintained as a private garden around offices for the cement company.

TOUR 20
BASSINGBOURN

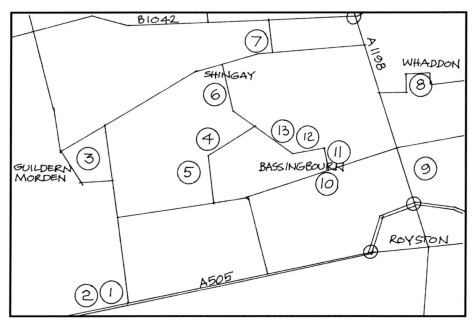

20.1 Odsey Grange   OS293380

The medieval manor house, situated on the county boundary with Hertfordshire, was acquired by a member of the Fordham family in 1793 and remains in their possession today.

The house was rebuilt in 1864 and the garden extended in 1912 with shrubberies. An extensive brick wall surmounted by wrought iron railings separates the south and west gardens from the surrounding parkland. The Park contains a family mausoleum in a clump of trees. Recent renewal of gardens includes formal walks between yew hedges, herbaceous borders and high brick walls covered on both sides with roses. To the north of the house on sloping ground bounded by a long barn is an imaginative layout of iris beds and ornamental trees.

20.2 Odsey House   OS296380

Adjacent to Odsey Grange this tall elegant Georgian house, c.1720, was built as a Sporting Lodge for the Duke of Devonshire with extensive stabling. Several fine mature beech trees are underplanted with a mass of spring bulbs. To the front of the house is a formal area laid out with circles of clipped box. An attractive archway leads to the north garden, which is also formally laid out with clipped yews and box lined paths incorporating an existing orchard, in open flat countryside.

20.3 Guilden Morden Hall   OS285439

Surrounded by fine deciduous trees this C15th house, rebuilt after the Peasants' Revolt in 1381, stands within one of the largest and best preserved moats in the county. An estate map of 1797 by J. Prickett marks an orchard within an outer moat, a garden within the inner moat and extensive groves to the north and east of the moats. Photographs of 1900 show a brick bridge over the moat and well planted gardens, with fruit trees and roses.

20.4 Abington Pigotts, Abington Hall   OS304445

The Hall was built on a new site in 1829 by Lt Col G.E.Graham who created a small park to the south-west soon afterwards.

A fountain to the east of the hall is shown on the first OS map with a lawn leading to a ride through The Woodlands. From 1907 until 1920 the Hall was used as the rectory. There is an enclosed kitchen garden and today the garden to the south of the Hall contains shrubs and mature trees overlooking the park.

20.5 Abington Pigotts, Downhall Manor   OS304438

The medieval manor house, now replaced by a C19th farmhouse, stood within a complex moated site, most of which survives. Also surviving is a remarkable timber-framed gatehouse dating from the late C13th to C14th. To the west, the old water mill has recently been restored.

An estate map dated 1804 shows an inner moat around the Hall and to the south within an outer moat a garden of six rectangular-edged plots.

In the meadows further south of the Hall a cross avenue of trees is shown running east west but these do not appear on the OS map dated 1887.

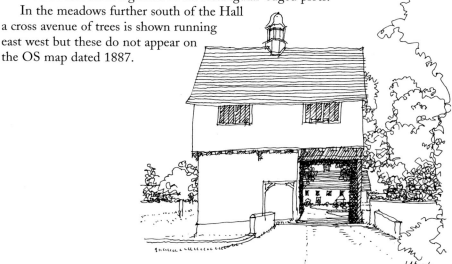

Downhall Manor – Gatehouse

20.6 Shingay cum Wendy, South Farm OS308463

This is a late 17th century Tudor farmhouse with an adjoining range of medieval and Victorian farm buildings forming a large courtyard.

The 10 acre garden surrounds the buildings and is protected by extensive shelter planting. Hedging is clipped into exotic outlines with views across the surrounding flat landscape. There is a conservatory and an extensive vegetable garden with 100 unusual varieties and species. Anna Pavord writing in *'The Independent'* noted "In the series of vegetable gardens there are more different things to eat than I have ever seen to eat in one place before". Well-established flower beds are arranged around the bog garden. There is an interesting irrigation system throughout.

20.7 Shingay cum Wendy, Preceptory of The Knights Hospitallers OS308472

In the mid C12th the manor of Shingay was given to the Knights Hospitallers who made it their administrative centre for all their lands in the area.

The site eventually contained a manor house, chapel, two dovecotes and other buildings, all within an extensive moat. The latter widened at its south-eastern corner to form a small lake across which visitors glimpsed the house. After the Dissolution of the Monasteries in 1540 the buildings were converted into Shingay Hall. The house was pulled down in the late 18th century, the church in 1697 and the ruins of its replacement chapel removed in 1836. There are foundations of buildings and the extensive moated site can still be discerned. Some old fruit trees still remain in the south-west corner.

20.8 Whaddon, Rectory Farm OS353466

The present C17th house stands on a moated site east of the church. The entrance to the garden has recently been planted with mixed trees. Rising behind the house to the south are large chestnuts that make a striking backdrop to the cluster of tall chimneys. A timber footbridge gives access across the moat to cornfields to the south. To the east of the house and adjacent to the drive is a red brick, slate-tiled turreted dovecotee. To the north of the farm are tightly arranged barns.

20.9 Kneesworth Hall OS350441

The Hall lies to the south-east of the village, just east of the Roman Ermine Street. Its predecessor, a much altered and enlarged early C17th house, together with a small 46 acre park, was purchased in 1900 by Sidney Holland, 2nd Viscount Knutsford. He rebuilt the house in 1903-4 to designs by Roland Plumb and enlarged the parkland.

The entrance drive to Kneesworth Hall winds through parkland, crossing a stream and climbing towards the Hall, which is hidden by large yews before being revealed round a bend. Some of the low brick walls around the rose garden remain. Now Kneesworth House Hospital, it is used to care for young adults, continuing the work of the 2nd Viscount whose memorial is to be found in Bassingbourn churchyard.

20.10 Bassingbourn Village College   OS331436

Bassingbourn Village College is situated west of the village and is surrounded by open countryside. It was designed by Wilfred Wingate the county architect, and opened in 1954 by R.A. Butler.

The site covers 22 acres and is enhanced by avenues of limes and hornbeams, as well as other mature trees in the grounds. Flower beds and borders of shrubs and roses surround the college. Several pieces of art and pottery were given to the college by artists who exhibited work at the 1951 Festival of Britain. On the facade of the hall is a striking sculpture by Harold Daw, representing a youth with symbols of the arts and sciences. In the garden to the north of the college are four statues, brought here in 1953. They were previously sited on the roof of the Court House at Castle Hill, Cambridge (now demolished).

20.11 Bassingbourn, Manor Farm   OS331440

Manor Farm has a typical Queen Anne façade but its origins are a 17th century timber building. It lies next to the village church on the south side and a path leads from the garden across the churchyard to the south porch. Behind a yew hedge in the front garden is a thatched dovecotee still in use. The rear of the house is joined to a large Tudor tithe barn which forms part of a courtyard. To the south of the house, a pair of lofty horse chestnuts overlook a pond containing a range of water plants. Large garden areas extend to the east of the tithe barn enclosed by beech hedges.

20.12 Bassingbourn, John O'Gaunt's House   OS329453

Now visible only as crop marks from the air, this was one of the most remarkable late-medieval gardens of England. It was created between 1461 and 1470 by John Tiptoft, Earl of Worcester, and resembled the early Renaissance gardens of Italy which he had recently visited. Tiptoft's house stood on a high mound within a moat giving long views to the adjacent hills to the north and south. Around it are moated compartments with ponds and pathways. A long raised causeway linked it to the village.

20.13 Bassingbourn, The Mill House   OS327444

The Mill House is north-west of Bassingbourn on the road to Shingay. During the last twenty years the owners have designed a garden of about one acre around the house, incorporating an existing orchard in the open flat countryside. A wall encloses a secret garden containing a box hedged rectangular pool. A pergola from the north of the house supports an abundance of climbing roses and clematis. The garden is filled with many fascinating plants which grow well on this exposed site.

TOUR 21
WIMPOLE

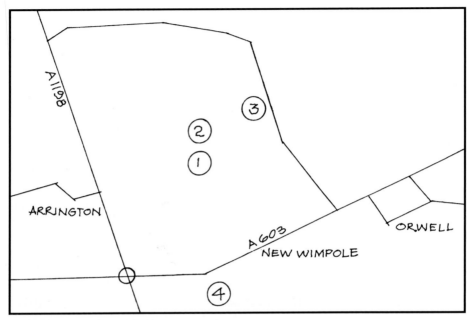

21.1 Wimpole Hall, The Park   OS330505

This magnificent building, standing in 20 acres of garden and 500 acres of formal and landscaped park with walled gardens and an estate farm, is now owned by The National Trust. The park dates from 1302 and the Hall was built in the mid C17th with alterations by Gibbs, Flitcroft, Soane and Kendall.

Owners of Wimpole have always noted the topographical junction of the flat clay lands to the west of Cambridge with the rising chalk ground which can be traced south-west to the Chilterns. From the Hall each vista is distinct. To the south the land opens out towards the hills beyond Royston, but to the north and east the land rises into undulating wooded hills. Around the Hall there is parkland dotted with trees, with farmland and woods beyond.

The earliest reference to the park is indicated on a 1638 estate map showing two deer parks to the west of the old manor house, the High and Low Park, marked by banks which still survive as do some of the walnut trees which separated them. Sir Thomas Chicheley replaced the manor house in 1640 with a new mansion and formal garden. A formal avenue 90 feet wide was planted south towards the road. The Earl of Radnor acquired Wimpole in 1683 and Kip's engraving shows the extensive improvements to the garden which were carried out. A water garden was laid out to the south-west of the Hall and ponds to the south-east. To the north fish ponds were added with clumps of trees to the north. Johnson's Hill, the high point to the north was linked to the Hall by a new avenue.

Between 1720 and 1725 Lord Harley employed Charles Bridgeman, who added more avenues in the parkland and simplified Radnor's north garden. He planted a grid of limes and horse chestnuts to the west of the Hall, and by cutting through another avenue allowed Whaddon church spire to become an eye catcher. Bridgeman's most dramatic alteration was the two mile long South Avenue with parallel lines of elms 50 feet apart across a space of 90 yards. The avenue continues around an octagonal basin and then to the Great North Road. The avenue was felled in the 1970s following Dutch Elm disease, and has been replanted with limes grafted from trees on the estate.

'Capability' Brown proposed alterations to the formal avenues between 1765 and 1775, mainly those to the north-west of the hall. Radnor's fish ponds became lakes with islands and were crossed by a Chinese Bridge which has now been restored. In 1774 James Essex reworked Sanderson Miller's proposals for a Gothic tower on Johnson's Hill, which consists of 3 circular towers in various stages of ruin. 15 years later Brown's pupil William Emes relocated the kitchen garden to its present position and the park was extended further to the south-west where new plantations sheltered it from the road.

In 1801 Humphry Repton proposed further informality in the planting by extending and bulking up Brown's belts of trees around the perimeter of the park. He laid out the drive to the east via Cobb's Wood and then looping to the south to the Cambridge Road near Orwell. The west gates to the park at the village of Arrington and the stables were designed in 1851 by Kendall. The park was extended in the mid C19th and planting continued until 1910. Since the estate was given to the National Trust a considerable amount of new planting and restoration work in the park has been undertaken and a series of planned walks have been established. Rare breeds of animals now graze the fields in the park.

21.2 New Wimpole, Wimpole Hall Garden OS330505

Benjamin Hare's map of Wimpole in 1638 shows the manor house surrounded by a rectangular moat and approached through a pair of gatehouses. Later in 1640 after Sir Thomas Chicheley replaced this building with his new house, a rectangular formal garden was laid out around the hall on the north-south axis. After 1683 the Earl of Radnor extended the northern garden with parterres and fountains, intersecting hedged alleys and wrought iron gates with assistance from his gardeners, George London and Henry Wise. Kip's view of 1707 shows the water garden to the south west of the Hall. The banks can still be noted in the grounds. To the west is a long walled vegetable garden and orchard.

Following the rigid layouts of Bridgeman's avenues, successive gardeners removed much of the formality around the Hall. Robert Greening was the 1st professional gardener to be employed by the Earls of Hardwicke. By 1750 the formality of the north garden was done away with and a new lawn was made with a serpentine walk around the perimeter passing through regular clumps of trees. Greening moved the walled garden to the east of this new layout to enable him to grow apricots, cherries, nectarines and greengages with the help of a heated hot wall.

In 1789 William Emes removed the shrubberies to the north of the hall, filled in the ha-ha and created a new walled garden in its present position to the north-east of the hall, demolishing the gardens of Bridgeman and Greening. A map of 1825 made by the land agent Robert Withers shows Repton's proposals for an enclosed garden to the north of the house and a formal garden between the two main wings. During the remainder of the C19th shrubberies were planted in the pleasure gardens to the north and east of the Hall and some of the original conifers remain today along the path to the walled garden.

The last private owner of the Hall was Mrs. Bambridge, Rudyard Kipling's daughter. With her husband, she maintained the garden and planted many daffodils between 1920 and 1950. A small Dutch formal garden edged with box hedges and a simplified version of the Victorian parterres have been laid out to the north of the Hall by the National Trust. In 1987 a rose garden was planted with evergreen shrubs on the site of Kendall's conservatory which was taken down during Mrs. Bambridge's time.

The walled kitchen garden of 2 acres is undergoing restoration. The glasshouse was designed by Sir John Soane in 1793 and the gardener's house added in 1805. An outer wall of this garden was added in the late C19th and is no longer complete. Walnut trees form a National Collection in the garden at Wimpole, continuing the tradition of the walnuts planted between the original two parks recorded in 1638.

21.3 New Wimpole, Wimpole Home Farm   OS330505

Between 1790 and 1806 Philip Yorke, 3rd Earl of Hardwicke commissioned various work at Wimpole Hall by Sir John Soane. Yorke was passionately interested in farming and the estate soon became well known for its progressive agriculture. Soane designed the agricultural buildings for Yorke's model farm. This was built to the north-east of the Hall so that Yorke could keep his eye on the farm.

Soane's plan of 1796 incorporated a large barn, cow stalls, stables for the working horses, pigsties, cart sheds, a slaughter area and a dairy. A series of deer pens were built as the herd at Wimpole suffered a rare disease in 1794. In 1860 an octagonal dairy and farm-house were built

Although the layout as proposed by Soane was not built to his plan, and several individual buildings have been demolished, what remains gives a good impression of a model farm located within the park.

The byre and the fold yards represent the need for shelter for cows. But as more cows were kept, a middle range was built and the rick yard was made into fold yards for the cattle. The cartsheds are open fronted and built for 8 carts and 2 waggons, but by 1834 space for 15 carts was required. The barn was completed in 1796. It now houses the museum, and is thatched with double entrances opening on to threshing floors. The stables for the 15 working horses were also used for ploughs and cart traces.

The fields immediately around the Home Farm are now used for grazing rare breeds of farm animals which are in danger of extinction.

21.4 New Wimpole, River Cam Farmhouse   OS341488

This C17th timber-framed house was purchased by the present owner in 1978. It had stood empty for 10 years with a demolition order on the property and was bought together with two acres of ridge and furrow meadow. A small tributary of the river Cam runs through the grounds. The existing elms died and new shelter planting was undertaken. A garden was created containing a yew enclosed rose garden, a knot garden, a bog garden and a fine curved herbaceous border with a central camomile garden with honeysuckles and tropaeolums enclosed by yew hedging. A gap in the perimeter shelter belt allows a view across the landscape to Whaddon church.

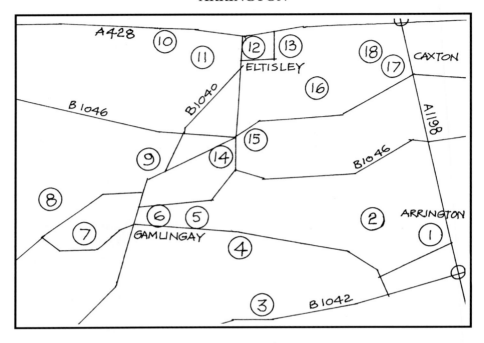

22.1 Arrington, Village Garden   OS328503

This ⅓ acre garden was created by the villagers of Arrington in one day in the spring of 1993 (without the help of Anneka Rice). The site, owned by the National Trust, had previously been a meadow and was used for the annual village fete. The original idea was to create a safe place for children to play, and for people to meet in quiet and pleasant surroundings.

After two years planning (and with local support) the whole village turned out to help on 23rd March 1993. Having cleared the site, flower beds were prepared and plants arrived from local gardens. It had been decided that only plants which encouraged wild life would be used. An area of meadow turf would be left unmown for wildflowers to emerge. At the rear of the garden, a children's play area was constructed.

Behind the attractive iron railings a notice board gives information about the garden, with a list of sponsors on the reverse side. The maintenance is undertaken by villagers. One is prompted to ask why no other village in the county has copied this idea.

22.2 Croydon Wilds

OS304514

A new house on the remote Wilds was built here in the early C17th by the Cage family who then owned most of the parish.

It was placed centrally within an exactly square moated garden which had terraced walkways along two sides of the interior and raised mounts at the corners, The house was demolished in 1957 but the moat survives.

22.3 Tadlow House

OS279476

A charming 2.5 acre garden has been created around a former rectory built in 1832 by Downing College.

The garden originally consisted of a kitchen garden to the north-west and to the south a lawn edged with mixed tree planting and path. The entrance drive from the road to the west of the house is beneath mature cedar and beech trees. The east garden has formal flower beds, roses and herbs, and is enclosed by a yew hedge. To the south is a meadow with a view towards the churches of Ashwell and Steeple Morden across the River Rhee valley. The west garden consists of a circular shrubbery with a fine judas tree leading to an orchard on the site of an earlier kitchen garden. A formal pool with summerhouse and sympathetic plantings completes the new layout. There is a Spring flower walk, with many bulbs in grass beneath flowering trees.

22.4 Hatley Park

OS275510

Originally a medieval deer park, developed in the C17th and C18th but mainly in the mid C19th into a large landscaped park, in the centre of which stands a late C17th house.

The formal gardens lie to the south of the house and lead to a fine chestnut tree avenue. There is a ha-ha with balustrading and circular pool between yew hedges, and two large topiary yews. To the east lies a formal rose garden with low box hedges, and to the west in the centre of the pleasure garden is an extensive lake with two islands. To either side of the frontage of the house are clipped box hedges, and a tree lined drive from the west lodge passes the house and continues to the thatched lodge. A path near the rose garden leads to the village church on the edge of the park. Along the northern boundary is a recent ha-ha. There is a large walled garden in the park to the west of the house.

22.5 Gamlingay, Merton Grange

OS248521

This is an early C18th brick house with garden and walled kitchen garden situated to the east of a small park, approached by the main drive from the west lodge entrance through an avenue of beech and chestnut trees. The park contains fine limes but one hundred elms were lost to Dutch elm disease. There is a ha-ha between the garden and the park. The service drive leads to a stable block, and nearby a small gateway gives access to the east garden.

The south façade of the Grange supports a large timber Victorian conservatory with barrel vault roof. To the south lawns lead to a *Cupressus leylandii* hedge around a swimming pool and clumps of shrubs are edged with low clipped laurel. Further from the house is an orchard and formal circular rose garden. North-west of the house is an overgrown topiary garden, with magnolias and bamboos near a walled garden, and further along the boundary an ornamental oval moat.

22.6 Gamlingay, The Emplins   OS242525

Between 1475 and 1491 Thomas Bird leased the manor from Merton College, Oxford, and built The Emplins which became the rectory, which is situated to the east of the church. It survived the destructive fire that swept through the village in 1600. The garden has been created by the present owners. In front of the house is a profusion of shrubs and herbaceous plants and to the rear are informal beds with low hedges. Herbs and old fashioned roses intermingle with other plants creating a gentle, floral display throughout the summer months.

22.7 Gamlingay Park   OS226518

The park comprises extensive earthwork remains of an early formal garden which was laid out when a house was built for Sir George Downing in 1712, but abandoned in 1776. Downing was married when fifteen to his cousin, who was two years younger. Upon his return from a 'Grand Tour' he refused to live with or acknowledge his wife. Her petition to the House of Lords for a divorce failed, and they lived apart. He became MP for Dunwich and in 1711 inherited 7,000 acres at Gamlingay. The new house cost £9,000, and was three storeys around three sides of a courtyard with a large circular drive to the south.

The gardens were laid to the north and sloped down to a trapezoidal lake, with three long terraces linked by ramps. Beyond the lake was a large formal garden with the main vista through woodland on the axis of the house. There was a small area of maze-like serpentine paths near the house. Near Drove Road north of the main garden area is the 'Full Moon Gate', the sole surviving feature of the C18th buildings. There is an estate plan dated 1801 in Downing College. This describes the labyrinth in the west of the wood "enclosed by a brick wall with paths 10 feet wide and grassed with Hornbeam hedges on each side 10 feet high". Also marked on the plan are the positions of statues of a Roman Gladiator, two pyramids, a Figure of Diana, Fame on a Pedestal, an Urn, Mercury, a Gothic Gate and an Obelisk. These were located as eye catchers in rides through the wood. The Downing family owned property in London in the area of the Prime Minister's formal residence.

22.8 Tetworth Hall   OS305557

This is an early 18th century red brick Queen Anne house in parkland on a 'sandy' ridge, built in 1710 for John Pedley MP (died 1722), with late C18th additions when the park, formal gardens and woodland walk were laid out.

Today the woodland walk has been developed with fine collections of rhododendrons, azaleas and other acid soil loving plants. Groups of oak and sweet chestnuts form a shade canopy over large pools and a bog garden. Spectacular clumps of Himalayan lilies over ten feet high follow the rhododendrons. The west lawn has rose beds and diamond brick-edged beds planted with cotton lavender, with a wide herbaceous border to the north. A central flight of steps leads down from the lawn to a grass terrace. There are plantings of cornus and magnolia species in rough grass beyond and also a vegetable garden. Fine views overlook the Bedfordshire countryside.

22.9 Waresley Park OS245545

In the spring of 1792 Humphry Repton was called in to advise on the improvement of 'Waresley Park in Huntingdonshire, a Seat of William Needham Esq.' Originally a deer park, Repton thought this could be improved by concealing the boundaries and removing the paling fences. The house was to be improved by changing the "nondescript Georgian style to a 'Gothic appearance', then planting special trees in the park and further improvements to the approach to the house".

Repton produced his Red Book in the summer of 1792. The estate comprising 832 acres was offered for sale in 1932, when it was divided into three properties. A new large villa of 1934 with a round towered centre overlooks the Repton landscape which still retains the earlier kitchen gardens. Parts of the old deer park are now cultivated. The new drive to the villa is lined with *Cupressus leylandii*, and a steeple chase course is laid out through the park.

22.10 Croxton Manor OS245596

Croxton Manor lies at the far end of the village high street facing the remnants of the village green. The late medieval timber framed pink building was once the manor house for Westbury hamlet. From the C16th until the early C19th, it was the home of Dr. Edward Leeds, retired master of Clare College, and his descendants, mostly merchants and lawyers. The gently undulating garden has recently been restored and includes a knot garden of santolinas and box in gravel with willow pyramids, a conifer bed, raised vegetable plots protected by a yew hedge, a winter garden of dogwoods, herbaceous borders and a landscaped pool. The garden is edged with railings and views directly into Croxton Park can be enjoyed from the house.

22.11 Croxton Park OS251595

A small landscaped park to provide the setting for a new house was created in 1760-61 on the edge of the village by Edward Leeds, whose family had lived here since the 1570s. In 1825 the last of the Leeds sold Croxton to Samuel Newton, grandson of a Liverpool merchant, who removed the village, laid out a much larger park, formed a triangular lake and extended the house. Also of this period is a walled kitchen garden, an ice house, stables and a gamekeeper's cottage. In the park, immediately north-west of the house, are the earthworks of a circular enclosure and of former ponds. These are all that survive of the late C16th formal gardens here.

22.12 Eltisley, The Old House OS269597

East of the village church is the early C17th timber framed house built for Thomas Disbrowe. His son married Oliver Cromwell's sister and inherited this house.

In the grounds was the holy well of St. Pandionia the daughter of a Scottish king, which survived until the late C16th. The ditches, ponds, banks and prospect mounds are probably the remains of a C17th formal water garden. The principal feature is an irregular area enclosed by a ditch in the shape of a reversed 'J' which follows the churchyard fence. Two rectangular ponds are to the east of the house.

22.13 Eltisley, Pond Farm OS273597

Pond Farm is situated to the east of the triangular village green. This early Tudor timber framed building stands on a raised site surrounded on three sides by a tree lined moat. The elevated lawn in front of the farm house is held by a brick retaining wall. Between this and an outer wall is a broad expanse of grass which runs into adjacent arable fields. In earlier times this space was occupied by a range of farm buildings. The pond between the road and the outer wall has sadly disappeared.

22.14 Great Gransden Hall OS264556

Situated to the west of the village, Great Gransden Hall is a brick house built in the middle of the C17th and later remodelled in the early C18th.

It was built on the site of an earlier house near an ornamental moat. The Hall looks south into the park which is crossed by Abbotsley Brook. The 1879 sale particulars show a walled kitchen garden to the east (now developed for housing), pleasure grounds with cross paths near the Hall and formal island flower beds in lawns. To the north of the village street stands an orchard on higher ground.

22.15 Great Gransden, Rippington Manor OS271556

This is an Elizabethan brick manor house built c.1550 and it was occupied by one Julius Caesar, when he was physician to Queen Mary and Queen Elizabeth I. The Caesars were descended from Caesar Aldemare of Padua, and had settled in England by 1550.

The south terrace leads down to a large walled garden with clipped yew hedges enclosing a well in the centre. Further to the south is a moat. There are two fishponds and an avenue of chestnuts, with a dovecote in an adjacent field.

22.16 Great Gransden, Hardwicke Farm OS288575

On the route of the old Caxton to Gransden road is an 1810 rendered farm house with a large brick barn and other outbuildings forming a large courtyard

To the west lies a grove of poplars planted by prisoners of the Napoleonic wars. There are two ponds, one either side of the drive. The garden was created by the present owners during the last twenty five years by renovating the derelict farm buildings round a courtyard, and by the removal of extensive railway carriages which had been used as pigsties. The raised central path of the courtyard garden is edged with lavender. Many plants are grown in large pots.

To the south of the house is a central path edged with catmint and standard roses leading to an old apple tree covered with a climbing rose. A wide gap in the boundary *Cupressus leylandii* hedge gives views towards Hayley Wood. Herbaceous borders are filled with many poppies, sages and catmints.

22.17 Caxton Hall   OS301583

Situated some distance to the west of Ermine Street, Caxton Hall has a long access drive between two houses in the centre of the village.

This drive, lined with mature trees leads to the C17th brick house. The garden is intersected by the Bourn Brook which is crossed by a footbridge to a wrought iron gate giving access to Peter Street. Herbaceous plantings against the wall include many alliums. There are mature trees including several golden conifers.

22.18 Caxton Moats   OS295588

The date and function of this earthen castle with its moats, barbican and outworks, have been a matter of some dispute. It is probably a temporary fortification, built in the 1140s to block the old Caxton and Eltisley road during the revolt led by Geoffrey de Mandeville.

The only horticultural interest lies in the arrangement of low mounds and ditches to the south-east, locally nicknamed 'The Asparagus Beds'. Their actual purpose is unknown although they are likely to be much later than the castle.

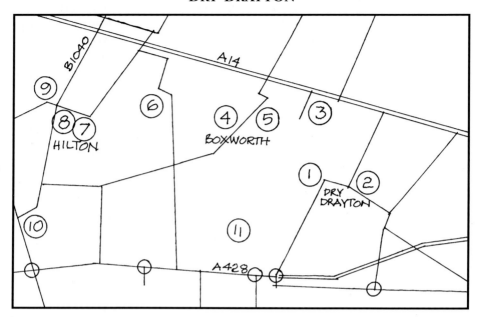

23.1 Dry Drayton, The Old Rectory   OS379621

The Old Rectory was built in 1830 and stands in extensive grounds. To the north and east were extensive shrubberies with many trees. and a pond crossed by a small bridge. The walled kitchen garden was to the west of the Rectory and was divided in two parts. To the west of the walled garden is a circular icehouse of gault brick with a round headed arch at the entrance. The icehouse is contemporary with the Rectory. The shrubbery walk to the south of the house enjoys views across a small field to Sheepclose Spinney.

23.2 Dry Drayton, The Park   OS382619

Until it was demolished in 1817, Drayton Park was the major house in the village. There are few records of the house until 1655 when it was occupied by John Sedgewick. Between 1713-1730 the house was probably the residence of the Dukes of Bedford and kept in good order. In 1795 the property was sold to the Rector of Dry Drayton who died in 1808. His son did not live there and the house was later demolished

In 1740 an estate map of the Dukes of Bedford shows an avenue to the south of the park and the prospect and gardens which would have been newly laid out after the house was built. All that remains today in a field east of the village church is the garden moat and the adjacent platform. Park Street has been re-aligned in the village.

23.3 Lolworth, The Grange   OS373642

The Grange is situated at the end of a drive, approached through brick pillars with wrought iron gates. It was built in1867 on a large scale with a patterned tiled roof.

To the south east are the remains of a trapezoidal medieval moat complete in 1842 when it was shown on the tithe map. The grounds consist of several gardens among mature trees – cedars, Scots pine, copper beech, Wellingtonia and limes. There is a loggia with climbing plants on the south side of the house. The garden has now been simplified. The 1938 sale particulars showed paths which are now grassed over and the complex layout of flowerbeds on the lower lawn have been removed.

23.4 Boxworth House   OS349646

Formerly the Old Rectory, the house stands in extensive grounds of 10 acres which include the old medieval street and part of the old village green.

The OS map of 1888 shows a kitchen garden, a plunge pool and canal with boat house. The property now includes part of the old orchard on medieval ridge and furrow and to the north east, Browns Leys Grove, the remains of an extensive elm wood which had cross rides. There are fine specimen trees – evergreen oak, plane and chestnuts – which today shade the canal.

23.5 Boxworth Manor   OS352646

The Manor House is predominantly of C18th date but incorporates an earlier, C17th building. It was taken over in 1882 by Captain Edmund Henry Thornhill (d.1936) and his son Edmund Bacon Thornhill who together created the present flower and kitchen garden.

These new gardens were based on those at the family home at Diddington (see 25.3), and Mr. Petfield, Head Gardener at Diddington, planned the work. By 1882 this was a small farmhouse garden and was enlarged eightfold and laid out by the head gardener. In 1902 the elder Thornhill planted a copy of the maze at Hatfield House south of the Huntingdon Road near a spinney called 'The Thicket'. By the end of 1914 the maze was overgrown and eventually it was grubbed out after the Second World War. Today the garden has fine specimen trees and herbaceous borders but many trees and shrubs were removed because of overcrowding. Immediately to the south of the road opposite is a small vegetable garden on the site of an earlier workshop, with lawns enclosed by low brick walls and piers.

23.6 Conington Hall   OS320665

Conington Hall, built in about 1700 by a member of the Cotton family, stands in some 70 acres of parkland.

Originally it had only a walled garden and a group of fishponds to the north. The parkland was created gradually after 1800, the south quarter before 1836, the rest in the later C19th century. This involved the removal of part of the village of Conington.

The fishponds and the walled garden survive; the latter now contains fine hothouses, glasshouses and a fruit room. The Hall is approached through a grove of tall trees in the park and pleasure grounds. The 'Wilderness' of 10 acres to the north of the Hall has a central vista with two rectangular fish ponds which survive today. There are mature trees and yew hedges to the south of the Hall.

23.7 Hilton Maze   OS295664

One of three turf mazes remaining in England, the Hilton Maze on the village green, north east of the village church, was cut in 1660. It is 53ft in diameter. In the centre is a stone pier with cornice and ball sundial. It was created by William Sparrow, to whom there is an inscription on the pier : "Ad hoc William Sparrow departed this life

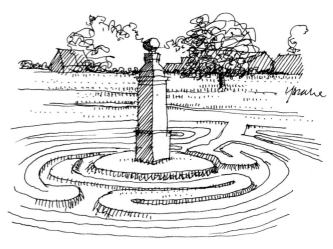

Hilton Turf Maze

on the 25th of August anno Domini 1729, aged 88 years". The central rings of the maze were obscured to make way for the memorial and in 1800 was recut incorrectly. In 1967 it was again recut, correctly, by P.G.M. Dickinson, the Huntingdon historian, restoring the original network of passages.

23.8 Hilton Hall   OS292664

Hilton Hall is an early C17th brick house to the north-west of the village green. Its first owner was Robert Walpole who died in 1699. His second wife was Susan Sparrow, the widowed mother of William Sparrow who built the Maze at Hilton.

To the south of the Hall there is a fine square, late C17th two storey brick dovecotee, with a pyramidal roof. There is also a small pond and extensive orchard. A recent owner was the writer David Garnett (died in 1981), whose second wife was Angelica Bell, the daughter of Duncan Grant and Vanessa Bell. Garnett's first novel *'Lady into Fox'* became a best seller. Another novel, *'Go She Must'*, gives a good picture of life in the village during the 1920s. D.H. Lawrence, one of his friends, teased him for living in a 'Hall'.

23.9 Hilton House
OS289665

Thomas Jeffrey's map of 1768 shows a building on the site of Hilton House which may represent the present building.

The 1888 OS map indicates a garden to the north of the house with trees and shrubs around a narrow lawn with a perimeter boundary walk. In 1922 the house was bought by Dr. Sidney Peters (MP for Huntingdon from 1929 until 1945) who found the grounds in a derelict state. With the help of his father-in-law, he restored the Victorian layout with a rose garden, herbaceous border and beds for annuals. At the time of his death in 1976 the garden had deteriorated once again. His son returned to Hilton House and the garden was recreated with ponds and fountains, a Chinese bridge and architectural follies, in keeping with the original layout.

23.10 Papworth Everard, Papworth Hall
OS288626

Papworth Hall was built between 1810 and 1813 for Charles Madryll Cheere and incorporates details Cheere saw on his Grand Tour, including some from temples on the Acropolis, Athens.

The grounds consist of three broad avenues that radiate from the Hall. One leads east to the Italian garden which is bounded by a moat with a lead statue as a centrepiece. At one time there was an icehouse nearby, and cages for rare birds between the Italian and kitchen garden. A breed of exotic pheasant was named after Cheere. The estate was bought in 1896 by E.T. Hooley who made a new drive lined with lime trees giving access from Ermine Street, and built a new lodge in the classical style. In 1909 he was bankrupted and the estate became the Cambridgeshire Tuberculosis Colony in 1918. In 1927 Papworth Village Settlement was established and it is now owned by Papworth NHS Hospital Trust. The grounds and mature planting of the previous owners have been sympathetically extended in recent years.

23.11 Childerley Hall
OS357615

Childerley Hall, comprising house and separate chapel, is set in parkland between the sites of two former villages of Great and Little Childerley. The property was acquired by Sir John Cutts in the reign of Henry VII. Charles I was confined to Childerley Hall by Oliver Cromwell for one night in June 1647.

The Hall is approached from the A428 at Childerley Gate along a drive 1.5 miles long. The Hall overlooks the large original C16th rectangular garden to the south which is bordered by a moat on three sides with flat top banks or walkways and viewing mounts at two corners. Originally the four acre garden was divided by paths into smaller knot gardens, mazes and arbours but these have not survived.

The present owners have since 1957 restored the garden, which was then a wilderness. The terraces, banks and corner mounts have been restored and there are fine collections of plants, shrubs and trees, especially an extensive collection of roses. There is a walled kitchen garden to the east and a secret garden to the west of the Hall.

TOUR 24
GODMANCHESTER

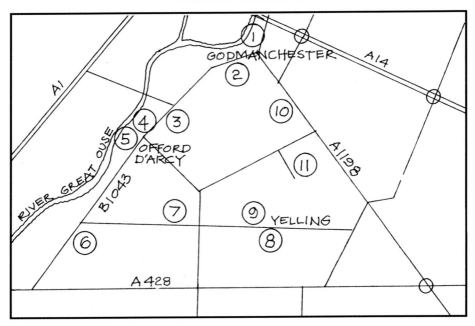

24.1 Godmanchester, Island Hall   OS245705

Built in 1749, this is a fine well preserved brick house with a garden which includes the island in the River Ouse. The house and gardens have been sympathetically restored by the present owners. In 1941 the house was used by the Women's Auxillary Air Force which built Nissen huts in the garden.

Sensitively taking account of the position of several fine existing specimen trees, the garden has been restored and looks mature. A Chinese timber bridge connects the island to the garden leading the visitor's eye through avenues which in turn reveal Port Holme, the largest single area of meadowland still surviving in this county. An avenue of Huntingdon elms is in course of regeneration. To the east of the Causeway an open field was formerly the site of the kitchen garden.

24.2 Godmanchester, Farm Hall   OS244700

This red brick house was built for Charles Clarke, Recorder of Huntingdon and a Baron of the Exchequer, in 1746. During the Second World War the house was used as a training centre for British secret agents, and after the war ten leading German nuclear physicists were interned in secrecy.

The south lawn with ha-ha leads to a town park of 24 acres with a central lime avenue laid out when the house was built. The park has a perimeter walk along the hedgerows. There are enclosed gardens to the west with roses, herbaceous borders and shrubs, laid out over an earlier walled kitchen garden. Opposite the Hall, on the north side of West Street, is a landscaped garden with pairs of gates and a claire-voie which reveals a canal bordered by poplars with outlet to the River Ouse. The canal and south avenue are on the main axis of the house.

24.3 Offord Cluny, Manor House   OS220672

An early C18th brick house sited on the east of the High Street, which was built for a member of the Deane family on the foundations of an earlier manor house.

Offord Cluny, Manor House orchard

An 1806 plan of the parish shows the site owned by Thomas Sismey. The grounds to the east of the Manor House are named 'The Lawn' and the 'Image Ground'. The first OS map of 1886 shows a park to the east of the House with a shrubbery walk to the south and a pond, with Manor Farm immediately to the south. The garden continues to the west of the High Street with trimmed hollies in an orchard beyond a claire-voie. The 1901 OS map indicates a new walled kitchen garden to the north of the house. The original garden wall has a gate flanked by brick piers with cornices and ball finials.

24.4 Offord Darcy, The Limes   OS218665

Situated between the High Street and the village church, this rectory was built in 1870 for the Rev. William Thornhill.

A long rectangular shaped garden to the south of the house is divided by paths often with shrubs planted to one side, with several low box hedges. Conifers, mainly giant redwoods and pines, evergreens, and deciduous mature trees still remain. There are ponds to the north of the house.

24.5 Offord Darcy, Manor House   OS216664

Richard Nailour built this house in 1606-1608 to the south-west of the church almost on the east bank of the River Ouse. In the mid-C19th the house was occupied by William Priestly, miller and farmer, who introduced French wheats to Huntingdonshire.

The house stands in the north-west corner of a small park enclosed on two sides by long brick walls. Manor Farm to the south has a dovecote adjacent to the drive. The gardens around Manor House were reduced by the construction of the Great Northern Railway lines to the west, and now have island shrub beds with a mature giant redwood.

24.6 Paxton Hill House   OS206625

This is an early C19th country house built for Edgar Hanbury with a later Victorian addition to the north-east.

Situated on the summit of a small hill to the north of Gallow Brook and standing within 46 acres of grounds, it has magnificent views to the west over the River Ouse shimmering 120ft below. The grounds are enclosed by a thin strip of perimeter planting. There is a lodge to the north with an avenue of trees leading to the house. To the south east of the house is an extensive kitchen garden with glasshouses enclosed by further shelter belt planting

24.7 Toseland Hall   OS234625

This symmetrical small Tudor Hall with tall ornamental chimney stacks, was built in 1600 by Sir Nicholas Luke. To the west of the Hall is a group of restored Elizabethan buildings including a thatched timber barn and stables. Nearer the Hall lies a pool, once a horse pond, now filled with fish and surrounded by a rockery. To the east is an extensive orchard. Nearby was Graveley aerodrome runway. The Hall was protected during the Second World War by a large red light fixed to top of one of the chimneys.

24.8 Yelling, Church Farm House   OS262624

Immediately opposite the church lychgate stands Church Farm, a fine red brick farmhouse of the late C17th with a five bay frontage with classical pilasters and pediments.

The small front garden to the street has a pair of chestnuts either side of a straight path bordered by flower beds leading to the front door. The west border is supported by a retaining wall with steps leading down to a large thatched barn.

24.9 Yelling, The Old Rectory   OS261625

Situated to the west of the village church, the Old Rectory is approached through white wrought iron gates.

A gravel drive sweeps round beneath lofty mature trees to the south of the long-fronted Rectory. A stable block lies to the north-east, and a small orchard with a pond. On the large lawn to the west of the house is a fine cedar of Lebanon. The lawn slopes away from the Rectory and is protected from the road with its high curving bank by a shelter belt of laurels. The Rev. Henry Venn, BA Jesus College, 1725–1797, when exhausted retired to Yelling and wrote *'Complete Duty of Man'*, his volume of sermons.

24.10 Papworth St. Agnes, Lattenbury Hall   OS270660

The Hall was built between 1800 and 1810 as the new parsonage for the Rev. H.G.Sperling on a spur of high ground some distance to the west of Ermine Street within a park of 55 acres including 26 acres of woodland. The drive passed a small lodge originally surrounded by tall elms. To the west of the Hall was an extensive walled garden with vegetable plots surrounded by low box hedges, and a large apple store. A stable block was to the north of the Hall. The Hall was demolished in 1965, but the parkland survives with many fine trees on its sloping site.

24.11 Papworth St. Agnes, Manor House   OS268648

This 1585 stone manor house to the north of the village, was built for Sir William Mallory, descendant of Sir Thomas Malory who wrote *'Morte d'Arthur'*. The garden has a dovecote and extensive walls, to the north a moat with water and to the east a dry moat and pond; all this is part of a larger but never completed garden layout with prospect mounds at corners of the moat. The house was built on the site of an older manor house which stood within a rectangular moated site. This moat was remodelled and became part of the garden of the house. As only part of the house was completed only part of the garden was laid out. By the C17th and C18th the garden receded towards the house. The eastern Elizabethan garden is now pasture land.

TOUR 25
KIMBOLTON

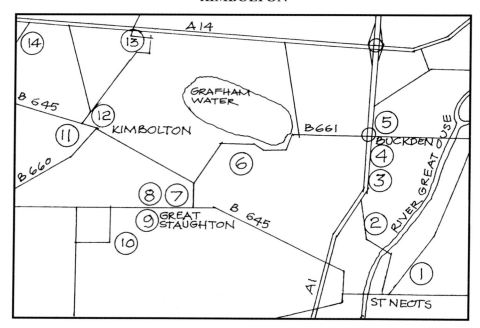

25.1 St. Neots, Priory Park OS195613

This public park extends over 80 acres to the north of St. Neots. The house, built for Owsley Rowley in 1792 and later altered in the C19th, was situated on high ground in the north-east corner.

There is the boundary shelter belt planting, and some individual trees remaining from medieval field boundaries, and clumps of exotic introductions. The garden had a shrubbery walk screening a quadrant shaped walled orchard. There are views across the Park to the River Ouse to the west. The house was demolished in 1965 to make way for a new housing estate and the park handed over to the Local District Council. In the 1930s the occupant was George Fydell Rowley who was noted for his eccentricities. He was violently opposed to motor cars and expected his guests to arrive in horse drawn vehicles or they were not invited again.

25.2 Little Paxton Hall OS187629

Little Paxton Hall is situated to the north west of the village church. Rebuilt in 1738, it incorporated parts of an Elizabethan house built by Bishop Reynolds of Lincoln for his son. The Hall could be approached from the south through a fine avenue or from the original Great North Road to the west. It is an imposing property originally with extensive kitchen and flower gardens set in 53 acres of open pasture land. The sale particulars of 1811 record the large orchard and a well stocked dovecotee. In 1920 the whole estate of 1702 acres was sold and divided into 27 lots. In 1989 the Hall was renamed Bethany House and converted into a retirement home. There is now a large garden to the front of the house.

25.3 Diddington Hall   OS195660

Built in mid C18th for the Thornhill family to the south of the village church, Diddington Hall was situated in a well wooded extensive park depicted on the 1859 Estate map.

The original layout of the park is thought to have been carried out by Richard Wood, garden designer (?1716-1795). By 1884 the garden contained an extensive range of conifers and, in a three foot deep bed of sawdust, rhododendrons survived remarkably well. To the east of the Hall the elaborate parterre was filled with echeverias, sedums, mesembryanthemums and multicoloured coleus. There was a parterre with L shaped yew hedging at the four corners, and a sundial. To the south was an inner and outer walled garden with glass structures. Sadly, the Hall was demolished in 1962 and the garden was lost, but fine mature trees remain in the park.

25.4 Buckden, Stirtloe House   OS196669

This late C18th brick house stands in the north-east corner of a small landscaped park of 50 acres to the south and extending west to the Great North Road. This was part of a larger deer park. The house is approached through fine iron gates and gate piers. A claire-voie with iron railings to the north of the house gives views to Buckden Towers. There is a well-established seven acre garden with fine trees, redwoods and cedars, and a walled kitchen garden with trained fruit trees along a south facing herbaceous border. Between 1784 and 1790 the house was occupied by Lancelot, son of 'Capability' Brown.

25.5 Buckden Towers   OS193667

Formerly Buckden Palace, this was one of the many residences of 60 successive Bishops of Lincoln from the 11th century until 1840. Many royal visitors came to Buckden including Henry III, Edward I, Richard III, James I and the Prince Regent. Catherine of Aragon stayed for two years following the annulment of her marriage to Henry VIII.

What now remains, including the Great Tower and Inner Gatehouse is mainly of about 1480 and is part of the great rebuilding by Bishops Thomas Rotherham and John Russell. It all lies within a moat. The outer wall enclosed a large courtyard and a bowling green.

Inside this wall were a small deer park, an orchard and fish ponds – the whole site covering 15 acres. In 1640 Bishop John Williams restored the park and constructed a raised perimeter walk, shaded by yews and a having a viewing mound to the north. This was destroyed during the civil war and restored again in 1660. In 1870 the site was bought by Mr. James Marshall (of Marshall and Snelgrove), who demolished several buildings and constructed a Victorian house. In 1965 the property passed to the Claretian Missionaries. In recent years the gardens have been restored. The walnut tree avenue in the outer court has been partly replanted. Catherine's garden has been recreated with medieval knots and mount.

The medieval orchard and nuttery has been replanted. A new pleached lime avenue separates the garden from the deer park and four fish ponds which were converted into a lake in the C17th have been stocked with fish. One magnificent oak dating from the C17th survives in the park and two London Planes dating from the 1660 restoration, one planted on the viewing mount, still stands. In summer it is difficult for visitors within the park to realise that they are actually in the centre of Buckden.

25.6 Great Staughton, Gaynes Hall   OS148663

Gaynes Hall was built by George Byfield at the end of the C17th for the Duberly family, and stands on high ground with fine views to the south within a wooded park.

In 1798 Humphry Repton was commissioned by Sir James Duberly to submit plans and remarks for the improvement of Gaynes Hall. In Repton's Red Book there are various marginal comments by the owner disagreeing with Repton's ideas. Today the C17th garden walls remain to the east of the Hall. The moat, which formerly surrounded the Hall, is fragmentary, but has the northern arm partly filled with water and spanned by a bridge. There are still remains of an outer moat to the south and east of the Hall with a smaller moated enclosure at the north-east corner. The entrance lodge and drive to the north have the remains of a fine avenue to the Hall.

Repton's suggestions for views to the churches of Little Staughton, Keysoe and Great Staughton were carried out. Part of the park to the east is now the site of a prison. The Red Book sold in April 1998 for a record price.

25.7 Great Staughton, The Old Vicarage   OS125646

The Old Vicarage is situated to the north-east of the village church which lies east of the River Kym.

Built in 1852 by Mr. H.B.Wilson (later prosecuted by the Ecclesiastical Courts for his views in *'Essays and Reviews'*) the house is approached through a mixed tree-lined drive to the west of a small park. A footpath leads from the west of the house through the park to the church. The garden to the west of the house comprises lawns and to the north a kitchen garden is divided into four quarters by paths.

25.8 Great Staughton, Place House   OS124648

Immediately to the north-west of the church, on the north side of the road, is Place House, originally built on the site of a moated grange of the Charterhouse by Sir Oliver Leader (1539) when he acquired the Rectory Manor. Here he imparked a large area of land, which led to riots by the adjoining tenants. The house was originally surrounded by a formal moat, which is now partially filled in, and brick walls to the south. There is a further moated enclosure to the west of the house and in the corner of the adjacent field a rectangular mound with rounded edges. Nearer the house are clipped yew hedges.

25.9 Great Staughton, The Manor/Garden Farm   OS124643

Staughton Manor dates from 1539 and was later extended in 1768. It stands in the remains of a 500 acre park with the main drive from the east near the village school. The pair of fine stone gate piers with rustication and bands of Greek key motifs with swags above can be seen across the park. As one approaches the church, the park can be seen with mature planes and limes and extensive ridge and furrow.

To the north of the Manor is the stable block with a central arch. Further east a private footpath runs along a tributary of the river to the churchyard. This continues as a ha-ha around the grounds to the south of the Manor. After the First World War the owner Mr. Howey, laid out a track for his model railway in the park and garden over a mile in length. This half sized model railway was later given to the Dymchurch Railway in Kent, which Mr. Howey founded in 1921. The east garden was developed in the 1930s as a sunken garden with suspension bridge and adjacent ponds with rockeries (now overgrown).

To the west of the Manor stands a fine walled kitchen garden of about three acres at Garden Farm. A gardener's cottage is built centrally along the north wall. This garden employed 7 gardeners before the First World War. Today the garden is used partly as a farmyard, but 2/3rds of the C18th brick walls still remain with original copings.

25.10 Great Staughton, Old Manor Farm   OS116631

Here stood an interesting fortified manor house built c.1274 by Adam de Creting, which for almost four centuries was the home of the Cretings and Wautons. The house was in disrepair by 1705 and soon after was abandoned as a ruin.

The remains were used to build the walled garden at Staughton Manor. Around the house was a motte and bailey with entrance from the east. This castle formation stands above a large rectangular space enclosed by a wide and fairly deep moat. An inner moat to the south has an extension to the north-west which were once fish ponds. Parts of the moat still contain water. There are fine pollarded sycamores along the dry outer moat.

25.11 Kimbolton Castle   OS102676

The first castle on this site was built in 1197 by Geoffrey Fitzpiers, Chief Justiciar to King John. Between 1534 and 1536, Catherine of Aragon spent the last years of her life here.

In 1585 a garden of 10 acres is first indicated on an estate map although it is possible that that Anne, Dowager Duchess of Buckingham, had a garden at Kimbolton in 1470. From 1615 to 1950 the property and vast estate was owned by the Montague family, Dukes of Manchester. By 1687 inventories recorded a Great Garden and the Little Fountain Garden. Three sides of the Castle were laid out with terraces. The Great Garden to the south consisted of a lawn flanked by a double row of lime trees, and beyond an oval pond. The garden, enclosed by two brick walls, was ornamented with 66 stone flower pots.

Vanburgh was asked to remodel the south facade which had collapsed and to "consider how to dispose the Stairs down into the garden, so as not to break too much into the Terrace". He also noted the canal which was "now brimful of water and looks mighty well". An unnamed visitor in 1727 mentioned "the gardens are 18 acres, with a canal in them. The park is 800 acres, with fine ridings". Joseph Spence, a landscape gardener, in 1757 gave suggestions for improving the grounds by opening up views from the Castle; these were partly carried out. The gatehouse is by Robert Adam 1765, and the estate wall and new kitchen gardens (now a housing estate) date from this time. In 1880 an eastern avenue of Wellingtonias was planted. which still flourish today, with underplanting of young trees for the future.

Kimbolton Castle

After the First World War parts of the estate were sold. Today the castle is a school which has restored the Castle and its interior and has slowly bought back some of the land originally owned by the Montagues. The grounds are now a mix of parkland and playing fields. The folly on Warren Hill overlooks the castle.

25.12 Kimbolton, The Cemetery   OS101680

This is situated to the north of the village church and reached by a well-maintained footpath passing medieval cottages and then over a humped backed cast iron bridge over the river Kym which flows round the north of the town. The site comprises 1.5 acres with access through fine wrought iron gates and railings between the decorative brick Mortuary Chapel and the Lodge. It was laid out c.1860 with a central and perimeter walk. The original plantings of conifers – cedar of Lebanon, redwoods, cypresses, yews and incense cedars – are now mature specimens, forming a botanical collection still to be admired by visitors on their Sunday walk.

25.13 Spaldwick, Site of Bishop's Palace   OS128728

A medieval palace of the Bishops of Lincoln once stood in a D-shaped site surrounding the village church, bounded on three sides by the existing roads and a deep hollow to the west.

Until the 1920s the remains of a series of terraces and scarps existed; and extensive earthworks have been destroyed by modern ploughing. In the north-west corner is a circular mound 15m in diameter and to the east are three marshy depressions, possibly linked rectangular ponds with a fourth small pond to the east. All may have been the gardens attached to the Palace, as was the custom with other medieval palaces of the Bishops of Lincoln.

25.14 Keyston, The Parks, Old Manor House   OS045754

The site of a former Manor House lies in a field to the east of Keyston church. By 1589 the manor was held by Robert, Earl of Essex, who was forced to sell that year to pay his debts to the Crown. It was granted to Thomas Emerson in 1614 by James I and was occupied continuously until the early 19th century when it was pulled down.

A wide ditch around the Manor House which never held water, is stepped in order to maintain the appearance of a true moat. To the east a long depression, possibly a pond, and to the south-west a bank or dam may have been a fishpond or perhaps a lake in the Manor House garden. Double terraces to the north and north-west are likely to be the remains of a garden.

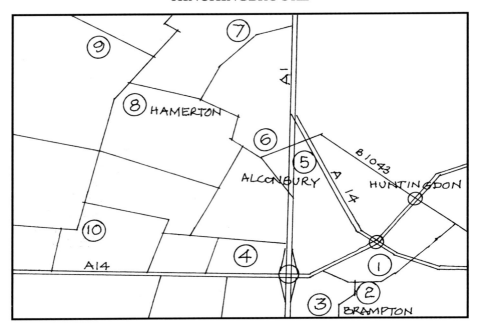

26.1 Huntingdon, Hinchingbrooke House   OS225715

In 1538 the land (the site of an Augustinian nunnery) was given to Sir Richard Williams (alias Cromwell). The property was extended in the late 16th and early 17th century. In 1627 it was sold by Sir Oliver Cromwell (uncle to the Lord Protector) to Sir Sidney Montague. By 1660 the owner was Edward the second Earl of Manchester, who had carried out elaborate work to the grounds which Samuel Pepys recorded in his diaries.

The entrance to the house is from a re-located C16th gatehouse through a courtyard with a circular lawn and clipped yew bushes. Extensive lawns to the east lead to a terrace with fine views across the landscape. To the west is open woodland with forest and exotic trees in which is situated a C19th cottage ornée with small box-edged garden with pool, terraced path and fine oak tree with wrought iron seat. A newly planted rose garden with lattice wall on the site of an earlier rose garden is now protected by a conifer hedge. The Japanese garden beyond the former kitchen garden has now been lost. Alconbury Brook has been made into a canal along the south-west boundary, and nearby is an allée 630 yards long planted with chestnuts and recorded on the 1757 estate map. Hinchingbrooke House is now a school.

26.2 Brampton, Pepys House   OS219709

Samuel Pepys was born in this farmhouse to the east of the village church. The front garden with its lawn and simple boundary shrub planting today gives little indication of the drama which took place in this garden in the mid C17th. Devotees of Samuel Pepys' diary will recall that on the 10th–11th of October 1667, Pepys returned to Brampton in a panic to try and recover the gold he had buried in this garden. Luckily after two attempts at night, he recovered his hoard.

26.3 Brampton Park   OS208704

This early C19th castellated house in Tudor style by Thomas Whitwell built for Lady Oliver Sparrow stands in 40 acres of grounds.

The 1824 estate map by Lovell shows proposals for the garden – a canal to the north of the house running east-west with a suspension bridge and statue at the far west end. Along the northern edge of the property cabinets (secret hedged enclosures some with statues) were made in shrubberies. There is a large walled garden to the west of the house. In 1834 Lovell was asked to produce a further layout omitting the canal and proposing instead a grand drive through the park with formal flower beds in extensive lawns. In 1907 the house was partly destroyed by fire, and a smaller house was built on the same site. This site is now RAF Brampton with numerous military buildings in the grounds.

26.4 Alconbury, Weybridge Park   OS182730

The moated farmhouse once stood within a deer park and a Royal Forest, and probably originated as the park keeper's lodge there. The house was rebuilt in the C16th and enlarged in the C17th when it may have been used as a hunting lodge for the Earls of Manchester. Certainly a map of 1651 shows the house in the centre of a radiating pattern of rides through the woodland there.

26.5 Alconbury, Manor Farm   OS185762

This early C17th brick house lies to the south of the churchyard, with associated farm buildings to the east.

The garden, which lies to the south of the house, is surrounded by a fine late C17th brick wall. Immediately on the garden side of the wall is a row of pleached limes. The garden is subdivided into small enclosed spaces. On the north front of the house is a large *Magnolia grandiflora*.

26.6 Alconbury, Alconbury House   OS195758

This small country house was built in the late C18th for Sir Peter Burnell, later Lord Gwydir, and enlarged in 1850 by Hodson and Vesey. The house is situated on a commanding site east of the village with the upgraded A1 in the valley below.

There are commanding views to the south and west through heavily wooded parkland, now reduced to 50 acres. Many elms were recently lost but a fine yew planted prior to building the house still remains. There is a short double avenue from the west with a drive through shrubberies to the house. From there a path leads, via extensive lawns around the house, to a walled garden with chamfered corners and a small pavilion along the south wall. To the north was an avenue from Ermine Street, now developed for a lorry park, which led to stables and other buildings. The house was used as a USAF Officers' Mess in the Second World War; Clark Gable and James Stewart were stationed at the nearby base.

26.7 Coppingford, Whitehall   OS178818

This large rendered brick house to the north-east of the village stands amongst mature trees. The garden is notable for a fine collection of trees and shrubs mainly evergreens and conifers, planted during the 1860s. Around a lawn to the south are giant redwoods, cypresses, phillyreas, yews and daphnes. This is very similar in range to the evergreens and conifers planted by the Rev. Strong at Thorpe Hall, Longthorpe, in 1860.

26.8 Hamerton, Garden remains   OS136797

To the south of the present Rectory, which was built in 1851 on the site of Hamerton Manor House, are the remains of an elaborate garden.

Sale particulars of 1669-83 state to the east of the sloping garden and "several yards behind it, are ponds of water, with a great garden, and other lesser gardens and faire orchards well planted with good fruit, consisting of about ten acres". The site consists of a broad rectangular area with a large mount, and terraces with walks and flower beds, all sloping away to a long 'L' shaped canal. To the east lies a trapezoidal area bounded by a low bank, probably a water garden with an island in the centre of a marshy area.

26.9 Steeple Gidding, Garden remains   OS132819

To the south of the redundant village church and adjacent to the site of a deserted village of Steeple Gidding are the remains of a C17th garden.

Soon after 1648 Sir Thomas Cotton demolished an existing house, built a new one and laid out an elaborate garden. The house was demolished in the early C19th but the outlines of the garden survive. A large raised platform has traces of cross-paths on it while below it to the south and east are the low scarps and banks of another part of the formal garden set above five rectangular ponds. The OS map of 1885 shows a double avenue of trees commencing from the southern most pond and crossing the landscape to the south for almost one mile. A short length of one side of this avenue still remains in arable fields today.

26 10 Leighton Bromswold, Manor House   OS116753

The archaeological remains of an extensive early C17th garden lie to the east of the church. An area 600ft by 300ft is enclosed on three sides by raised terrace walkways linked to two corner prospect mounds. Inside low depressions mark the sites of paths and traces of former shallow ponds exist in each corner. These gardens were created in 1616 by Sir Gervaise Clifton who also built a house to go with them. The house was demolished in c.1750 but its moated gatehouse still survives as the Manor House. Childerley Hall garden is of comparable size and layout (23.11).

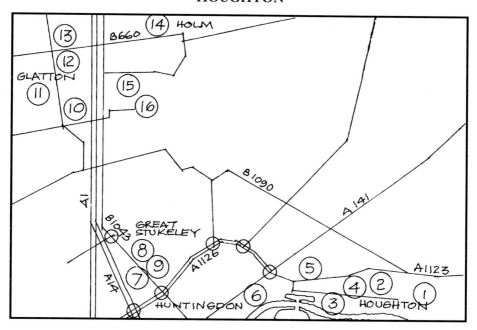

27.1 Houghton Grange   OS296720

Standing in 39 acres of parkland, reached by a 300 yard long drive of lime trees, this Tudor style red brick house was built for Harold Coote in 1897 by James Ransome.

The entrance drive is guarded by two lodge cottages. The sale particulars describe the gardens to the south and west of the house which stands on a terrace overlooking the valley of the River Ouse. The south terrace leads down to formal flowers borders and lawns for tennis and croquet and then to a sunken pool garden enclosed by yew hedges with rose banks on the outer curved sides. To the west is a sunken Dutch garden enclosed by high yew hedges, rose garden with tiled paths, a pretty thatched teahouse and a rose pergola. Thriving orchard and vegetable gardens with extensive glass houses are sited amongst espalier fruit tree paved walks. The grounds were extended in 1905 to include a further 6 acres south of the Thicket Path, closer to the river. This is now a Poultry Research Station.

27.2 Houghton Hill House   OS293723

Early in the C19th wealthy people chose the location of the village of Houghton to build new houses on elevated land which commanded fine views to the south. From 1840 this invasion commenced and still continues today. Houghton Hill was ideal for such a purpose and in 1841 Gilbert Ansley built his home, surrounding it with a park of 89 acres.

The house subsequently passed through several hands and in 1967 Lord Catto bought the property together with 16 acres, all that remained of the original park, and regenerated the garden which by then had fallen into disrepair. A view to Hemingford Abbots church was opened giving prominence to a mature cedar of Lebanon in the grounds. Extensive new gardens were laid out including a lake and a small park formed on the north side with a curved entrance drive. An open air swimming pool with guest house from restored stables and an octagonal fountain have completed the improvements.

27.3 Houghton, The Manor   OS284723

This is a fascinating two storey large brick house designed in 1905 by the Rev. F. J. Kingsley-Backenbury Oliphant in an Elizabethan vernacular revival style where no detail has been overlooked.

The garden is to three sides of the house, which stands at the edge of the pavement along Thicket Road. The garden has a terrace near the house with castellated yew hedging, and a flight of steps to the south lead down to a lawn with circular beds filled with small plants giving the effect of upturned saucers on a green beige cloth. Recently the garden has been simplified but the yews remain and the perimeter planting along the side footpath to Love Lane has now matured.

27.4 Houghton, The Elms   OS285722

Built in 1868 for George William Brown this large three storey Victorian house stands in 8 acres of grounds along the Bridle Road. Brown was a partner in the family firm of millers – Brown and Goodman.

Brown took a great interest in the garden, planting fine conifers, pines and many bulbs. Today the trees have reached maturity and provide one of the few examples of Victorian garden layouts in the county. There are monkey puzzles, cedars and cupressus towering above cercis, euonymus, berberis and pyracantha which are arranged in island beds filled with standard roses and edged with bedding plants. The large conservatory with its semi-circular glass roof is on the south side of the house and in good repair. In the spring snowdrops and aconites are followed by drifts of daffodils and then bluebells. All is well maintained by Intervet Laboratories.

27.5 Wyton, River View   OS267727

The garden created for a famous heavyweight boxer complements a late C20th brick house with two storey columns, imitating the American Southfork vernacular so often seen in fenland villages.

Pillars of well manicured *Cupressus leylandii* trees, imitating punching bags, each with variegated euonymus skirts, line both sides of the curved entrance drive. There is a wide range of conifers either side of the drive, with looser planting with monkey puzzle tree and various grasses near the house.

27.6 Hartford House OS257727

A mellow red brick Georgian house adjacent to a quiet lane that leads to Hartford church. Hartford House stands on the bank of the River Ouse, once a favourite spot of the poet William Cowper. In the early C19th the gardens, orchards and pasture covered some 6 acres. Later in that century when the house became the residence of Charles John Desborough, a Director of Barclays Bank in Huntingdon, the gardens contained many fine conifers, two enclosed gardens and a long avenue of trees leading to a viewing mound overlooking the river. The whole garden was enclosed by a brick wall. Today the walled kitchen garden and other parts of the grounds have been developed for housing.

27.7 Great Stukeley, Finings OS223742

The 1930s house owned by a recent Prime Minister on high ground in the village is surrounded by a two acre garden, and is protected from the elements by a shelter belt and a woodland with poplars, hornbeams and whitebeam. To the north of the house are recent shrubberies with large drifts of spring bulbs. Three ponds are planted with water lilies and contain koi carp. There is a wild flower area and plantings of the rose named after the P.M.'s wife.

27.8 Great Stukeley, Wychwood OS221748

Along Owl Lane and behind a high hedge lies a garden of two contrasting moods. Immediately on entering the garden one is confronted by bright colours of annuals and herbaceous flower borders with golden cypress columns and a topiary magnolia. Then further away from the lane is an acre of lawn with large areas, like islands, full of native plants and wild grasses billowing in the wind, in complete contrast to the strong planting of the front garden. Here thrive poppies and ladies bedstraw amongst birches and rowans. Vegetables and rare poultry are also accommodated.

27.9 Great Stukeley Hall OS223748

The existing hall is thought to have been built for James Torkington whose family held the estate for 300 years. During the last century it was occupied by various families and finally by Howard Coote, who bought it in 1904. The 1888 OS maps show a small park to the south with peripheral planting and shrubberies around the Hall, and to the west a large walled kitchen garden. 1870 photographs indicate complex flower beds in the south lawn. By 1924 the garden had been formalised with a terrace and ha-ha overlooking the park. The path layout in the kitchen garden has been lost and immediately to the south-west a new chestnut avenue has been planted. Today this avenue borders a new road to the Hall. New detached houses have been built to the north side of this tree-lined access.

27.10 Sawtry, The Manor OS168838

This 1820 brick house is situated to the north-east of the village green. The garden is enclosed by a new brick wall built to allow evergreen oak branches to grow through it.

The south garden has a lawn with specimen trees, shrubs and conifers. To the east along the road frontage, behind a hawthorn hedge are alternate golden and dark green conifers. To the north is one of several ponds still remaining in a large field owned by the manor in 1880, called Park Pond. The northern part of the field has now been developed for housing. Manor House has now lost the view across its field or small park.

27.11 Conington, Round Hill   OS155852

South of Glatton and 1.5 miles west of Conington church on an eastern spur is a partly moated pentagonal enclosure within a medieval deer park accessed by a footbridge from the east. The 1613 map shows a circular garden in a wooded area divided by cross paths possibly edged with hedges. At the centre was a lodge, now demolished. To the west was a symmetrical ogee space edged with trees. The whole area was probably intended for a house to be built by Sir Robert Cotton (1586-1631) who lived at Conington Castle. A sketch made in 1912 shows a two-storeyed gate lodge with a pediment above a large recessed circular arch. The site is no doubt the subject of the old rhyme: "Glatton round hill, Yaxley stone mill And Whittlesey mere Are the three wonders of Huntingdonshire".

27.12 Glatton, Allways   OS155861

The writer Beverley Nichols lived at Allways, a thatched cottage in Glatton, between 1928 and 1936.

During this period he developed the garden to the south of the property into a series of spaces. His secret garden, wood, the rockery and some of his planting interests – bamboos, roses, honeysuckles – can all be found in the garden today. The orchard and vegetable garden to the west as depicted on the garden plan drawn by Rex Whistler have been sold for two housing plots. During his stay at Glatton the garden was often opened to raise funds for the church. Here Nichols wrote his trilogy of books *'Down the Garden Path', 'A Thatched Roof'* and *'A Village in a Valley'*. He called his cottage 'Allways' perhaps after Irving Berlin's hit song of 1925 or because it was situated near cross roads.

27.13 Glatton Hall   OS155862

This is a rendered house to the east of the parish church standing on sloping ground with a drive from the south. The garden comprises a lawn surrounded by mature conifers and deciduous trees with clumps of bamboo, and a pond amongst the trees. To the west is the walled kitchen garden. Extending to the north-east is the property's small park with fine mature trees and perimeter shelter belts to the north and south.

27.14 Holme, Holmewood Hall   OS193883

A large Tudor style red brick house was built between 1873 and 1877 for William Wells MP, by William Young of Lancaster on the site of an earlier house of 1644. The hall stands at the eastern corner of an extensive park originally approached from the

Great North Road to the west. The 9 acres of pleasure grounds around the hall today comprise sunken tennis lawns over-shadowed by mature trees, and to the south a lawn with parterres intersected by a gravel walk and separated from the carriage drive by a handsome wrought iron screen rising from a dwarf brick wall. Then a curved ha-ha with views to the north and flights of steps lead to higher lawns with fine trees. Beyond are the remains of a rose garden with yew and box hedges leading to the extensive walled kitchen garden (now sold for housing).

A gatehouse to the left of the Hall with a semi-octagonal stair turret re-uses double doors dated 1631, restored with geometric carved panels. The first floor was used as a game larder with built-in game racks. The brick screen wall and entrance to the garden has an 1877 shaped gable

Holmwood Hall – garden gate

over an arched doorway with a terracotta plaque above with cherubs. The Hall is covered with virginia creeper and magnolias.

27.15 Conington Castle   OS180857

This C16th house for Sir Robert Cotton (1586-1631) stood in parkland with an entrance lodge and gates along the Great North Road. It was visited by Ben Jonson who described the house as "one of his favourite country houses".

Between 1803 and 1815 the Castle was restored by Cockerell and the grounds laid out by Lapidge (a draughtsman employed by 'Capability' Brown). The undulating parkland is crossed by a stream flowing east with several footbridges. The drive from the entrance lodge passes across the stream to the south-west corner of the Castle. To the east are stables which form a court with a central lawn. Further to the east, in a depression in the ground, south of Church Lane, was an extensive walled kitchen garden, with a long rectangular fish pond along the south wall, and shrubberies either side of the stream south of the pond.

The formal gardens were to the north of the house and bounded by a raised terrace walk. In 1798 stone octagonal summer houses were built at either end south of this terrace in which Sir Robert Cotton placed antique stones, and a further fish pond was made in the lawns. To the north-east of the park is an ice house on a moated site. The fishpond and kitchen garden to the east no longer exist.

27.16 Conington, Bruce's Castle   OS183845

All that remains of this important garden is a quadrangular moat, densely wooded, to the east of Bruce's Castle Farm. The castle was noted as no longer standing in 1586. The ancient manor house of the Bruses stood within a moated enclosure and was probably built by Bernard de Brus soon after 1242. It was described in 1279 as the court of the manor with a garden and spinney of 6.5 acres. The house was surrounded within the moat by gardens and yards; to the west was a vineyard, somewhat to the north was the garden, and between the house and the gatehouse was a herb garden. A 1595 map indicates the site with an extensive 'Flowery Close' to the west divided with avenues of trees into a chequerboard pattern. To the east was a small 'Hopyard'.

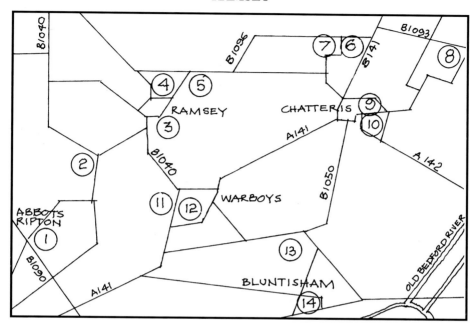

28.1 Abbots Ripton Hall   OS213783

Extensive pleasure grounds and ornamental gardens, developed from the 1950s by
Humphrey Waterfield lie to the south and east of the 18th century hall remodelled by
Salvin in 1856.

The gardens are on the site of a medieval garden which contained an eel pond and
mound, and a Victorian garden. Abbots Ripton Brook runs through the garden
feeding ponds and a lake with a Chinese pavilion on the far side. A brook crossed by
a Chinese bridge leads to a lawn with a thatched Gothic summerhouse and is crossed
again by a 1764 brick bridge. A memorial urn to Humphrey Waterfield (d.1971) is
adjacent to a canal and a fountain backed by a tall yew hedge near the Hall.
Outstanding herbaceous borders 100 yards long lead to a chestnut avenue, at whose
mid-point is a gothic crossing in trellis by Peter Foster (Surveyor of Westminster
Abbey), built in 1979 to replace diseased elms. Silver-leaved plants border the north-
west boundary wall, and a rectangular medieval pool is near a small mount at the
south west corner. There are kitchen gardens with plant houses.

Lanning Roper advised on the design and planting between 1960 and 1970, and
the Chinese and Gothic timber buildings are by Peter Foster. Fine East Anglian elms

survive, and there is a new arboretum with a collection of oak trees, white flowering shrub borders and circular rose garden. All lie within the bounds of a medieval deer park with Holland and Wennington Woods to the north in which mature cedars are still growing.

28.2 Upwood House OS258828

Upwood Manor House stands to the west of Upwood High Street in extensive grounds including The Warren. Originally the property of the abbots of Ramsey, it came to the Cromwell family after the Dissolution and in 1578 Henry Cromwell partly rebuilt the house.

The well-timbered grounds are screened from the road by a high brick wall and a belt of trees. A short avenue drive leads to the house. In 1920 the sale documents listed a sunken tennis lawn, herbaceous borders, shrubbery with woodland walks, and a walled kitchen garden well planted with a choice variety of fruit trees in full bearing. Parts of the garden have been sold for individual houses.

28.3 Ramsey Abbey House OS295854

Using part of Ramsey Abbey dating from the C12th, is a three storeyed house within a park to the south-east of the town. C19th alterations to the house were carried out by Blore and Soane.

The original C13th gateway to the south of Abbey Green and an ice house (in course of restoration) on a moated site near Booth's Hill still remain. An early C17th map of Ramsey Abbey estate shows orchards within rectangular enclosures around the house. The original C19th garden enclosed with a stone balustrade lay only to the south and east of the house. Later this was extended to the west. The garden contains fine mature specimen trees on lawns, a rustic garden pavilion and stone fountain.

In shrubberies to the north was a pond and rockery with a path edged with topiary yews which led to the entrance of a walled kitchen garden (now undergoing restoration by the Cambridgeshire Gardens Trust) with a stone gateway by Blore. There is a stable block adjacent to the walled garden. The main entrance to the garden is through the gatehouse, (owned by The National Trust) and is now part ruin. The house is now a school. The park is partly used for playing fields, and another school has been built in the south-east of the park.

28.4 Ramsey, Bodsey House OS295874

Bodsey House is situated along the Toll Road 1.5 miles north of Ramsey church. Originally on a small island in the fens, Bodsey was given to Ramsey Abbey on its foundation in 969 and became a hermitage until the Abbey was dissolved in 1539. After the Reformation the property was converted by the Cromwells into a manor house.

The original moat to the south still remains and the house today is surrounded by reclaimed marshland. The house stands adjacent to the road and has a garden to the east and south divided into two parts by a wall with a gate. The garden adjacent to the road is protected by a beech hedge and contains several conifers and shrubs.

28.5 Ramsey Forty Foot, The Elms OS308880

A small new house, situated to the west end of The Forty Foot Dyke, overlooks a recently created 2 acre water garden incorporating two disused clay quarries originally used for making bricks. The two lakes are landscaped with water-lilies and the banks are covered by a wide range of trees and shrubs. The lakes are divided by a grass causeway with a timber summerhouse affording views to both lakes. English elms still survive along the south boundary.

28.6 Doddington Hall OS401906

Doddington Hall, formerly The Rectory, is an admirable example of a large Victorian villa which was built in 1872 by W. Smith, and stands in two acres of attractive gardens. The Rectory replaced a C15th building and in 1852 the east side of the house was stated to have "one of the most delightful gardens in the kingdom".

The Ordnance Survey map of 1886 indicates an entrance from the west through mature trees, with an enclosed kitchen garden with fruit trees to the north, and in the south-east corner a sunken lawn with raised grass terraces on two sides. Recent sale particulars mention an attractive fountain in the front entrance and a small maze along a path which leads through shrubberies, alongside pools and under mature trees.

28.7 Doddington, Alpha Cottage OS399907

Doddington sits on fenland's largest island after Ely and is only 25 feet above sea level. Alpha Cottage, in New Street is to the south of the clock tower, which was erected in 1897 to commemorate Queen Victoria's diamond jubilee. The cottage was built in 1850 by John Yorke for the Watts family.

An early photograph indicates timber picket fencing at the back edge of the pavement and bushy conifers well established within the front narrow garden. Today the front garden contains three clipped topiary toadstools as high as the ridge of the two storey cottage and smaller topiary is emerging from behind a new picket fence.

Doddington, Alpha Cottage topiary

28.8 Manea, Remains of Charles I Garden OS480894

Manea lies in the centre of a tract of fenland of which the drainage was taken over by Charles I from the Earl of Bedford and his Adventurers, when they were facing ruin.

The King is thought to have planned a model town or village here, to be known as Charlemont. The entire Bedford Levels were to be converted into rich winter pasture, and in the centre, attached to the obscure village of Manea was to be built a royal palace, an

English Versailles. The town was to be designed by the King himself and approached by a grand canal cut from the River Ouse. Venice and St. Petersberg had both emerged from swamps and if the outbreak of the Civil War had not occurred the scheme might have commenced. A small hill south of the village still bears the name Charle Mont, which is now obscured by recent development.

28.9 Chatteris, New Road Cemetery OS399685

There are two cemeteries in New Road, Chatteris, both to the north of the road, and a further burial ground existed to the south of the road opposite the General Cemetery (Meeks Cemetery).

The New Road Cemetery (The Parochial Cemetery) is the more easterly in New Road. This cemetery was started in 1856 and covered an area of six acres with an entrance lodge and two mortuary chapels (Church of England and Nonconformist). These were located halfway along the central drive. Although the original site was a narrow rectangle the paths were curvilinear in layout. The road frontage is still lined with plane trees planted when the cemetery was opened in 1869. Similar to other cemeteries of this date, trees were planted for botanical interest and were enjoyed by local residents on a Sunday afternoon's stroll. Only the remnants of one chapel remains today, several paths have been lost and the cemetery has been enlarged on the western boundary.

28.10 Chatteris, Manor House OS397855

The Manor House is situated in Wenny Road, north of Tuck's Gate. The house is late C18th with extensive outbuildings and a cupola of the same date.

By the middle of the C19th three large fields to the east of the manor were planted to form a small park, with strip boundary plantations to the north and south. In the north of these fields is a mid C19th brick ice house amongst the trees. There is a semi-circular drive to the house through an early C19th long brick wall.

28.11 Warboys, Manor House OS304799

Situated to the north of the village church the Manor House is a mid C17th red brick house with two Dutch gables. The house was built by Sir John Leman, member of the Fishmongers' Company and Lord Mayor of London 1616-1617.

The garden lies to the south of the house, and is divided into two areas by a yew hedge. It contains herbaceous borders and a gravel brick edged path and lawn. There are fine views extending to the fields beyond. Earlier in the C20th the house was let to Virginia Woolf.

28.12 Warboys, The Moat House OS304798

Formerly The Rectory, this 1830 gault brick house with an orangery stands on a terrace with an openwork balustrade. The garden consists of 3.5 acres. To the south is a large fish pond with two islands reached by foot bridges. An ice house to the rear of the house and a timber gamekeeper's larder of 1830, octagonal in plan, were both originally thatched. A former coach house lies to the north with a walled kitchen garden and orchard, now landscaped with herbaceous beds and shrubberies for easier maintenance.

28.13 Somersham, The Bishops Palace   OS355770

The site of the medieval palace of the Bishops of Ely lies to the south of the village of Somersham. From the early C12th it became an episcopal residence of some importance, being relatively close to Ely and at the end of the first stage of most journeys made by the Bishops of Ely on their way to London.

About this time the Bishop created elaborate gardens around his palace. Two large lakes supporting duck, swan and heron, one either side of the approach to the building, created an impressive first view. To the side small enclosed gardens were surrounded by a moat. Behind the palace further gardens lay either side of a raised causeway, known as Lady's Walk, with views across various parts of the garden. Ornamental fishponds, a terraced walk with gardens below, further raised walks, a small water garden, and an orchard completed the layout which was surrounded by a large deer park. The site is now farmed, and apart from remains of brick walled gardens there is little evidence of the former glory. However, aerial photographs show the outlines of the ponds, terraces and water gardens as cropmarks, and evidence of the spacious layout can be realised from the existing field boundaries.

28.14 Bluntisham House   OS368745

Formerly the Rectory, this early C19th house stands on the site of an earlier C18th house. An 1814 account of the garden in the *'Huntingdon Gazette'* states "the principal eclat of this happy spot, is derived from its lawns and gardens, excellence of which few on so small a scale ever equalled, numerous illusions, labyrinths, mazes unvisited by the sun, paths winding into bowers, and cool grottos stored with scraps, conspire to please and surprise in these fantastic regions".

The present garden is about 3 acres with a lawn running down from the house to the new brick pier and railing fence, which enables a view to extend from the house uninterrupted across the meadows on the other side of the road to the river in the distance. In the rear garden is a Gothic arch said to have come from either Ramsey Abbey or the local church. The picturesque gardener's cottage on the west side has a timbered gable with triangular window. Part of the extensive kitchen garden was sold in 1935 for the building of a Meeting House. In spring the lawns are edged with sheets of hardy cyclamen. Dorothy L. Sayers, the crime fiction writer, lived in the house, as a young girl, when her father was Rector.

TOUR 29
ISLE OF ELY

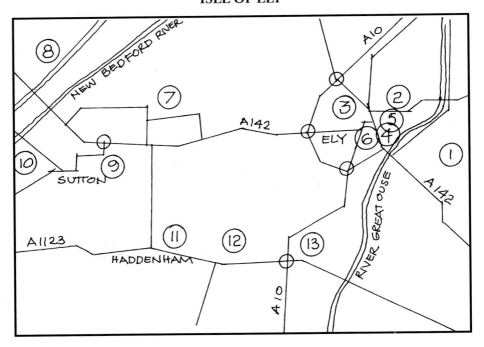

29.1 Ely, Quanea Hill   OS573797

Quanea Hill is situated at Middle Fen to the south-east of Ely. The house stands on a small hill overlooking the garden, which is laid out on the sloping banks. The west garden has a grass terrace leading to extensive rose beds and the steeper slopes are planted with ground cover plants. The north garden is protected from cold winds by an avenue of poplars which frame the east end of Ely Cathedral across the fen in the distance.

29.2 Ely, Prickwillow Road, No. 43   OS546806

A Victorian mansion dating from 1850 with a small drive is situated behind a screen of trees to the north of the road. The Ordnance Survey Map of 1888 indicates a larger garden than exists today with an oval lawn to the west and greenhouse with two plots to the north. The sale documents of 1985 mention a crinkle-crankle wall to the east and an underground apple store. Today the garden contains a large range of plants, collected by the present owners. The herbaceous borders are filled with interesting perennials and there is a vegetable garden and several fruit trees.

29.3 Ely, Egremont Street, No. 31 OS537806

Originally the site of one of many extensive orchards around the city, the garden at 31 Egremont Street still keeps part of the old orchard as an integral area of the garden. The present owners have skilfully divided this 1 acre garden into a series of separate spaces, keeping earlier division walls as part of the layout. The central garden is a productive vegetable garden with a central path edged with box. To the west are several trees with roses climbing through them and from here are fine views towards the cathedral. Nearer the house, the scale is more intimate with a lawn surrounded by herbaceous plants and a young Gingko and tulip tree are growing well, obviously enjoying the good soil and the protection from the cold east winds.

29.4 Ely, Abbey Park OS543801

Abbey Park lies south of the Cathedral precincts on sloping land between The Gallery and Broad Street, and is divided by an east-west path.

To the north is an enclosed meadow with several mature trees sometimes referred to as the Dean's Garden. The remaining area to the south is grassland with a mound – Cherry Hill, the remains of a C12th castle belonging to the bishops of Ely. Speed's map of 1610 shows Cherry Hill surmounted by a windmill, and a print by Samuel and Nathaniel Buck in 1743 shows Cherry Hill with the name Mill Hill surmounted by a stump. In 1779 James Bentham, a minor canon of Ely, planted the whole mound with trees, walnut, pear and probably some cherry and built a path which wound to the summit. Here he placed a classical column bearing the inscription (in Latin): "That these might benefit another age".

In 1872 John Bacon, Clerk of Works to the Dean and Chapter, noted that : "large parties would sit on the grass in circles while they enjoyed the red, the white, and the black heart cherries" on Cherry Sundays which were celebrated in Ely in July each year. In 1897 Dean Merivale according to a further inscription: "Planted an oak in the grove". At the turn of the C20th a summer house was placed on Cherry Hill. In 1982 the path and hill were cleared of vegetation and the column restored.

29.5 Ely, The Bishop's Palace OS540802

This was originally the Deanery and has recently become the Bishop's Palace. It is a large house built into the Great Hall of the monastery which lies south of the remains of the cloisters.

Against the north wall of the Bishop's Palace, close to its east end are the remains of the Monks Kitchen which is now the rose garden with lawn and garden seat. The garden to the north of the palace is divided into 'rooms' by ancient walls. The rose garden is divided by low box hedges forming a parterre, to one side a lawn with fine specimen trees and an herbaceous border, then a wild flower area and vegetable garden.

29.6 Ely, Old Bishop's Palace

OS539803

Two brick towers were built by Bishop Alcock between 1486 and 1500 at the east end of the green, and were later joined by three sides of a courtyard c.1670 which replaced a C13th hall. The north entrance courtyard is simply planted with evergreens.

To the south of the Old Palace was a large garden including an extensive walled kitchen garden and glasshouse range. The Ely Cathedral records contain lists of plants in this garden on 25th October 1787, which comprise many half-hardy South African plants which had found their way to Ely. The walled garden no longer forms part of this garden. In the centre of the lawn is a plane tree planted by Bishop Gunning in 1674, which he had obtained from the Oxford Botanic garden and is now over 120 feet high, the largest plane tree in the county. There is also a fine cut-leaved plane tree and a Gingko. By 1985 the site was derelict and following the sale of the property to the Sue Ryder Foundation, the garden was cleared and is being replanted. Borders along the south front of the Old Palace are stocked with plants recorded by W. Ingram, the gardener in 1787. The pond is now cleared and is surrounded with sympathetic planting and the garden is enjoyed by patients and their relatives.

29.7 Witcham Hall

OS464801

Witcham Hall was built c.1700 and is a fine example of a Jacobean house. In 1840 it was remodelled in the Gothic style and has recently been restored.

The gardens are screened from the road by a high brick wall and the entrance is through an early 18th century wrought-iron gate, flanked by brick piers surmounted with stone urns with masques, swag enrichments and flame bursts from gadroon capping. A pathway leads directly to the hall between two topiary yews clipped to represent large salt and pepper pots. To the north and west of the hall are herbaceous borders and a Victorian 'earth closet' is retained in a corner of the garden. The octagonal thatched summerhouse is dwarfed by an enormous Scots pine tree which acts as a local landmark.

29.8 Mepal, Fortrey's Hall

OS444826

Fortrey's Hall lies to the west of the Old Bedford River and was built by the Fortreys, refugees from Brabant in the early C16th, and later co-adventurers with the Earl of Bedford (of Thorney Manor House, see 30.10) in the drainage of the Fens.

Samuel Fortrey, a London merchant, built the hall. Later, in 1631, he built the Dutch House at Kew. His son Sir James Fortrey died in 1719 and his romantic career is recorded on a wall monument in Mepal Church. "He enlarged Fortrey Hall with very considerable apartments and with Gardens and other improvements so as to make (in such a place) the admiration of the time". These have all disappeared.

29.9 Sutton House   OS449791

East of the village church stood the large Victorian house of the Vipan family (see Stibbington Hall 31.3) surrounded by a small park of 22 acres.

The house was approached by a carriage drive from the Lodge at Church Lane through an avenue of Wellingtonias. The pleasure grounds contained many ornamental trees and shrubs, which were separated from the park to the east by a ha-ha. To the north of the house was a large walled garden with a vinery and greenhouse. To the east was a tennis court with a dovecote and aviary nearby. The Vipans were interested in ferns and had established an extensive fernery at Sutton House. The house has now been demolished and in 1980 the site was developed for housing. A small part of the park, some 9 acres, has been refurbished.

29.10 Sutton, Burystead Farm   OS434789

Burystead Farm incorporates a late C13th – early C14th chapel of a former monastic range and the south wing was built in 1742. Burystead Manor was given to the prior and convent of Ely after the Danish invasions. After the Dissolution of 1541 it was transferred to the Dean and Chapter. During the C14th it was kept in hand by the prior and convent, and was considered the most valuable part of their property.

The farmhouse lies to the west of the village where the high ground of the Isle of Ely drops sharply under the slope of the hill along the road to Sutton Gault. The Burystead moat is to the east of this road and is 40ft in width. Within the moat the enclosed area is not raised but contains various irregular depressions. Around the moat are some mature trees which are possibly an indication that here was a C17th garden and moat. There would seem to be no reason for laying out such a large moat for defensive requirements at some distance from the Manor. A large mature cedar which still grows in the farm's garden offers a further clue to there once having been an extensive garden on this site.

29.11 Haddenham Garden remains   OS470755

The garden remains of Hinton Hall lie to the east of the village of Haddenham. The present Hinton Hall, a late 19th century building, stands partly on the site of the earlier house.

Prior to 1969 the earthwork remains of an elaborate garden, possibly late C17th or early C18th in date, lay on the rising ground to the south and east of the house. They included a former trapezoidal pond and cascade, a long canal, terraces and a fine avenue. It is possible that the gardens were laid out either by Thomas Towers who sold the land in 1693 or by David Rowland who then bought it. The canal and a parallel avenue were laid out to provide two different views from the house. The site was destroyed for agricultural purposes and only some of the avenue trees, limes and elms, remain.

29.12 Wilburton Manor House   OS486753

In 1851 Albert Peel invited A.W.G. Pugin to design him a house north of The Berristead which had been bought by his father, Sir Albert Peel, in 1817. It stands in a park of 25 acres which was planted soon after the house was built. The drive is lined with an avenue of lime trees with shrubs beneath. This avenue continues across

Berristead Lane. To the south of the house was a sunken parterre with a central stone sundial. Nearby are fish ponds and to the north of the house a walled kitchen garden and orchard. Today the house is a school and part of the park is used by the school. Along the Ely road are fine oaks older than the park which may have been part of the grounds associated with The Berristead c.1600.

29.13 Stretham, Juniper House   OS513745

Juniper House, formerly The Rectory, was built during the early C17th, remodelled in the C18th and stands in 1.5 acres of mature grounds, south of the village church.

Early photographs show a tennis court with mature trees, and the OS Map of 1887 shows a lawn to the west of the Rectory, edged with trees, mainly coniferous with a serpentine walk amongst them. These mature trees can still be appreciated today from the west of the village, but the sale particulars of 1994 include views of an overgrown garden. Former residents of the Rectory should be better known as they include Mark Ridley (1560-1624) who became physician to the Czar of Russia. His father was the Rector of Stretham. The Rector H.H. Baber (1775-1869) was at one time Keeper of the Printed Books at the British Museum.

Today the vicarage is called Juniper House and is the home of the National Autistic Society. The garden has been replanted with a wide herbaceous border with several pampas grass plants and the old cedar, mulberry, walnut, yews and holly are now well cared for.

TOUR 30
WISBECH

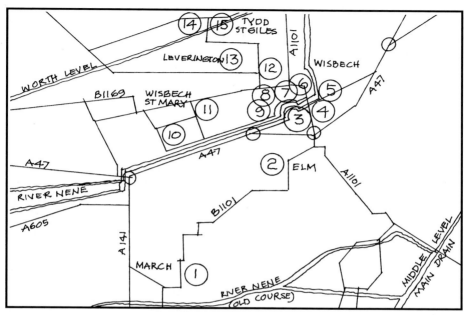

30.1 March, The Cemetery   OS420975

March Cemetery, in Station Road to the north of the town, was laid out in 1867 with a Cemetery Chapel and Mortuary spanned by a bell turret surmounted by an ashlar faced spire designed by G.W. Stephenson. From a distance the building looks like a parish church situated within a large graveyard.

The Cemetery is entered through cast iron gates with stone piers surmounted by large foliated finials, adjacent to a rustic stone lodge all by Stephenson. The chapel and entrance drive are on higher ground which slopes gently away towards the areas for burials. The site is approximately 5 acres. As at Chatteris (see 28.9), the trees, now mature, form a small but extensive arboretum of the newly introduced exotic species. The limes, copper beeches, giant cedars, cypresses, monkey puzzles, Wellingtonias, golden yews, and Scots pines contrasted with the formal avenue of Irish yews along the drive to the chapel and beyond.

30.2 Elm House   OS471071

Elm House was originally built in 1630 and the front façade was added in the late C18th century. The extensive garden was re-designed by Mr. Denys Bullard, MP for King's Lynn from 1959-1964. The house stands back from the road behind mature lime trees with hollies beneath, and a new cedar and monkey puzzle tree.

To the rear of the house is a grass walk between two wide beds of shrubs and herbaceous perennials with fruit bushes and vegetables behind the two borders. The whole is enclosed by brick walls which contained the original walled kitchen garden. The grass walk leads to a ha-ha and a vista has been established towards the young arboretum planted in the meadow adjoining the garden. The OS map of 1888 indicates ponds in the meadow where a bog garden is now being established. Further in the distance was an avenue between two ditches which was on the axis of the house. Would that the trees in that avenue of elms were still surviving.

30.3 Wisbech Castle   OS462097

There have been buildings on the site of Wisbech Castle since Norman times. Thurloe's House similar to Thorpe Hall, was demolished in 1816 to make way for the present Castle. The castle is on an oval shaped site surrounded by late Georgian terraced houses in the centre of Wisbech. It was built in 1816 by Joseph Medworth in a Regency style, incorporating a considerable amount of material from Thurloe's Castle. After Medworth's death the Castle was bought by William Peckover who immediately removed the northern part of Medworth's wall so as to open to the public an ornamental garden, which forms Union Place with a recently placed War Memorial.

The garden to the rear of the Castle is below street level and surrounded by evergreen planting, including a Chusan palm. Only one of two oval flower beds remain. Immediately behind the boundary wall are pleached limes. The lower garden allows access to underground vaults beneath the terrace walk, which is at ground level. In Thurloe's time the garden was grander with two curious looking obelisks, said to have replaced earlier monuments to persons buried in the grounds. The Castle was given to the Local Education Authority in 1969 by Mrs. Fendick in memory of her husband, who had been the Chief Education Officer for the Isle of Ely.

30.4 Wisbech, The Park   OS466100

In 1869, 19 acres were bought from the Ecclesiastical Commissioners for the creation of a public park in Wisbech. The Park was opened in 1870 and is situated to the west of Townshend Road

The Commissioners undertook to plant a lime avenue along the west side of the Park now called The Avenue. The main contributors to the cost of £3,769.18s.10d were William and Algernon Peckover, bankers, influenced by Octavia Hill who argued for the provision of open spaces in towns. Overlooking the south of the Park a new hospital was built in 1873 with a lodge and a detached residence for the surgeon. This was in harmony with the elegant houses existing along Townshend Road. A memorial column erected in 1871 to the late Richard Young, MP, still stands today near the bandstand which was opened on 9th July 1908.

The Park is divided by a path and privet hedge. The northern part comprises a fine arboretum, that to the south provides several sports areas, bowls, tennis, football, and a children's play area. A concrete platform along the privet hedge once served as a base for an army tank. Recently a garden, designed by Diane Maclean, has been laid out by the Nene Housing Society, incorporating tall timber poles arranged in groups of three adjacent to snake-like paving patterns.

30.5 Wisbech, Mount Pleasant Cemetery OS465106

In September 1877 the Local Board of Health purchased the new burial ground situated to the north of the Mount Pleasant Bank (a Roman embankment) for the sum of £2,250. A new cemetery was required under the Burial Act of 1854 as the Church cemetery would be filled in 3 years. It was noted in a London daily journal that "the Corporation's administration was being carried out on enlightened lines, which were worthy of imitation elsewhere".

In 1881 the Cemetery Chapel, the Cemetery Cottage and the gate piers were all built. The layout of the Cemetery is a rigid grid path pattern with a central drive, which is lined with conifers, evergreen laurels and pine trees. A fine Wellingtonia marks the first cross path where the path is edged with box hedging. The far end of the drive is marked with a further Wellingtonia surrounded by yews. Scots pines, a monkey puzzle tree, variegated hollies and copper beeches are further evidence of Victorian cemeteries planted as arboretums. A rose garden within a clipped beech hedge has now been included to the right of the drive.

30.6 Wisbech, Leverington Road, The General Cemetery OS459103

After many years' use, the Churchyard of St. Peters had become so crowded that a new site was required for burial. Three acres were purchased along Leverington Road for £950 in 1836, and the grounds were laid out with a classical Chapel in the centre designed by William Adams in 1848.

The Committee of Management set about planting evergreens and other trees and shrubs to make the site more like "a pleasure ground than a receptacle for death". This ambitious ideal was influenced by the Père la Chaise Cemetery in Paris and Highgate Cemetery in London.

A photograph taken in 1912 shows the cemetery intact with all its buildings standing, but by 1972 the grounds were overgrown with brambles and are now reached by a path beside a bungalow. The drive to the cemetery has been lost and a timber merchants

The Chapel, General Cemetery, Leverington Road, Wisbech

yard replaces the approach to the Mortuary Chapel. In 1974 the Local Authority acquired the site and sought to clear the grounds and demolish the chapel. Today only the Chapel walls stand, the roof has fallen in, and scaffolding stops the walls collapsing. All around the trees have grown to such size that they dominate the cemetery. Walker's print of 1849 depicted a simple classical chapel standing elegantly amongst mown lawns and small evergreen shrubs. Gone are the neat lawns and now primroses carpet the ground. A cedar, variegated hollies, Irish and English yews are dwarfed by sycamores and the original layout is completely lost. The graves of Samuel Smith, a local photographer, and Basil Lambert, a recent benefactor to the town, are only just discernible.

30.7 Wisbech, Peckover House   OS458098

Peckover House was built before 1727 and was known as Bank House. The Peckover family, who were bankers, owned the property from the second half of C18th. In 1948 it was given to the National Trust by Alexandrina Peckover.

The garden is to the north of the house and extends westwards at the rear of the stables and other houses overlooking the North Brink. The south front of the house supports a fine wisteria. The Wilderness walk to the rear of the house has evergreens underplanted with ferns, and the Gingko c.1800 (now reduced in size) and the tulip tree will soon be removed, but replacements have already been planted to take their place. To the west of the croquet lawn are fine trees, a Chusan palm, monkey puzzle and Californian redwood which are unusual in East Anglia. The central area is enclosed by brick walls with a small Orangery to the north. Either side of the central paths are hydrangeas and paeonies. A gap between topiary peacocks leads to a Victorian pool which has recently been restored.

Moving further west the garden opens out to a lawn with specimen fruit trees, cutting borders and a glasshouse filled with tender ferns. East of the Orangery a series of metal arches support climbing roses and honeysuckles. The border is laid out with Victorian formality. Throughout the garden are various structures (one saved from the family's kitchen garden nearby) and a rustic tetrastyle summerhouse. The whole planting displays the art of the gardener.

30.8 Wisbech, Sibald's Holme   OS455095

Sibald's Holme is a brick house, built in the early C19th and later altered by Algernon Peckover in an Italianate style with three storey bay windows. The house overlooks a bend along the North Brink.

To the rear was an extensive garden overlooking a small park. Early photographs indicate the Victorian garden with crescent shaped flower beds, circular rose beds, serpentine gravel paths, a sundial and vase on a pedestal, glasshouses with palm and cacti, palm trees, a folly and a bridge over the stream. There were views from the edge of the garden across the park to the two storey summerhouse. One fine copper beech tree dominates the garden today, and the glass house still survives; but the house is divided into two dwellings and new housing has encroached on the park. The adjacent brewery has also taken some of the rear garden. The small park to the rear has been developed for housing.

30.9 Wisbech, Elgood's Brewery   OS456093

Elgood's Brewery stands on a 5 acre site situated on the North Brink of the River Nene. This 200 year old Georgian Brewery was one of the first to be built outside London.

The gardens have been restored over the last 5 years and consist of 4 acres. The Elgood family have owned the Brewery for 120 years and many of the mature monkey puzzle, weeping holly and mulberry date back to their arrival. The lake (originally in Sibalds House garden) and main lawn still remain from the last century and new plantings have been developed to include a Japanese garden, a herb and knot garden, a rose garden and a maze planted with thuja and laurel. Much has been based on pre-war garden photographs which have been recently discovered and the whole has a feel of Victorian exuberance.

30.10 Wisbech St. Mary, Inham Hall   OS413076

Inham Hall was built in 1723 and is situated west of the school. The drive to the east of the Hall is through conifers and flowering cherry trees. To the north-west is a small park with horse chestnuts and limes. In front of the Hall is a large lawn edged with mixed borders either side which lead to a ha-ha at the edge of the park. The Hall is framed by mature deciduous trees. The garden to the west of the Hall is protected from west winds by tall conifers. The land to the east has been developed for housing. Immediately around and to the south of the Hall are extensive orchards.

30.11 Wisbech St. Mary, Manor House   OS421088

The Manor House at Wisbech St. Mary is dated 1791 in wrought iron on the north gable end.

Adjoining and flanking the house are shaped and curving forecourt walls with pilaster buttresses framing a doorway. To the south of the house is a lean-to timber glasshouse with an access through the curved wall. The front garden is dominated by two large topiary yews which frame and dwarf the house. These are further balanced by mature evergreen oaks. Luckily the fields opposite the Manor house to the west are still arable and not developed. There is a small park to the rear of the Manor with mature pollarded trees.

30.12 Leverington Hall   OS447112

Most of the old halls and manor houses in the Fenland parishes were pulled down in the early C19th. Leverington Hall is one of the few survivors. The Hall dates from c.1630 and stands opposite the church within a brick-walled forecourt with an entrance driveway through a pair of gate piers crowned with stone pineapple finials.

The main garden is to the rear of the Hall and is also walled. The wide lawn is edged with shrub and herbaceous borders either side and stretches towards the old raised Sea Bank to the east. Originally the lawn was divided into 4 quadrants by paths. There is a paved terrace along the east of the house with a small rockery and an ornamental pond nearby.

30.13 Leverington, Park House OS435119

Park House lies in Park Field to the north of Gorefield Road. This red brick house was built in 1720 and was owned by John Lumpkin until 1743.

The south front overlooks a small garden enclosed on both sides by brick walls ending with brick piers. The main garden was an orchard to the east and north with a further extension to the east. Between the road and the house is a paddock with a rectangular pond. Oliver Goldsmith is reputed to have written *'She Stoops to Conquer'* under the shade of a mulberry tree in the garden. The pond in which he may have visualized Mrs. Hardcastle "dragged up to her waist like a mermaid after her circumbendibus" can still be seen.

30.14 Tydd St. Giles, Paget Hall OS426167

Paget Hall (The Old Rectory) is situated in Cats Lane. The rectory was built in 1868 and designed by Sir Giles Gilbert Scott, for his brother Canon John Scott, who was then Rector of Tydd St. Giles. Paget Hall occupies the site of the former Rectory and is built on a raised terrace which is supported on solid blocks of reinforced concrete.

Part of the field in front of the Hall is an intake from the common. This has an access path across it to the west part of the garden, where there was a kitchen garden. The north side of the garden has a tree walk sheltered from the fen drain bank which is also the most northerly limit of the county.

30.15 Tydd St. Giles, The Manor House OS429166

Protected from the Fenland winds by mature oaks, poplars and cedars this late C16th manor house was restored by Howard Carter in 1926.

With energy and intrepid determination he set about improving the garden. A visit to the Chelsea Flower Show in 1948 inspired him to add interest to his garden. Carter was so impressed by George Whitelegg's rock garden display that year, complete with electrically operated waterfall, he ordered it to be delivered lock, stock and barrel to Tydd Manor. Later, he received a telephone call from Wisbech station telling him his garden was on the platform awaiting collection! After a lengthy discussion over the phone the garden was delivered. The rocks were divided into two and positioned in the south-west corner of the south lawn where they remain today. There is an interesting collection of trees growing to the east of the manor forming a small arboretum and the vegetable garden lies to the south of Kirkgate Road opposite.

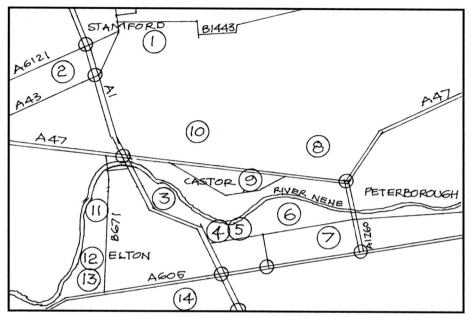

31.1 St. Martins Without Stamford, Burghley House OS048062

This important landscaped park created c.1555, surrounds a house built between 1555 and 1587 for Sir William Cecil, 1st Lord Burghley and Chancellor to Queen Elizabeth I, and lies to the south-east of Stamford.

In 1702 George London and Henry Wise were responsible for designing the goose foot layout of lime trees in radiating avenues from the house. This is shown on the Haynes plan of 1755. The house was remodelled by Lancelot Brown in 1756, including the layout of the forecourt. Between 1754 and 1779, he designed a new layout for the park for the 9th Earl of Exeter. The park today is the largest surviving example of Lancelot 'Capability' Brown's work in the country. The serpentine lake with a waterfall descending into a dell, the balustraded bridge with Coadestone lions, banqueting house, model farm and gamekeeper's cottage, carriage drive and park layout into Upper, Middle and Lower Park are all by Brown. Some of the radiating avenues still remain and individual sweet chestnuts date from the C16th planting. The large kitchen garden still has a collection of pear trees. The boathouse on the lake is in course of restoration. Nearby is the family Mausoleum.

The dell garden, originally an arboretum of North American trees, with restored ice house, is now a sculpture park with resident sculptor. The entrance court lawn to the house is edged with hybrid tea roses and to the south is a formal yew enclosed rose garden designed by Elizabeth Banks. The Orangery to the east of the house by Brown overlooks a small rose garden with central fountain. The whole park, now 1,500 acres, is enclosed by a dry stone wall with several fine entrance gates. In the south-west corner of the park is a golf course, and the park has been further landscaped to accommodate jumps for an annual three-day equestrian event.

31.2 Wothorpe Towers   OS025054

The old hill-top manor house at Wothorpe was rebuilt in the later C16th and surrounded by an elaborate set of courts and walled gardens including one with a zig-zag stream flowing through it. In about 1620 Thomas Cecil, elder son of Lord Burghley, replaced the house by a dramatic towered lodge which he used "to retire out of the dust whilst his great house at Burghley was a-sweeping". The existing gardens were swept away and new terraced walks and

Wothorpe Towers

parterres created, although many of the earlier walls were retained and still survive. The house was abandoned in the later C18th and is now a ruin. A splendid garden gateway with recessed seating niches lies to the east of the house.

31.3 Stibbington Hall   OS090987

Set in grounds of 19 acres this fine Jacobean stone house built in 1625 has a handsome stone gateway which leads into the front entrance court. To the west is a small park with drive through the perimeter planting, to the east are paddocks with a frontage to the River Nene and to the south a formal garden with central stone-edged lily pond in lawn surrounded by raised mixed planting.

Captain John Alexander Maylin Vipan came to live at the hall with his mother after 1880. He was a keen ichthyologist, and kept one of the finest collection of fish in captivity in his two greenhouses in the kitchen garden. His collection of butterflies and moths was one of the best in the old county of Huntingdonshire. In his other greenhouses he cultivated ferns and orchids, two of which were named after him –

Vanda vipanii and the hybrid *Cypripedium vipanii*. His collection of fish was transferred to the London Zoo a few years before his death in 1939.

31.4 Alwalton Hall   OS134960

Used as the Dower House by members of the Fitzwilliam family at Milton Hall this mid C19th house was reached from Milton along the Lynch Drive planted in the early 19th century.

This drive was planted in the picturesque manner and passed a farm house and lodge built from fragments from the demolished 17th century Dryden Lodge at nearby Chesterton. Recent owners have sold off building plots in the grounds. The house is approached by a tree lined circular drive and to the west are fine trees- cedar and plane – with herbaceous borders.

31.5 Alwalton Manor House   OS135962

The C17th Manor House is situated to the north of the village and is approached through a large court of fine farm barns. Overlooking the flood meadows of the River Nene, the garden is divided into a series of garden rooms by trimmed yew and beech hedges. The use of box hedging is particularly good here. To the north a woodland walk is being planted with extensive views over the Nene valley to Castor.

31.6 Peterborough, Nene Park   OS174979

In 1960 the New Towns Act included Peterborough as the final town to carry out a major expansion scheme. By 1988 the Development Corporation had acquired 1,500 acres along the River Nene valley and had developed outdoor facilities linked by a riverside footpath for about 7 miles.

The park attracts $^3/_4$ million visitors a year who enjoy the water sports centre, rowing, trout fishing and golfing to name but a few activities. In 1988 the Corporation established the Peterborough Sculpture Trust to site 26 major works in the park from its collection. These are to be found at Thorpe Meadows. With the new link road to the A1 from the north-west of Peterborough part of the Victorian shrubberies and the stone bridge of the Milton Estate now lie near the bluebell woods of the park. In September 1988, Nene Park passed to the Nene Park Trust.

31.7 Orton Longueville Hall   OS165964

The Hall, now a hotel, was set in twenty two acres of parkland to the south-west of the city of Peterborough which expanded under the New Towns Act, engulfing the picturesque village of Orton Longueville. Originally the seat of the Marquess and Marchioness of Huntly, the Hall was built in 1835 to the designs of H. Smith of London. Charles (10th Marquess) and his wife Maria were keen horticulturalists. Maria compiled an Herbarium of local wild plants.

They were both responsible for the introduction of rare trees to the estate, including the dramatic 700 yard long avenue of Wellingtonias along the south boundary, which were planted as seedlings in 1861. Mr. Harding, the head gardener showed many visitors the fine collection of conifers and was known for his patent method of measuring the height of the trees with his six foot staff. A gigantic Conservatory attached to the hall still remains. An article in the *'Cottage Gardener'*, July 1888 stated "The grounds are never more beautiful than when the numerous conifers are wreathed in fleecy snow, or resemble fountains and cones of silver by the hoar frost glistening on every spray and leaf". The grounds included rockbound dells and a wilderness full of ferns. There was a large rockery for alpines, a small Italian garden and a 4 acre walled vegetable and fruit garden with a central canal. In 1954 the hall and park were sold to Cambridgeshire Education Authority and a school building was built in the walled vegetable garden. The park is now a school surrounded by playing fields.

31.8 Castor, Milton Hall   OS145999

Milton Hall (which dates from 1594) is situated in an extensive park in which some original oak trees from an earlier Tudor Deer Park survive. The gardens and pleasure grounds of approximately 35 acres lie to the south of the Hall. There are views to the park from both sides of the house.

The Repton Red Book dated 1791 for Earl Fitzwilliam proposed a Gothic lodge and kennels designed as a ruined castle to the east of the house which still survive. The park is divided into Sheep Park (now the south lawn), Deer Park to the north, and Crickety Park. The stable block of 1690 by Talman is to the east of the house.

Immediately to the south of the house are a series of walled enclosures of irregular shape. The first is now laid out as a formal garden with a circular central pond, then the glasshouses remaining from an existing walled garden, followed by a practice yard for horses, which leads to an Italianate garden by Percy Cane with central fountain and summer house. In the west wall fine wrought-iron gates open towards the lake. A serpentine walk around the pleasure gardens leads to an Orangery (1791) by William Chambers set on a terrace amongst fine specimen cedar, plane, tulip, pine and Wellingtonia trees. An ornamental bridge over the River Nene to the south of the park is now in Nene Park.

31.9 Castor House   OS129983

This early C18th stone manor house with rendered front, was built for the Bishops of Peterborough. For over two hundred years the bishops were also Rectors of Castor, and lived in the house.

It is possibly due to their interest in gardens that the grounds of the manor house contained so many fine trees – cedars, silver limes, an extensive range of conifers and Judas trees. These were planted on higher ground which rises steeply to the east of the house and extends to the top of Love's Lane. This arboretum was laid out with serpentine paths, so there were no formal rides or main vistas with cross axes. To the north of the house is an extensive walled garden which recently was reputed to contain a cordon apple tree 15 yards long and still producing a huge crop of apples. The gateway which encloses the entrance court has cast-iron gates and overthrow between rusticated stone piers with ball finials. In the road face of each pier is a niche closed in by an iron railing

31.10 Upton, Manor House
OS111005

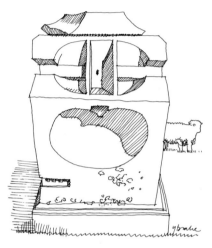

Upton Manor Sundial

The remaining wing of the late C16th manor house stands to the east of the hamlet of Upton. The two storey stone house was built for Sir Robert Wingfield, who sold the property in 1625 to the Dove family. Bishop Dove of Peterborough once lived in the manor house and is buried in the church. The house is said once to have been the home of Jane Seymour. It was also the birthplace of James Harington (1611-1677), the author of *'The Commonwealth of Oceana'* published in 1656.

The Manor House has a lawn to the south with a central flower bed and bordered by shrubs. To the west of the house is an orchard with mulberry trees south of the small village church. In the centre of the orchard is a mid C17th astronomical sundial in the form of a large stone block on a moulded base, almost 6ft high. It was erected by Bishop Dove. The east and west sides have divided rectangular concavities diagonally set with concave hemispheres. The side facing south has a deep heart shaped concavity and the southern face of the top is inclined and has a divided rectangular concavity with semi-circular ends.

31.11 Wansford, Stibbington House
OS076985

This late C18th house with roof belvedere and iron veranda stands in 3 acres of gardens to the south of the village.

At the gothic lodge a drive leads through a small park to a circular lawn in front of the house. To the west a terrace and sloping lawns lead to the site of an old paper mill with weir and sluices along the river Nene. Outlines of the rose beds in the lower lawn are still visible in drought. The garden was extended with river walks to the south. To the east is a lawn with several mature conifers which leads to the vegetable garden.

31.12 Elton, Berryleas
OS086943

This is a fine stone house built in 1930 for Sir Richard Proby, to a design by the architect Sir E. Guy Dawber in his sensitive neo-Cotswold style with mullioned windows and gables. On this site was The Old Rectory, a C17th house of Barnack and Ketton stone which was taken down in 1929. The Rev. F.W. Faber erected part of the boundary wall to the east of the entrance gates in 1843.

The house is surrounded by fine trees. A cedar on the lawn was planted by Faber who called Berryleas "that great Anglican parsonage". Clumps of trees and shrubs were planted between the house and the river; gravelled walks to these plantations afforded pleasant promenades to which parishioners were admitted. Sadly these have all been destroyed, as have the 12 trees planted by Faber and called by him after the names of the Apostles.

31.13 Elton Hall   OS088935

Elton Hall sits in 200 acres of parkland bounded by the River Nene to the north. During the 18th and 19th centuries the drive ran through the park to the neighbouring village of Warmington. Since the Norman Conquest there has been a house where Elton Hall now stands. Ancestors of the present owners, the Proby family, built a residence at Elton in 1666. There is supposedly a ghostly figure who appears by the small clump of trees close to the house. The ghost is said to be that of Robert Sapcote who did not like losing at cards and robbed his guests on their way home if he had lost too much money.

Very little remains of what was the original garden. A 1730 Buck drawing shows a formal garden laid out to the north-east of the house. Late 18th century sketches show the grounds with lawn, trees and shrubs. The formal gardens and pleasure gardens were laid out in the 1890's by Edward Milner and in 1913 by Colonel Douglas Proby to designs by his son-in-law, A.H. Hallam Murray. Only some mature trees, the box parterre and four conical yews on the south side of the house remain.

The main structure of the gardens as you see them today, the paths, lawn, lily pond, well head and rose garden wall all date from 1913. The rest of Murray's planting, which included the rose garden and bowling green, together with the 1890's planting of a geometric pattern of yew on the main lawn, had all been lost by 1979. The new layout of hedges, lime and box avenues, gates, orangery, hermitage, rose and shrub gardens and wilderness have been laid out by the present owners. Fine avenues through the park extend into the surrounding estate. The walled garden is occupied by a garden centre.

31.14 Washingley Hall   OS135886

Washingley Hall is to the west of the village of Stilton near to the remains of a castle. The house was built in the C17th, remodelled and enlarged in the C18th on the site of an earlier property.

The house was approached through a fine pair of wrought iron gates supported on stone pillars surmounted by eagles which still stand today. The drive terminated in a gravelled forecourt. The house was demolished after 1934 but the layout of the drive and garden walls can still be seen in the grass. To the east of the house the walls of the kitchen garden still remain and the fishponds are beneath the mature trees which once formed the pleasure grounds. The curved garden wall foundations from the south front of the house can also be found in the grass. These stone walls had arched recesses with seating. A paved terrace leads directly onto the extensive south lawn. It is interesting to note that during the early C18th Charles Bridgeman bought an inn for his wife in Stilton, and may have been involved in the garden at Washingley.

When Lord Cobham acquired the property, the south gardens contained clipped yews around flower beds, and there was a summer house and lily pond. The south garden would have been bounded by the moat. The stable block to the west is now a farm. All these are within a park with fishponds, pheasantry and stew ponds.

Washingley Hall

TOUR 32
BARNACK

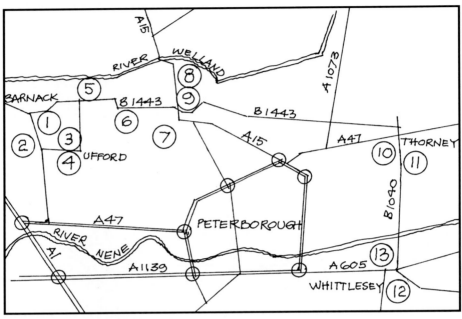

32.1 Barnack, Kingsley House   OS078049

Kingsley House, formerly the Old Rectory, lies south-west of Barnack Church and is named after the Kingsley family. Charles Kingsley was a member of this family and wrote *'The Water Babies'* in 1863. Originally the house was built in C14th but was altered in 1792 and by the Victorians in 1861.

The house is approached by a curving drive from Millstone Lane to the west, while a second entrance with circular drive leads to the church. The large walled garden is laid out with a sunken lawn with rose beds, lawns and trees to the south, and has a similar garden layout with sunken lawn as shown on an 1810 west view. Kingsley House is now divided into two private houses but still retains the exterior Kingsley knew.

32.2 Barnack, Walcot Hall   OS079042

In 1671 on the death of Bernard Walcot, Walcot was bought by Sir Hugh Cholmondeley who built the present house in 1678.

Situated on slightly higher ground than the garden, the hall has fine views across the landscape to the east. Garden walls and terraces to the south and west are possibly part of the 18th century improvements carried out in 1767. The grounds are entered from the lodge through fine C17th gate piers to the north of the hall. The stable block lies to the east. To the south are the gardens with a canal and vista to Ufford in the east. The view from the west of the hall is through an avenue of lime trees which leads to a disused entrance on the Great North Road. The grounds to the north of the hall adjoin the 'Hills and Holes', abandoned early quarry workings. In the garden are two temples and a rotunda.

32.3 Ufford Hall   OS091044

Ufford Hall was built between 1734 and 1751 by George Manners, the third son of the 3rd Duke of Rutland, on the site of the old manor house of Uphall. The Hall is situated on the west side of the road to Bainton with stable block to the north.

Ufford Hall

There is a park of 34 acres to the west of the Hall created from paddocks owned by William Symonds in 1799. An interesting perimeter walk in the southern shelter belt of the park leads to the church via an enclosed covered gateway, a mixture of Gothic and Jacobean but probably C19th. The Hall has views across open land to the east and the garden to the west is mainly lawns with a ha-ha at the edge of the park. A walled kitchen garden is to the north of the stable block.

32.4 Ufford, Old Rectory   OS091043

The rectory has a C19th external appearance but conceals C14th roof timbers inside. It was the home of Mary Paley between 1850-70, the daughter of Rev. Thomas Paley, Rector of Ufford cum Bainton, who wrote about: "the rambling old house, its front covered in red and white roses, a lawn, forest trees, long herbaceous borders and green terraces of the wonderful Victorian garden". She subsequently married Alfred Marshall, the economist, and spent the later years of her life at Balliol Croft, 6 Madingley Road in Cambridge (see 6.7).

32.5 Bainton House   OS094063

Situated to the north of the village, this C16th/17th stone house overlooks a mini park to the south-west towards the Stamford road, and is reached from a lodge via a drive passing through the park.

The garden covers almost two acres with a ha-ha at the edge of the park and to the west a spinney. There is a wild garden and in spring there is a fine display of bulbs.

32.6 Helpston, John Clare's Cottage OS112054

The poet John Clare was born in 1793 in a small stone-built thatched cottage along the road to Ailsworth. In 1811 he moved from Woodcroft Castle to Burghley House as a gardener's boy. There is a dovecote on the north side of the property, the last of three that existed when the whole of the village was purchased by the Fitzwilliams under Elizabeth I. Today the cottage is adorned by fine hanging baskets and low growing climbers. Between 1824-1825 Clare kept a journal in which he made several references to his garden – what plants flowered, trees that grew there, cuttings he collected from the wild and established, and also plants and seeds given to him.

32.7 Etton, Woodcroft Castle OS140045

Situated in the remote fenlands north-west of Peterborough are the important remains of a moated C13th castle with a later Elizabethan range.

The grounds include sweeping lawns and mature trees in front of the castle. To the rear is a small rose garden. The site is now surrounded by a shelter belt of trees along the approach roads, and the grounds are somewhat unkempt but secluded. John Clare, who lived nearby at Helpston, worked as a gardener at Woodcroft Castle but became "tired of wading thro' the moat each day so left".

32.8 Northborough Manor OS151075

This stone manor house and gatehouse range were built in 1334 by Roger de Norburgh, who was Bishop of Lichfield and Coventry and later became Lord High Treasurer of England under Edward III. In 1572 John Claypole built the dovecote; his grandson married Oliver Cromwell's favourite daughter, Elizabeth, when she was 16 years old and then came to live at Northborough Manor.

In 1960 the waterway access to the south of the property was drained, earlier access to the village had been by the Roman canal (Car Dyke) at the east side of the village. In 1960 Roy Genders rented the manor and proceeded to restore the building. The layout of the garden immediately to the south of the hall is his design. He wrote over 300 gardening books and articles during his stay at Northborough. The house then became a restaurant and recently the present owners have completed the restoration and brought the garden layout back to the plan established by Genders.

Today the planting with low hedges of lavender and santolina around a formal layout is evocative of medieval garden layouts, and the east garden has a sympathetic timber trellis walk for growing vines with a central urn. An avenue of weeping willows leads to a live willow seat by Andrew Basham near the vegetable and cutting garden.

32.9 Glinton, The Manor House OS156059

Situated east of the village church this ashlared house built in 1630-1640, probably for the Wildebore family, has fine curved gables on the west front.

The west garden within a low yew hedge contains both conifers and deciduous trees. In the centre of the lawn is a topiary Irish yew and other yew topiary at the edge. There is a walled garden to the south and east of the house with cross and perimeter paths and some specimen trees. To the north is a large range of farm buildings also with curved gables.

32.10 Thorney Abbey House   OS280040

This stone house with a central chimney was built in 1660 by the same builders as at Thorpe Hall (see 33.8), but to a smaller scale, for John, Earl of Bedford. His father Francis, the 4th Earl of Bedford, took the lead in organising the work and finding the money to solve the problem of making below sea level lands dry and fertile, upon the advice of Cornelius Vermuyden.

To the west of the house is a raised stone balustraded terrace with central steps leading to lawns and specimen trees. The entrance is from the street to the south-east of the stable block, through a gateway with stone piers and globes similar to those at Thorpe Hall. The west garden wall has a timber gate between a further pair of stone piers with globes in the brick wall which leads to a five sided walled kitchen garden with diagonal canal. A stone gateway with pediment leads from the kitchen garden to the park, known as Abbey Field, which surrounds the house on three sides. Immediately within the park on the north side next to the Peterborough Road is Thorney River. Boat houses in the park were connected by canals to the river.

32.11 Thorney, Thorneycroft   OS284039

This Victorian house to the east of the road going south to Whittlesey from the village has a small garden bounded by a raised bank and ditches sympathetically planted with evergreens, box hedging, conifers, laurels and yews. The road frontage is compactly planted under dense tree canopy. This is a rare example of a garden stocked with Victorian favourites available during the last century. Here is a good impression of what so many gardens during the last century must have looked like before perennial and ground-cover plants became the vogue.

32.12 Whittlesey, Portland House   OS270969

The remains of a north entrance gateway, flanked by a pair of fine gate piers surmounted by stone vases and a pair of stone gate piers surmounted by eagles in a suburban front garden are all that remain today of Portland House. The original structure dated from 1600 and was enlarged later in the C17th. Frances Stuart married Lord Jerome Weston when she was fifteen years old. Three years later her husband became 2nd Earl of Portland and it was he who probably built the house. He later received 2,000 acres of land around Whittlesey as a gift from King Charles II. Francis died in 1694 and is buried in Westminster Abbey.

Before demolition of the house after the Second World War, an RAF aerial photograph shows the south garden which was enclosed by a stone wall. From the central bay of the house two diagonal paths radiated from the terrace which overlooked a lawn with mature trees along the southern boundary. To the west were fruit trees and to the east a rose garden enclosed by a privet hedge. The front garden to the north had a Ginkgo and an acacia tree either side of the diagonal flagged stone drive.

32.13 Whittlesey, Sudbury Court   OS264976

Situated to the north of the town on the line of the old Roman 'Fen Causeway' this recent sheltered housing accommodation was built on the site of a market garden and today is surrounded by drab post-war semi detached houses.

Anthony Walker (architect) has created an inward looking village and John Dejardin (landscape architect) has extended and enhanced the variety and scale of the architecture with planting throughout. Paths wind through a series of varied spaces formed by trees, shrubs, ground cover plants and rolling grassed areas. The rear areas have a wilder appearance and are planted with faster growing species to screen unsightly surrounding houses. In addition to the communal landscaped areas are three allotments and a greenhouse for keen gardeners.

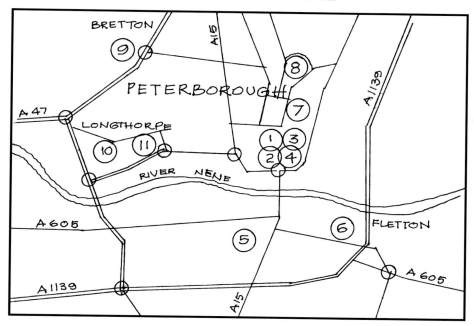

33.1 Peterborough, Cathedral Precincts

OS195986

St. Peter's Cathedral is acknowledged as one of the finest Norman cathedrals in Europe. It is surrounded by medieval walled precincts covering 30 acres which constitute a green heart for the modern city. The precincts contain the site of Medeshamstede 'the first monastery in all Mercia' founded c.674, and the subsequent late Saxon defensive Burh, which was monastery and community combined. The remains of a Norman motte and bailey, Tout Hill, are in the Deanery garden. The Benedictine monastery was surrendered in 1539 and established as a cathedral in 1541. The precincts are identified as follows:

1. Gallery, Galilee or Minster Court.

This entrance court has witnessed great pilgrimages, riots and battles, the funeral processions of Katherine of Aragon and Mary, Queen of Scots, arrived here and Cromwell's soldiers rode in to sack the Cathedral in 1643. Eayre's map of 1718 shows orchards/gardens in the north-west corner of the court, and the 1st OS map of 1886 shows the present layout of green wedges, shrubs and gravel paths.

2. The Cloister, also known as Laurel Court.

The cloister dates from the C12th and was demolished in 1643. It was then let as a nursery garden to John Glover on condition "that the tenant should supply laurel leaves and evergreens for decorating the Cathedral on the principal feast days". The cloister is crossed by a diagonal path.

3. Cemetery areas north and east of the Cathedral.
The north cemetery dates from the C7th but the present gravestones are mostly 18th century. With its trees and wide borders, planted in 1823, little seems to have changed in the last 150 years. The Monks' cemetery is to the south-east of the Cathedral and has graves of bishops and other notables. This area (which conforms to the St. Gall plan, where it is referred to as 'Paradise') has trees and wild flowers.

4. The Six Prebendal houses and their gardens.
Monastic buildings to the south of the Cathedral were converted into houses with gardens for six canons as a result of the 1541 Reformation. The 1886 OS map shows the gardens as Victorian, with shrubberies, walks and formal flower beds.

33.2 Peterborough, The Bishop's Palace   OS195986

Formerly The Abbot's gardens which stretched down to the River Nene and in 1302 Abbot Godfrey de Crowland's Herbarium with double moats and bridges was planted at a cost of £25. Early 19th century engravings show the palace garden as "bosky and well-treed" with landscape paths; and Rock's engraving of c.1840 has sheep on the lawn, with Reptonesque flower beds near the building, some of which still survive. The C20th saw the River Nene channelled and the Bishop lost his watery garden. The water meadows were filled and the herbarium lost under a car park. But in 1896, Bishop Carr Glyn appointed Edwin Lutyens to extend the Palace. This new south-east wing overlooks the vegetable garden and is complemented by a Jekyll garden layout with fruit trees and herbaceous plants with a central path. The Refectory vegetable garden to the south was originally divided from the Palace by a high wall. With its wall now removed this vegetable garden becomes an extension to the Palace garden. It still retains its 1886 layout with many of the box hedges still intact. Two thirds are still a productive garden, the remainder is given over to orchard.

33.3 Peterborough, The Deanery Garden   OS195986

The present deanery contains a core of medieval buildings and the changes to the garden are well documented. Eayre's 1728 map shows two large fish ponds which were later filled in by 1825. The front garden was an orchard and Tout Hill was in the bishop's deer park. The deer park disappeared in C19th development of Peterborough. Well documented as an early Victorian Picturesque garden of great note, Dean Turton maintained a fine garden in the 1840's, and at the end of the C19th Dean Barlow made the walk, walls and arches that remain in the eastern part of the garden. The cemetery areas and the Deanery garden retain an overwhelming Picturesque atmosphere.

Today car parking in the entrance court has reduced the edges of the island bed. Within the garden only one third of the vegetable garden is worked, the remainder is grass and orchard. Much of the perimeter landscape remains but along the northern herbaceous border ground elder has taken over and will be difficult to maintain. The 'dell' created in the moat of the castle is overrun with tree seedlings as are the slopes of Tout Hill. The mature copper beech dominates the east lawn but the nearby Judas tree, cockspur thorn and mulberry are old and add to the air of general decline in the garden.

33.4 Peterborough, The Vineyard OS195986

The Cathedral Vineyard is situated to the east of the cathedral along the eastern boundary of the precincts. The earliest garden history reference is for the vineyard. Abbot Martin de Bec "gathered together many monks for the worship of God and planted a vineyard" according to the *'Chronicle'* of Hugh Candidus dated 1147. This was maintained throughout the C15th, and this strip of land has been cultivated ever since. John Harvey's plan of 1981 records two garden areas of medieval origin in the southern part of the vineyard. Eayre's map of 1720 shows the northern part partly treed and partly open and the southern part laid out in more formal manner with an orchard. The boundary of the Vineyard has remained the same since the middle part east of the Cathedral was added to the Monks' Cemetery c.1214-22. By 1886 an extensive Picturesque garden enclosed by stone walls had been planted. Sadly to the south of the garden two bungalows have been erected with vehicular access and a timber fence divides the garden.

33.5 Peterborough, Fletton Tower OS190976

Built in 1840 by William Lawrence, a local solicitor, this romantic Tudor style stone house with a central tower over the entrance porch stands hidden behind high brick walls, surrounded by rows of terraced houses and factories in Peterborough.

Access was from the Oundle Road to the north via a tree lined drive with a lodge to a gateway leading to the gardens. Another drive served the property from London Road to the east. The garden was originally laid out in a series of rectangular compartments around the house. At the turn of the century it became the home of L.P. Hartley, the author of *'The Go-Between'* and the *'Eustace and Hilda'* trilogy. Today the north avenue has been built over and several of the compartments have been sold. The east drive has been abandoned to a factory estate. The entrance to the house is now from the south.

33.6 Peterborough, The Cemetery OS197996

Broad Road Cemetery is to the south of The Park. It was one of the new cemeteries urgently required in the 1850's and was laid out on a series of rectangular spaces connected by a central broad road from the two lodges on the eastern boundary. This separated the consecrated from the non-Conformist portions, and either side of this road two chapels were built – a Church of England Mortuary Chapel and a Non-Conformist Mortuary Chapel. These were joined by an arch over the road which was surmounted by a spire. The burial areas are divided by walks planted with a wide range of trees – limes, yews, hollies, evergreen oaks, weeping ash, Monterey pine and sycamores. The gravestones are on raised plots along the western boundary. Sadly, the chapels were demolished in 1960.

33.7 Peterborough, The Park   OS196998

In 1879 the Peterborough Land Company produced a new large residential layout for two hundred acres, over an area in the north of the city encompassing a new park of 22 acres. This was possibly the first scheme of town planning in the city "for the residents of the new development who paid an annual fee to use it".

The Park was located in the centre of the new housing and planned in the shape of a scallop shell. It was divided into four quadrants and at the centre was a circular lawn with a bandstand. The cross paths were planted on either side with conifers with shrubs beneath. The perimeter planting has mixed conifers and deciduous trees sometimes besides a raised perimeter path. This path still exists today with its serpentine route. Along the south boundary is a row of glaucous cedars with annual bedding schemes either side of Princes Gate. In the south-west corner of the Park is an oval sunken garden adjacent to a rose garden edged with lavender, possibly the site of an original pond for swans. A range of pavilions serves those playing tennis, bowls, golf and putting. The original timber framed aviary survives. A new toddlers playground with paddling pool has recently been provided.

33.8 Bretton, Cotton End   OS160996

Cotton End is a warden controlled sheltered housing scheme for the elderly along Bretton Way in Peterborough. It was designed by Matthew Robotham & Quinn in 1983 and John Dejardin, the landscape architect. The design of the two storey housing is a horseshoe shape, overlooking the adjacent Recreation Ground to the south.

A pathway winds its way through a series of varied spaces formed by trees, shrubs and ground cover plants and rolling grass areas. These are arranged in a soft informal manner ensuring a relaxed atmosphere, with the views and spaces changing in scale and form in keeping with the movement of an elderly person. The living rooms look into the central area and therefore here the landscape is more varied and colourful. There are clipped evergreen trees which look like lollipops behind parallel hedges in rows of different height and species.

33.9 Peterborough, Fletton, St. Margaret's Road, No. 22   OS200975

Recently the owner has created a meadow-like effect in a small garden by using a wide range of perennials and grasses. The idea of bringing an idealised countryside under the control of a gardener is gaining momentum. Thus by avoiding regular mowing and encouraging perennials and annuals, little rainfall is required and no fertilisers are needed.

The perennials used include verbascums, achilleas, knautias, red clovers, and asters thereby achieving a long season of interest. The grasses included festucas, calamagrostis, stipas, mosquito grass and deschampsias for their clump forming habits. The few gaps are filled with camassias, alliums, and nectaroscordums; violets and lupins also are successful for seeding. This meadow is 18 x 22 ft and the plants grow much higher than the average lawn.

33.10 Longthorpe Tower   OS165984

A tower was added c.1300 at the north-east corner of an already existing house built by William de Thorpe in 1263. The Tower is square in plan with turrets on the corners and its walls are 6-7ft thick. Wall paintings in the Great Chamber on the first floor were discovered after the Second World War. There is a garden to the south of the Tower which comprises a lawn bordered by conifers and shrubs of recent planting. Before the encroachment of recent development there was a rectangular stone pigeon-house to the south-west of the Tower, and early sketches indicate an orchard with clipped shrubs.

33.11 Longthorpe, Thorpe Hall   OS172987

This three storey stone house was built between 1650 and 1656 for Oliver St. John, Lord Chief Justice of the Common Pleas for Oliver Cromwell. Although there have been modifications to the detail of the internal arrangement of the garden, its basic layout reflects the original design of the mid C17th.

The house stands within a rectangle of gardens, the whole being enclosed by a high stone wall contemporary with the house, its four corners surmounted by large stone urns. There are two entrance courts, one a road (mid Victorian) to the north and the other a water access from the River Nene to the south. The gates to these two courts are of elaborate design, the piers finished by pairs of lead falcons.

The principal garden lies to the east front, St. John's original layout was changed by the Rev. Strong in 1850 to an Italian design. Steps lead down from a stone terrace to a parterre of stone-edged beds. At the same time a raised walk to the north was treated as an informal shrubbery walk by the Victorians. To the south, the raised walk, originally a bowling alley, is now a broad gravel path with banked sides. In the south-east corner is an 18th century stone summerhouse set against the wall. This marks the eastern end of an axis established in the 1850s which runs across the gardens south of the house. An elaborate arch from the old south wing was placed in line with a gateway on the west wall to line up with the summerhouse.

The south garden walls were sold in 1789, and have been replaced by recently planted hornbeam hedges. The formal flower beds are planted with trees, shrubs, perennials and bulbs available by 1656.

To the south-west of the stable yard, a garden originally laid out by the Rev. Strong in c.1850 has a brick summerhouse and a rose garden around an oval pool –

originally a plunge pool for his children. By 1924 the house had been acquired by the Meaker family, whose roses have recently been replaced by healthier late 20th century ones.

Beyond the rose garden is the kitchen garden, now a garden centre, but the central herbaceous borders backed by yew hedges still remain. The earlier kitchen garden included an orchard and is now used by local model railway enthusiasts.

Outside the high stone wall is a line of mature conifers and deciduous trees visually extending the garden inside to the park outside. Pairs of seating niches along the outer face of this wall were possibly inspired by similar niches at Wothorpe Towers. Thorpe Hall is now a Sue Ryder Home, and recently the garden has been restored to reflect the owners' garden styles.

SELECTIVE BIBLIOGRAPHY AND SOURCES

Bendall, A. Sarah, *Maps, Land & Society*. Cambridge University Press, 1992

Bird, R. & Haycraft D., *The Gardens of Cambridge* Covent Garden Press, 1994

Burke's & Savills, *Guide to Country Houses, Volume III, East Anglia* London, 1981

Clark, R., *Cambridgeshire* Pimlico, 1996

Desmond, R., *Bibliography of British Gardens* St. Paul's Bibliographies, 1988

Gray, R., *Cambridge Gardens* The Pevensey Press, 1984

Headly, G. & Melenkamp, W., *Follies Grottoes & Garden Buildings* Arum Press, 1999

Mitchell, E., *Notes on the History of Four Cambridge Commons* Private, 1985

Oosthuizen, S., *Cambridgeshire from the Air* Alan Sutton Publishing Ltd, 1996

Pevsner, N., *Bedfordshire, Huntingdon and Peterborough* Penguin Books, 1997

Pevsner, N., *Cambridgeshire* Penguin Books, 1996

Taylor, A., *Archaeology of Cambridgeshire, Vol 1: South West Cambridgeshire* Cambridgeshire County Council, 1997

Taylor, A., *Archaeology of Cambridgeshire, Vol 2: South East Cambridgeshire and the fen edge* Cambridgeshire County Council, 1998

Taylor, C. C., *The Cambridgeshire Landscape* Hodder & Staughton, 1973

Taylor, C. C., *The Archaeology of Gardens* Shire Publications, 1983

Taylor, N., *Cambridge New Architecture* Leonard Hill, 1970

Way, T., *A study of the impact of imparkment on the social landscape of Cambridgeshire and Huntingdonshire from 1080 to 1760 Oxford B.A.R. 1997 Cambridgeshire Parklands* Cambridgeshire County Council, 1990

Anglesey Abbey, Peckover House, Wimpole Hall National Trust Guides

Cambridgeshire, Huntingdon & Peterborough Life Cambridgeshire Life Ltd.

Country Life Magazine

Gardens in England and Wales 1927–2000 The National Gardens Scheme

Historical Monuments in the County of Cambridgeshire, Volume I West Cambridgeshire HMSO, 1968

Historical Monuments in the County of Cambridgeshire, Volume II North East Cambridgeshire HMSO, 1972

Historical Monuments (England) Huntingdonshire HMSO, 1926

Journal The Garden History Society

Kelly's Directories of Cambridgeshire

Register of Parks and Gardens of Special Historic Interest in England: Part 5 – Cambridgeshire English Heritage

The Cambridge Review

The Garden Journal of the Royal Horticultural Society

The Gardeners' Chronicle

The Good Gardens Guide Ebury Press

The Victoria History of the County of Cambridgeshire and The Isle of Ely Oxford University Press

The Victoria History of the County of Huntingdonshire The Saint Catherine Press, 1936

For those interested in a particular park or garden, the Cambridgeshire Gardens Trust has extensive references in its archives that can be consulted by contacting the Trust's Secretary.

INDEX